Contributions to Economics

More information about this series at http://www.springer.com/series/1262

Anastasios Karasavvoglou • Zoran Aranđelović •
Srđan Marinković • Persefoni Polychronidou
Editors

The First Decade of Living with the Global Crisis

Economic and Social Developments in the Balkans and Eastern Europe

Springer

Editors
Anastasios Karasavvoglou
Eastern Macedonia and Thrace
Institute of Technology
Kavala
Greece

Zoran Aranđelović
Faculty of Economics
University of Niš
Niš
Serbia

Srđan Marinković
Faculty of Economics
University of Niš
Niš
Serbia

Persefoni Polychronidou
Eastern Macedonia and Thrace
Institute of Technology
Kavala
Greece

ISSN 1431-1933 ISSN 2197-7178 (electronic)
Contributions to Economics
ISBN 978-3-319-24266-8 ISBN 978-3-319-24267-5 (eBook)
DOI 10.1007/978-3-319-24267-5

Library of Congress Control Number: 2015960847

Springer Cham Heidelberg New York Dordrecht London

Printed on acid-free paper

Springer International Publishing AG Switzerland is part of Springer Science+Business Media (www.springer.com)

Contents

About the Book

It has been almost a decade since the global financial crisis first struck. Almost all countries in Eastern Europe and the Balkans continue to struggle toward recovery; they either suffer from severe recession or strive to sustain growth. Public debts are plunging dangerously together with hypertrophy of the public sector. There is still widespread corruption and a huge share of the informal economy. Youth and long-term unemployment are huge across the region.

The majority of the countries in the region have similar historical and cultural heritage. Moreover, they share the same political orientation to the European Union; they are members or candidates or aspire to set off on the path of European integration. They also have many common economic problems that cannot be neglected in the European integration process, e.g., low capacity to handle competitive pressures and the market forces in the single European market.

A failure to generate sustainable growth goes together with the inherited economic structure. Some of the countries are making efforts to reshape or invent a mix of policies that may tackle structural weaknesses and catch up with their peers and more developed societies.

Economic crises never come as they were before; they are multifaceted phenomena. Moreover, what were common features of all historical crises, the same as the ongoing one, are distortions in the flow of information and the way that people interact.

One strand of economic literature set up formal modeling of informational frictions, like uncertainty, asymmetric information, ambiguity, etc. The other one brings into the research focus complex social interactions. Economic disturbances come regularly with a diminishing of trust in people and institutions. A couple of decades ago, this fact started to attract the attention of academia. The concept of social capital has been introduced into different academic discourses and disciplines, within different interpretations and conceptions. Social capital can be defined as the sum of current and potential resources associated with a network of permanent interrelations of acquaintance and peer recognition. It is the glue that ties individuals and makes societies stronger. The more fragile the economy is, the more damaging is the impact on social capital.

The region assembles economies more vulnerable to external shocks. An orientation to functioning market economy, trade and capital account liberalization, and macroeconomic stability made the region susceptible to developments in the European core. This is why sovereign debt crisis in the Eurozone directly contributed to a second wave of recession. This is just a short list of issues that need to be addressed in order to direct the region into a bright future.

The 6th International Conference EBEEC 2014, held in Niš, Serbia, in May 2014, was a regional scientific event that attracted interest of more than a hundred scientists from all over the region and beyond and proved to be the right forum for discussing flaming issues that concern both academia and policy makers in the field of economic and social development of South East Europe and Balkan countries. This volume is a selection of 13 chapters, each tackling the main theme of the book from different perspectives. The scope of the chapters varies from cross-country analysis to single-country focused research or case studies. Some chapters have a rich methodological background, but some are more or less descriptive. Nonetheless, we hope that the book will be equally interesting to both educated readers and the general public.

We begin with a brief description of the overarching logic that underlies the selection of the topics in this volume and their sequence. Our choice was to start the book with discussions about more general economic themes. Vladislav Marjanović and Zoran Aranđelović discuss alternative strategies for structural transformation of the Serbian economy, as a policy instrument aimed to generate sustainable growth. The authors measure intensity of structural changes according to the coefficients known as the Michaely index (based on Gross Value Added) and Lilien's coefficient (based on employment data), and consequently they measure sectoral productivity. The chapter is a good review of past structural transformations. Structural transformations in Serbia have occurred with different dynamics and intensity in the last decade. The tertiary sector has recorded the highest contribution to total productivity, while agriculture has had the greatest negative reallocation effects, i.e., negatively influenced total productivity, opposite to manufacturing which has had positive effects. However, the positive effects are mainly the consequence of lost jobs. It underlines necessity of reindustrialization, as well as official support of leading and pulling sectors.

Abovementioned structural reforms are further discussed in the chapter by Sofija Adžić and Dragan Stojić. This chapter explores the trend of deindustrialization and its causes and clearly advocates for the strategy of reindustrialization of the Republic of Serbia. Following the European concept of endogenous, autopropulsive, self-sustainable, and inclusive development, the authors found clustering and poles of generic growth two most effective initiatives that could possibly lead to technological development and improvement of industrial competitiveness.

The last two chapters deal with agricultural issues. Sotirios Papadopoulos, Eleni Zafeiriou, and Christos Karelakis explore Greek farmers' choice among alternative farming systems. The authors employed multinomial logistic regression, based on survey data. The study confirms that a typical Greek farmer chose between conventional, organic, and integrated type of agriculture based on his expectations about what is going to be a dominant form of agriculture in the future. Further on, the very expectations are driven by sample population's characteristics like age, education, available subsidies, and whether farming is a premium or secondary source of income in each particular case.

In the final contribution to this part, Matteo Belletti and Elvira Leksinaj investigate impacts of remittances on technical and economic efficiency of Albanian agriculture, and particularly the farm income generation. Opposite to the finding of some earlier studies, which claim that migrants' remittances directed to the rural population are used by households to escape from agriculture, the authors found that because of predominance of small-scale production units (orientation to auto-consumption), net loss in the agricultural workforce, which comes from emigration, has no negative effect on farm income. It is hidden unemployment that compensates for the losing of hands.

Part II brings into the focus social capital, which is an increasingly studied issue in both economics and sociology. It seems that the marriage of pure economics with bordering sciences contributes to richer apparatus and better understanding of "economic" phenomena. Our choice to open this part with a study done by Anna Tokalaki, Anastasios Michailidis, Maria Partalidou, and Georgios Theodossiou is twofold. Firstly, the chapter has more general coverage of the concept of social capital, and serves as a good introduction into the next chapters, so that a reader will easily make a slip in discussions on specific topics related to social capital. Secondly, the empirical part of the chapter deals with the impact of the crisis and crisis resolution measures on the different dimensions of social capital in Greece, which is plausibly the part of the region most hardly hit by the crisis. The study is based on questionnaire survey done in the Thessaloniki prefecture in the region of Central Macedonia. The results are rather conclusive; there is a positive correlation between social capital and educational level and cultural differences, as well as between the income of a group and perceived social capital. The economically disadvantaged have less social capital stock because of insecurity and uncertainty related to the outlook of their lives. Moreover, while on average the stock of social capital in Greece has been perceived lower since the economic crisis, a part of social capital within the primary relationship (family, relatives, and friends) has increased.

The next chapter, written by Theodore Koutroukis and Spyros Roukanas, deals with the immediate aftermaths of the global crisis and the latest policy response in Greece. It is a study of political and social drivers of reforms and study of negotiations between a strong and unified foreign coalition and a weak state that found itself in necessity to advocate the interests of fragile Greek society. The content of proposed reforms makes the issue *par excellence* economic one, since the reforms tackled the fiscal consolidation, public services supply, labor market, etc. However, the authors were primarily interested in the peculiarity of social framework in which negotiations around Troika-Greece memoranda took place. There were strong deviations from social dialogue practice that were justified by the emergent nature of reforms that reduced negotiation capacity of social partners. In this specific case, Troika's monologue has replaced the European social partnership model. The authors advocate for rebuilding balance between capital and labor in Greek society.

In Chap. 7, Marija Džunić and Nataša Golubović deal with the links between social capital, corruption, and the level of economic development in Western Balkan countries. The chapter starts with a rather complete review of referent literature on the concepts of social capital and corruption, which makes it a rich source of knowledge that can be used in further analysis. The empirical part of this study tested a linear regression model that indicated that cross-country variations in GDP per capita may be explained by proxies of corruption perception, trust, and civic participation. The findings are further supported by ANOVA results. The analysis clearly indicates that countries with the highest level of corruption are also those with the lowest level of generalized trust and, consequently, those that have the slowest economic activity.

The concept of trust has been investigated one more time in the provocative chapter written by Panagiotis Mitrokos, Aristidis Bitzenis, Ioannis Makedos, and Panagiotis Kontakos, but this time with a focus on tax ethics. Conclusions are based on primary data collected through a questionnaire survey in Greece. The authors underline the damage in the Greek economy due to the recent expansion of the shadow economy and corruption. Rather low tax ethics of Greek tax payers is assigned not only to the various economic determinants but also to the combination of social, political, and cultural factors. Among the most prominent features, authors listed non-equitable tax system, economic structure that is dominated by small businesses and self-employment, a lack of trust in the governmental institutions, and finally, consumerism and individualism that override a set of values like altruism, sense of collective success, and national consciousness.

This part closes with Sofia Anastasiadou's contribution that in a way continues with previous discussions, trying to find the explanation for another socioeconomic trend looking through the more or less similar set of features of Greek society. The chapter is an econometric study of causes that could possibly explain the country's plague, unemployment and, consequently, "brain drain." Migration of high skilled labor from Greece toward more developed countries has been tested with the confirmatory factor analysis (CFA), based on the collected primary data. The instrument of questionnaire was spread out among the Greek student population from two universities. The students were asked to rate their attitude and justification for their choice. The structure of the questionnaire was designed to test the significance of four possible groups of reasons: political, economic, career opportunities, and psychological reasons. All four groups proved to be significant.

Part III takes up the issue of the external sector, the position of national states, and development issues. The Western Balkans countries are all small and open economies, and this makes them extremely vulnerable to external developments and prone to imported type of economic disturbances. This part opens with the chapter written by Odysseas Spiliopoulos and Dimitrios Petropoulos. It is the sole chapter in this part that explores foreign trade considerations. The prime focus of the chapter is on the institutional framework that governs trade of goods and services among countries in the Western Balkans and between the region and the European Union.

Alexandra Horobet, Lucian Belascu, and Ana-Maria Barsan investigate the choice of exchange rate regime, currency volatility, and its influence on foreign capital flows. This is an extensive and profound analysis of exchange rate volatility evolution during the last decade among eight countries from Eastern Europe and the Balkans. The authors experimented with numerous computational procedures in order to catch fully stochastic nature of exchange rate volatility (rolling standard deviations of daily logarithmic return, Hodrick–Prescott filters, and ARIMA models). The period of analysis spans last 15 years, which was enough to capture tranquil times that precede the recent financial crisis, turbulent crisis times, and post-crisis recovery. Time series analysis indicates a clear-cut reaction of all currency markets on global financial turbulence, as well as an incomplete spillover of volatility shocks among the local markets. A sharp increase in currency volatility was the case of common occurrence, with a difference in time persistence, that could be assigned either to the type of exchange rate regime or direct or indirect intervention measures taken by the monetary authorities to smooth currency volatility.

In Chap. 12, Srđan Marinković and Ognjen Radović explore the recent history of unilateral interventions conducted by national monetary authority in the Serbian currency market. Albeit single-country oriented one, the study has a potential to show a broad picture of exchange rate management among the countries in the region. The study is a logical complement of the previous more general discussion, since it takes explicitly into account the efforts that monetary authorities have made to manage exchange rate dynamics. The authors employed Markov-switching regressions in order to describe the time-varying nature of the exchange rate volatility. The employed models explain the driving force of switching between calm and turbulent regimes. The study found official FX interventions able to smooth daily volatility, but also raised doubts that the central bank intervened in response to detrimental past exchange rate trends rather than solely in response to excess volatility. High and rather pervasive level of financial euroization made macro-prudential stability the prime goal of official foreign exchange intervention.

The book closes with the chapter by Costin-Alexandru Ciupureanu and Mihai Daniel Roman. The chapter brings attention to the region's second most important source of foreign financial resources, workers' remittances. It is an econometric study that explores the impact of workers' remittances on poverty reduction in four largest economies in Eastern Europe and the Balkans, Ukraine, Poland, Romania, and Turkey. The countries in the sample are not homogeneous. Different levels of economic development and different paces on the road to the European Union make some of them even able to attract foreign labor force. The authors tested determinants of poverty level represented by poverty headcount and poverty gap, alternatively. The multiple linear regressions adapted level of unemployment, GINI coefficient, and GDP per capita as control variables. The results confirmed strong effect of workers' remittances on poverty reduction, i.e., a 10 % increase of remittances led to approximately 5 % decline in the share of people living in poverty.

At the end, we would like to acknowledge strong appreciation of the efforts made by the reviewers of the papers. Their inputs were extremely valuable for the final quality of the volume. We would also like to thank the participants for supporting the conference and University of Niš for hosting this event. Many thanks to our colleague Fotini Perdiki for editing the volume papers. Last but not least, we acknowledge the joint financial and administrative support of University of Niš and Eastern Macedonia and Thrace Institute of Technology.

Kavala, Greece — Anastasios Karasavvoglou
Niš, Serbia — Zoran Aranđelović
Niš, Serbia — Srđan Marinković
Kavala, Greece — Persefoni Polychronidou
November 2015

Part I
Structural Changes, Sustainable Growth and Sectoral Policy

Sectoral Analysis of Structural Changes of the Republic of Serbia

Vladislav Marjanovic and Zoran Arandjelovic

Abstract The practice of "structural experimenting" and inattention to structural disproportions is impermissible in the modern conditions of macroeconomic management. In order to properly determine the direction of restructuring of an economy, there should be conveyed a detailed sectoral analysis. It should provide us with knowledge about which sectors should be specially stimulated in the future, in order to accelerate the economic development of a country. It certainly does not mean that other sectors should be neglected, because such wrong decision would bring deeper structural disparities in national economy.

The restructuring of the economy is momentarily one of the most complex macroeconomic issues of the Republic of Serbia. In the order of activities, first of all, there should be identified the leading sectors of the economy of Serbia, which are the framework of its economic development. Also, there should be identified potential "pulling" sectors, that would give way to future structural changes and future economic structure of Serbia. The structure of economy of Serbia should be "adjusted" in such way that should even in the long run provide a stable economic growth, and to lessen the disbalance of the balance of payment, to increase the competitiveness of the economy, to decrease the unemployment, and finally, to increase the social standard of living.

Keywords Economic structure • Sectors • Structural transformation • Sectoral productivity

JEL Classification Codes 011 • 047

V. Marjanovic, Ph.D. (✉) • Z. Arandjelovic, Ph.D.
Faculty of Economics, University of Nis, Trg kralja Aleksandra ujedinitelja 11, 18000 Nis, Serbia
e-mail: vladislav.marjanovic@eknfak.ni.ac.rs; zoran.arandjelovic@eknfak.ni.ac.rs

A. Karasavvoglou et al. (eds.), *The First Decade of Living with the Global Crisis*, Contributions to Economics, DOI 10.1007/978-3-319-24267-5_1

1 Introduction

Both theory and practice pay great attention to economic structure issues. Economic structure, observed with equal seriousness, in both developed and undeveloped countries, indicates a very complex problem that has to be permanently examined and controlled.

The ratio between the production of a concrete branch, sector or region, and the production of a concrete national economy, varies over time and it is subjected to different internal and external impacts. Every country in the world tends towards its optimal economic structure, i.e. the structure that will enable relatively high rates of growth in the long run, along with full employment, low inflation, and favorable structure of balance of payment with a stable exchange rate. However, it rarely happens that a national economy attains an optimization of economic structure, which makes this issue current, especially in modern economic conditions.

A great number of internal and external factors has an impact on defining the economic structure of a country. The most important internal factors are: the abundance of factors and resources, accumulation, economic system, economic policy; the most important external factors are: import and financial dependency of a country, political and economic circumstances in external environment, possibilities of integration into world economy, inflow of FDI, etc. (Arandjelovic and Marjanovic 2011). The state and the well-conceived economic system must strongly affect the creation of economic structure, because without such economic structure management, it would be even more distant from its optimum.

Structural transformation of Serbian economy has entered the phase of intolerable slowdown. It reflects not only on the structure of production and income, but also on the structure of foreign trade, with negative effects on the current balance. If such trend continued, it would fast bring the economy to the phase of regress, and even deeper structural disproportions. So, there should be actively initiated a process of restructuring, with an active role of the state, in that sense.

The paper will, firstly, pay attention to "the transition" of economic structure of the Republic of Serbia in general, and then there will be followed a precise measuring of the intensity of structural changes, as well as the productivity of certain sectors in a longer run. Thus, relying on very simple quantitative analyses, the authors will try to show a direction of structural changes in the Republic of Serbia, and after that, to come to certain conclusions related to present and future vertical economic structure.

2 Economic Structure of Serbia in the Process of Transition-Transition of Economic Structure

It is hard to predict the direction, the intensity and the speed of structural changes, because many factors have an influence on them: offer and demand, technological changes, preferences, economic policy, and especially specific and different starting positions of a country which has begun its trip on the unknown road of transition. It is completely clear that the economies in transition had very little information about the future development and structure. After harsh initial transformational crisis (transitional recession) in the second half of 1990s, almost all economies in transition came to the acceleration of economic development. This kind of growth positively affected structural changes, and such structural changes along with changes in technology and consuming preferentials, are the key elements of transition into market economy (Kauffmann 2005). Moreover, structural changes that follow the logic of comparative advantages and the context of adequate policy of innovation and imitation, are important for the development of economies in transition and their process of catching-up other developed EU economies.

Generally speaking, the economic structure of all transitional economies has changed a lot and is still changing, no matter that most of these countries have completed their transition from centrally planned to market economies that are already full members of EU. The ex-socialistic system has obviously favorised industry, and discriminated bussines services, for which it was believed not to have created the added value. The opening of transitional economies has also brought changes in the sector of external trade, and the inflow of FDI has additionally changed the economic structure from the production of labour-intensive products to production of capital-intensive products.

The change in structure of production, trade and prices, leads also to the increase of social product per capita, which further changes the structure of demand to medium term. All these factors bring to new reallocations of resources among sectors and to their development.

Changes in sectoral productivity along with production innovations and changes on the level of demand, provoked many changes in the composition of output. The countries who most recently joined EU, affected the development of EU in various directions. Taking into account a unique EU market, it is obvious that structural changes and growth of social product of transitional economies, affect the economic structure and growth of the remainder of EU. The acceleration of investment from EU-15 in newly joined countries and the growing intensity of the mutual trade, have changed the structural composition of production and employment in the whole Europe. In addition, it has also started developing the sector of services that had been neglected for decades among newly joined members.

Thus, structural changes that have occured in the recent history in EU have four important elements:

1. changes in sectoral composition of industry,
2. changes in structure of trade,
3. relative increase of service sector,
4. change of prices structure and exchange rate (Welfens and Wziatek-Kubiak 2005).

Institutional modernisation and economic "attaining" of developed European economies of newly joined countries, led to disintegration of structural relationships not only in EU-15, but also in newly joined economies. It appears a new structure led by technological progress and adapting relative prices to the international environment. The opening up and the liberalization of former socialistic economies influenced the exchange of knowledge, the diffusion of technology and the exchange of goods and factors.

All these significant processes are followed by intensive reallocation of resources and the change of productivity in various sectors, and in that way they influenced the structural changes. Great changes in the structure of GDP and employment of the newly joined countries, had been closing up (and are still closing) their economic structures towards the EU structure. The industry sector had especially dealt with the process of "opening up" and with the international competition, so perhaps the greatest structural changes occured in this sector. The service sector, however, due to increase of demand and relative prices, gains significance, hence there is an increased supply and great structural changes in this sector of economy. Since the structural changes in general are the precondition for real (convergence), the obligation to implement Copenhagen and Maastricht criteria, as well as the the Lisbon strategy, crate new challenges for new members. The problem that really exists is to find an optimum between the gain of further convergence of structures of "old" and "new" members on one hand, and preservence of stability of prices and the real exchange rate on the other.

Today's economic structure of Serbia is a consequence of a great number of factors, most of which are related to the period of 1990s. The inherited state of the economic structure and disoriented structural transformation that after 2000 should have been "organized" unfortunately has not stopped, and the transitional recession that does not favor the quality of structural changes in Serbia has been lasting too long.

The economic structure of Serbia leans towards "non tradable" sector in which there are not many chances for the international game, at least for now. However, much serious issue is that the expansion of the service sector seems that it does occur due to stagnation of the industry sector, which in the case of Serbia is of crucial significance for solving the unenviable balance of payment situation. For now, we are to raise one more question: why did economic structure of Serbia get such contours. It is certain that enormous political risk, i.e. frequent critical political environment, great corruption, administrative inefficiecy and bad legal system, are the important factors that affect such economic structure. If we add to this an incorrect economic policy which approves bad privatisation policy, consumption without strategy and control, and inadequate system of distribution which does not follow the motion of sector productivity, the situation becomes more worse. If we would proceed further in the analysis of cause and effect of the economic structure of Serbia, the critical tone would become louder and louder, and pouring oil on fire for now would be finished with new world economy crisis, which additionally brought down the foreign demand and decreased insufficient export of Republic of Serbia.

3 Importance of Certain Sectors in the Future Development of Serbian Economy

3.1 Intensity of Structural Changes of Republic of Serbia

Structural transformation in Serbia had been occurring with different dynamics and intensity in the last few decades. That dynamics depended on the whole spectral of internal and external influences. The part to follow will focus on the period after 1990 and will follow structural changes in this period of two decades. In this analysis, perhaps the best solution is to "break" this long period in to sub periods, the first, 1990–2000, and the second 2000–2008. Such division is good, because in the first sub period had occurred unpredictable economic shocks with long-term economic and other consequences, which still can be felt, so to a great extent it affected the economic structure which had transformed by some unusual logic, determined by the disintegration of the state, the economic system, the sanctions, the wars and the transition.

A long time period (2000–2008) can be observed as "more peaceful", except for the global economy crisis. In fact, conditions for structural transformation of economy had been relatively normal and there have not been some specific economic shocks as in the previous period.

In order to discuss the intensity of structural changes, it not sufficient to only follow the rates of growth of GDP of certain sectors which is necessary, but not the sufficient condition for structural changes. So, as more complete and better indicators are used the coefficients of structural changes. This paper uses *Michaely* index, but the mathematical expression that determines it, can be also noticed as *Lawrence* index:

$V = \frac{\sum_{i=1}^{n} \left| d_{i(1)} - d_{i(0)} \right|}{2}$, where $d_i = \frac{q_i}{\sum_{i=1}^{n} q_i}$, and $\mathbf{q_i}$ the share of sector $\mathbf{i}$ in the total output of the concrete economy.[1]

The conclusions that we can underline this time are the following. The longer the period, for which we calculate the intensity of structural changes, the higher the coefficient (closer to 1). It means, considered in long-term, the structural transformation is more intense. Considering the two sub periods in Table 1 (1990–2000 and 2000–2008), we notice that in the first the coefficient V is lower ($V_{90\text{-}00} = 0.2340$, and $V_{00\text{-}08} = 0.3434$), i.e. the intensity of structural changes is higher in the second

[1] e.g. in paper N. Crespo, M. P. Fontoura, "Integration of CEECs into EU Markets: Structural Change and Convergence", ISEG-UTL, Lisboa, 2004, that is *Lawrence* index; by M. Korosic that is index of structural changes; in paper A. Dietrich, "Does Growth Cause Structural Change, or is it the Other Way Round?", A Dynamic Panel Data Analysis for Seven OECD Countries, Friedrich-Schiller-University, Jena, 2009 that is *Michaely* index.

Table 1 Intensity of structural changes of Republic of Serbia

i	d_{90}	d_{00}	d_{04}	d_{05}	d_{06}	d_{07}	d_{08}	$\lvert d_{i(00)}-d_{i(90)}\rvert$	$\lvert d_{i(08)}-d_{i(00)}\rvert$	$\lvert d_{i(05)}-d_{i(04)}\rvert$	$\lvert d_{i(06)}-d_{i(05)}\rvert$	$\lvert d_{i(07)}-d_{i(06)}\rvert$	$\lvert d_{i(08)}-d_{i(07)}\rvert$
A. Agriculture, hunting, forestry and water works supply	0.1624	0.0703	0.1537	0.1384	0.1313	0.1132	0.1165	0.0921	0.0462	0.0132	0.0061	0.0156	0.0028
B. Fishing	0.0007	0.0014	0.0005	0.0005	0.0003	0.0003	0.0003	0.0133	0.0011	0	0.0001	0	0
C. Mining and quarrying	0.3883	0.6142	0.0167	0.0163	0.0163	0.0153	0.0151	0.2259	0.4109	0.0003	0	0.0009	0.0002
D. Manufacturing			0.1769	0.1672	0.1680	0.1647	0.1580			0.0083	0.0006	0.0028	0.0058
E. Electricity, gas and water supply			0.0340	0.0339	0.0328	0.0314	0.0302			0.0001	0.0009	0.0012	0.0011
F. Construction	0.0791	0.0704	0.0365	0.0353	0.0361	0.0373	0.0370	0.0087	0.0334	0.0011	0.0007	0.0011	0.0003
G. Wholesale and retail trade, repairs	0.1780	0.1053	0.0986	0.1139	0.1195	0.1340	0.1356	0.0727	0.0303	0.0132	0.0048	0.0125	0.0019
H. Hotels and restaurants	0.0277	0.0129	0.0099	0.0090	0.0079	0.0079	0.0075	0.0148	0.0054	0.0007	0.0010	0	0.0003
I. Transport, storage and communications	0.0735	0.0710	0.0950	0.1111	0.1365	0.1533	0.1634	0.0025	0.0924	0.0139	0.0219	0.0145	0.0087
J. Financial intermediation	0.0263	0.0467	0.0362	0.0383	0.0408	0.0442	0.0476	0.0204	0	0.0018	0.0022	0.0029	0.0029
K. Real estate, renting and business activities			0.1529	0.1497	0.1484	0.1421	0.1422			0.0027	0.0012	0.0054	0.0001
L. Public adminis-tration, defense, compulsory social security			0.0716	0.0681	0.0627	0.0585	0.0560			0.0030	0.0046	0.0037	0.0021
M. Education	0.0117	0.0108	0.0348	0.0325	0.0300	0.0290	0.0282	0.0009	0.0174	0.0020	0.0021	0.0009	0.0007

N. Health and social work	0.0038	0.0029	0.0525	0.0502	0.0452	0.0422	0.0408	0.0009	0.0379	0.0020	0.0043	0.0026	0.0012
O. Other communal, social and person. serv. activities	0.0484	0.0310	0.0225	0.0220	0.0212	0.0202	0.0200	0.0174	0.0110	0.0004	0.0007	0.0009	0.0001
P. Private house-holds with employed persons			0.0012	0.0012	0.0014	0.0014	0.0013			0	0.0002	0	0.0001
V								**0.2348**	**0.3430**	**0.0364**	**0.0297**	**0.0658**	**0.0164**

Source: own calculation based on the Statistical office of the Republic of Serbia data

period, which is, perhaps, logical, taking into account already mentioned bad economic situation with the continual economic shocks which characterized this decade. Perhaps this locked a proper structural transformation, i.e. slowed the intensity of structural changes.

If we observe these coefficients at the annual level, we can notice that they are lower in the short-term period, so it can be concluded that the structural changes in Serbia in the last few years had been minor and cyclic. The lowest coefficient we measured for 2008 and it equals only 0.0164, which coincides with little economic growth and critical period which conditioned the structural changes to be minor.

Now, observing the period 1990–2000 and single sectors, the highest sector's growth of share in the total GVA of Serbia, had industry in general (along with mining, quarrying, production of energy, gas and water), then financial intermediation and fishery. In fact, these are the only three sectors that notified the growth of share in creating the total GVA, while all other sectors in this period notified a decrease of that share. The greatest decrease notified agriculture, trade, public and other personal services. This points clearly to a critical situation in this period, which can be observed from the aspect of change of the economic structure, as a combination of two phenomena—industrialization and deagrarisation, taking into account that these two sectors marked the structural changes in this period. Although in normal circumstances, tertiary sector would notify some kind of growth, in the observed period it never happened, because of the above mentioned circumstances.

The period between 2000 and 2008 seems to have been more favorable for more intensive structural changes since there had been no critical challenges, however there also happened some unusual phenomena for this level of development. Unlike the first period with the industrialization, deagrarization and detertiarization, now the opposite processes take place—deindustrialization, agrarization and tertiarization.

It is unusual though, that the agriculture in this period notifies one of the greatest increases of share in GVA of the country, apart from transport and communication and trade which are part of the tertiary sector, and for which it is logical to increase their participation on the advanced levels of development of the country. The greatest decrease of share in the total GVA on the other hand, notify industry, construction, public and other personal services. Although the fall of industry's share is perhaps logical in this period of change of economic structure, in the case of Serbia it is huge and abnormal, and it cannot be compensated by the positive bounce of the tertiary sector.

In order to check the direction of structural changes of Serbian economy, we use another indicator, which counts on the ground of employment, which to a great extent depends upon structural changes. That is *Lilien's* coefficient, mathematically expressed as:

$LI_{1,2} = \sqrt{\sum_{i=1}^{n} x_{i2}\left(\ln\frac{x_{i2}}{x_{i1}}\right)^2}$, where $x_{i1>0}$, $x_{i2>0}$, and $\mathbf{x_i}$ is the share of sector **i** in the total employment of the country. One can notice that coefficient **L** follows the dynamics of the coefficient **V**, i.e. that employment follows structural changes.

When the coefficient **V** is higher, higher is also the coefficient **L**, i.e. when changes in the economic structure are greater, greater are the changes in the structure and the dynamics of the employed. In the case of Serbia, as well as in the case of V coefficient, coefficient L is also higher in the 2000–2008 period (Table 2), when the intensity of structural changes had been higher.

The highest increase of sector share of the employed when the first period is in question (1990–2000) notify service sectors, as health and social services, education, real estate, state government and transport, and the lowest decrease trade, construction, agriculture, industry and tourism.

In 2000–2008 period the highest increase of share notify trade, real estate, business and state government, and the lowest decrease industry, financial intermediation and agriculture.

3.2 *Sectoral Productivity in Republic of Serbia*

It is high time to introduce productivity into the analysis. The goal of the analysis which is to follow is to determine those sectors that mostly contribute to the total productivity of the economy and those whose contribution is the least. The period for which we calculated productivity applies to 2004–2008 (period before crisis).

If we mark the output growth rate with an $\hat{X}$ (GDP or GVA), then mathematically we can present it as $\hat{X} = \frac{X_1 - X_0}{X_0}$. Then, $X_0 = \sum_i X_0^i$, where X_0^i is the level of output of sector **i**, (i = 1, 2, 3, . . .n).

Let $\theta_0^i = \frac{X_0^i}{X_0}$ be the share of sector **i** in the real output in the initial period, and $\varepsilon_0^i = \frac{L_0^i}{L_0}$ the share of sector **i** in the total employment of a country, where $L_0 = \sum_i L_0^i$.

Now, if productivity of sector **i** we define as $\frac{X_0^i}{L_0^i}$, then the sector's productivity growth rate looks like this:

$$\xi_L^i = \left(1 + \hat{L}^i\right)^{-1}\left(\hat{X}^i - \hat{L}^i\right) \approx \hat{X}^i - \hat{L}^i. \tag{1}$$

After a bit rearrangement, an equation can take the following form:

$$\xi_L = \left(1 + \hat{L}\right)^{-1}\sum_i \left[\theta_0^i\left(\hat{X}^i - \hat{L}^i\right) + (\theta_0^i - \varepsilon_0^i)\hat{L}^i\right]. \tag{2}$$

The equation (2) can be divided in two parts (the expression $\left(1 + \hat{L}^i\right)^{-1}$ is neglected for now). The first part is sector's productivity growth rate conventionally

Table 2 *Lilien* coefficient

i	$x_{i\,90}$	$x_{i\,00}$	$x_{i\,06}$	$x_{i\,07}$	$x_{i\,08}$	L_{07}	L_{08}	L_{90-00}	L_{00-08}
A. Agriculture, hunting, forestry and water works supply	5.2410	4.7020	3.9637	3.7750	3.3956	0.009	0.0381	0.0554	0.3598
B. Fishing	0.0502	0.0635	0.0719	0.0736	0.0716	0	0	0	0.0010
C. Mining and quarrying	40.7615	40.2941	1.9476	1.6399	1.6323	0.0485	0	0.0053	0
D. Manufacturing			28.6024	27.3508	25.9268	0.0547	0.7410		2.2402
E. Electricity, gas and water supply			2.9676	3.1406	3.2053	0.0101	0.0013		0
F. Construction	7.8964	5.5274	5.8102	5.7758	5.7803	0.0002	0	0.7032	0.0116
G. Wholesale and retail trade, repairs	10.2184	7.0505	13.4403	13.6941	13.9658	0.0048	0.0054	0.9709	6.5247
H. Hotels and restaurants	2.6468	2.2481	1.6807	1.6952	1.6552	0.0001	0.0009	0.0599	0.1551
I. Transport, storage and communications	6.4877	6.8410	7.4850	7.6118	7.5908	0.0021	0	0.0192	0.0821
J. Financial intermediation	3.6279	3.8460	2.0370	2.1400	2.2944	0.0052	0.0111	0.0131	3.3831
K. Real estate, renting and business activities	4.4314	4.9380	4.5618	4.6506	5.2267	0.0017	0.0713	0.0578	0
L. Public administration, defense, compulsory social security			4.6927	4.7925	4.8613	0.0021	0.0010		0.0012
M. Education	7.7141	9.5643	8.5230	9.0324	9.3095	0.0304	0.0085	0.4420	0.0068
N. Health and social work	6.7516	10.1090	10.7165	10.9627	11.2420	0.0056	0.0071	1.6471	0.1269
O. Other communal, social and person. serv. activities	4.1728	4.5913	3.4994	3.6650	3.8424	0.0078	0.0086	0.0419	0.1218
L						**0.0043**	**0.0097**	**0.0200**	**0.0361**

Source: own calculation based on the Statistical office of the Republic of Serbia data

measured as $\sum_i \theta_0^i \left(\hat{X}^i - \hat{L}^i\right)$. The second part $\sum_i (\theta_0^i - \varepsilon_0^i)\hat{L}^i$ is called the reallocation effect, so if $\theta_0^i > \varepsilon_0^i$, the sector has greater share in output than in employment, which implies that it has relatively higher average productivity (UN Economic and Social Affairs 2006). The positive growth of employment in that sector will increase total productivity of the economy.

These mathematic formulations are sufficient to understand Table 3. The productivity is calculated based on the Statistical office of the Republic of Serbia data in the last few years (before great world crisis) and we came to the following results. The greatest contribution to the total growth of productivity of Republic of Serbia (for this time's period it amounts 35.673) comes from transport, storage and communication sector, which is a tertiary sector. That by far the highest percentage (11.02) follows manufacturing (9.41) and trade (7.78). If we go further into explanation of sector's productivity and divide it into two mentioned determinants, the highest average productivity notifies sectors of transport, storage and communication, then trade, and finally manufacturing. Observing the effect of reallocation, it is by far the highest in agriculture, then in manufacturing, and finally real estate and financial intermediation sector.

This factor reallocation is necessary to explain more thoroughly. In agriculture the reallocation effect in the observed period is the highest, but with the negative sign (−3.26), to which contributed a great drain of workforce from this sector. The drain of workers from agriculture negatively affects the total productivity growth in this sector, and the economy in general. So, there is space to increase productivity in agriculture by employing new workers in this sector, i.e. by preventing further drain.

On the other hand, the situation in industry is reverse ($\theta_0^i < \varepsilon_0^i$), so decrease in number of workers in this sector makes a positive reallocation effect, which further in the total result gives a positive growth of productivity of this sector. Similar situation exists also in trade, where every increase in number of employees would mean a decrease of reallocation effect and a decrease of the total productivity of this sector.

Transport, for which we noticed that it has the highest individual share in productivity growth of Republic of Serbia's economy, has a negative reallocation effect because it has $\theta_0^i > \varepsilon_0^i$, i.e. it is a sector that can make a relatively high productivity, but the negative rate of growth of labor force decreases that productivity potential, so any increase of employment rate would lead to further increase of productivity.

From other sectors significant for increase of total productivity of economy we are mentioning construction, financial intermediation and real estate business, of which the latter two tertiary sectors have positive reallocation effects because of the increase in number of employees, while construction acts likewise the processing industry, so for that reason it can be associated with secondary sector.

Other unmentioned sectors (tertiary and quaternary) individually have minor impact on the increase of productivity of Serbian economy and inconsiderable

Table 3 Sectoral productivity of Republic of Serbia

i	$\hat{X}^i$	$\hat{L}^i$	$\hat{X}^i - \hat{L}^i$	θ_0^i	ε_0^i	$\theta_0^i(\hat{X}^i - \hat{L}^i)$	$(\theta_0^i - \varepsilon_0^i)\hat{L}^i$	ξ_L	$\theta_0^i - \varepsilon_0^i$
A. Agriculture, hunting, forestry and water works supply	−5.01	−29.6	24.59	0.15	0.04	3.69	−3.26	0.43	0.11
B. Fishing	−12.95	−13.8	0.13	0.0005	0.0007	0	0.003	0.003	−0.0002
C. Mining and quarrying	13.15	−27.41	40.56	0.02	0.02	0.81	0	0.81	0
D. Manufacturing	11.97	−23.42	35.39	0.18	0.31	6.37	3.04	9.41	−0.13
E. Electricity, gas and water supply	11.52	−1.47	12.99	0.03	0.02	0.39	−0.01	0.38	0.01
F. Construction	27.19	−6.46	33.65	0.04	0.05	1.35	0.06	1.41	−0.01
G. Wholesale and retail trade, repairs	72.31	−4.22	76.53	0.10	0.13	7.65	0.13	7.78	−0.003
H. Hotels and restaurants	−3.27	−15.16	11.89	0.009	0.02	0.11	0.17	0.28	−0.011
I. Transport, storage and communications	115.54	−8.90	124.44	0.09	0.07	11.20	−0.18	11.02	0.02
J. Financial intermediation	64.86	11.55	53.31	0.04	0.02	2.13	0.23	2.36	0.02
K. Real estate, renting and business activities	16.57	26.77	−10.2	0.15	0.04	−1.53	2.94	1.41	0.11
L. Public administration, defense, compulsory social security	−1.99	−1.98	−0.01	0.07	0.04	−0.0007	−0.06	−0.06	0.03
M. Education	1.41	1.43	−0.02	0.03	0.08	−0.0006	−0.07	0.07	−0.05
N. Health and social work	2.54	−2.52	5.06	0.05	0.10	0.25	0.13	0.38	−0.05
O. Other communal, social and person. serv. activities	11.92	11.08	0.84	0.02	0.03	0.02	0.11	0.13	−0.01
								35.673	

Source: own calculation based on the Statistical office of the Republic of Serbia data

reallocation effects, and education and state governance have even negative growth of productivity.

Once again we are concluding that on the example of Serbia as well applies validity that the labor force from agriculture and industry, moves towards tertiary and quaternary sectors, but these sectors on the other hand are sectors with low productivity.

4 Conclusion

Structural transformation in Serbia has been occurring with different dynamics and intensity in the last decades. The paper will especially focus on the period after 1990, and follow the structural changes of the two decades. This long period is divided in two sub periods: first, related to the interval between 1990 and 2000; and second, the interval between 2000 and 2008 (pre-crisis period). Such division is good, because in the first sub period there were occurring very unpredictable economic shocks with long-term economic and other consequences that still can be felt. It had a great influence on the economic structure that was transforming by a strange logic, determined by the deterioration of the country, economic system, sanctions, wars and transition. The second sub period can be considered more "peaceful", except for the global economic crisis. In fact, the conditions for the structural transformation of economy were more normal, and until 2009, there hadn't been any specific economic shocks as in the first period.

For measuring the structural changes it was used *Michaely* index, though the mathematical expression that determined it could be found also as *Lawrence* index, and the conclusions that we came to, were the following: the longer the period for which we calculated the intensity of structural changes, the higher the coefficient (closer to 1). It means that observed in the long run, the structural transformation is more intensive, and the intensity of structural changes is greater in the long run period. If we observed these coefficients on the annual level, we would notice that they are lower in the short run, so it can be concluded that structural changes in Serbia in the last few years have been insignificant and cyclic. The lowest coefficient was measured in 2008, and it amounted only 0.0164, which coincided with low economic growth, and the period of crisis that caused the structural changes to be inconsiderable.

From 1990 to 2000, the greatest sector's share increase in the total GVA of Serbia had had industry in general (along with mining, quarrying, electricity, gas and water supply), then financial intermediation and fishing. In fact, these are the only three sectors that notified the increase of share in creating the total GVA, while other sectors in this period notified the decrease of that share. The lowest decrease notified agriculture, trade, other communal and personal services. Such situation clearly indicates a critical situation in this period that can be observed from the aspect of change of economic structure as a combination of two phenomena—industrialization and deagrarization, knowing that these two sectors gave way to structural changes in this period. Although, under normal circumstances, the tertiary sector should notify any kind of growth, it didn't happen in the observed period, because of the already mentioned circumstances.

The period between 2000 and 2008 seems to have been more favorable for more intensive structural changes, because there were no critical temptations. However, there occurred some unusual phenomena for such level of development. Unlike the beginning period, with the industrialization, deagrarization and detertiarization, all of a sudden started to occur deindustrialization, agrarization and tertiarization.

It's awkward, though, that agriculture in this period notifies one of the greatest increases in GVA share of the country, along with transport, storage and communications, and trade that belong to tertiary sector, for which it's logical to increase their share on the advanced levels of the development of the country. On the other hand, the lowest decrease of share in the total GVA, notify manufacturing, construction, other communal, social and personal services. Although the decrease of industrial share may be logical in this period of change of economic structure, in the case of Serbia it is huge and abnormal, and it cannot be compensated with the increase of tertiary sector.

In order to determine the direction of structural changes of the economy of Serbia, we used one more indicator that based on unemployment, which indeed depends on structural changes, and that's *Lilien's* coefficient. One can notice that employment follows structural changes. When the changes in the economic structure are greater, the greater are the changes in structure and dynamics of the employed.

The highest growth of sector share of the employed when the beginning period is in question, (1990–2000) notify service sectors, such as health and social work, education, real-estate business, public administration and transport, while the lowest decrease notify trade, construction, manufacturing, industry and hotels and restaurants.

In the period between 2000 and 2008, the highest increase of employment share notify: trade, real-estate business and public administration, and the lowest decrease—manufacturing, financial intermediation and agriculture.

In order to identify the sectors which contribute the most to the total productivity of the economy, we complemented the quantitative analysis with the analysis of sector productivity. The greatest contribution to the total productivity growth of the Republic of Serbia, comes from the sector of transport, storage and communications, that belongs to tertiary sector. This is by far the greatest percentage followed by manufacturing and trade. Again, the greatest average productivity notifies the sector of transport, storage and communications, then trade, and finally, manufacturing. The reallocation effect is by far the greatest in agriculture, then in manufacturing, and finally in the real-estate business sector and financial intermediation.

In agriculture, the reallocation effect in the observed period is the greatest, but with the negative sign, due to a huge drain of labor force from this sector. The departure of employees from agriculture negatively influences the total productivity in this sector, but also the economy in general. Thus, there is space for increasing productivity in agriculture by employing new workers in this sector, i.e. by preventing their further drain.

The situation with manufacturing is quite reverse: the decline in number of workers in this sector makes a positive reallocation effect, which gives a further positive growth of productivity in the total result of this sector. The similar situation occurs in trade, where each increase in number of employees decreases the reallocation effect and lowers the total productivity of this sector.

Transportation, for which we noticed that it has the biggest individual contribution to the increase of productivity of Serbian economy, has a negative reallocation effect, i.e. it is a sector that can make a relatively high productivity, but its negative labor force growth rate lessens that productivity potential, so each increase of the employment rate would bring to further increase of productivity.

Other sectors important for the increase of the total productivity of the economy are the following: construction, financial intermediation, real-estate business, of which the latter two tertiary sectors have positive reallocation effects due to increase of number of workers, while construction acts similar to manufacturing, so it could be joined to secondary sector.

Other unmentioned sectors (tertiary and quaternary) individually have little influence on the productivity growth of the economy of Serbia and low reallocation effects, and education and state administration even have negative growth of productivity.

Once again, we are going to say that in the example of Serbia, there is a rule that labor force moves from agriculture and industry towards tertiary and quaternary sectors, and accordingly, these sectors are the sectors with low productivity.

References

Arandjelovic Z, Marjanovic V (2011) The influence of material and system factors on the economic structure. In: Science and the world economic crisis. University of Nis, Faculty of Economics, Nis

Crespo N, Fontoura MP (2004) Integration of CEECs into EU markets: structural change and convergence. ISEG-UTL, Lisboa

Dietrich A (2009) Does growth cause structural change, or is it the other way round? In: A dynamic panel data analysis for seven OECD countries. Friedrich-Schiller-University, Jena

http://webrzs.stat.gov.rs/WebSite/

Kauffmann A (2005) Structural change and economic dynamics in transition economies. In: Structural change and exchange rate dynamics. Springer, Berlin

UN Economic and Social Affairs (2006) World economic and social survey 2006, diverging growth and development

Welfens P, Wziatek-Kubiak A (2005) Introduction. In: Structural change and exchange rate dynamics. Springer, Berlin

Advances and Difficulties in Serbia's Reindustrialization

Sofija Adžić and Dragan Stojić

Abstract The starting point of this paper is that for the completion of (post) socialist transition process is needed the realization of the strategy of reindustrialization of the Republic of Serbia according to the European concept of endogenous, auto-propulsive, self-sustainable and inclusive development. Development based on knowledge that is the essence of this concept, in Republic of Serbia in the last three decades, was promoted several times as strong development orientation. Implementation has not started for several reasons, from which in the forefront the cultural-political tendency is easy to define and much easier leaving the determination. The processed material is divided into two parts. In the first part, the emphasis is on causes of deindustrialization in the Republic of Serbia. The second part deals with three generic development alternatives and policies of their realization with emphasis on phenomena that encourage or block the generating and implementation of technological and business innovation in the structure of industry in the Republic of Serbia. The performed analysis shows that networking and clusterization of enterprises and agricultural farms, apropos the development of poles of generic growth are the key mechanisms by which with process of integration of research, high education and production in the local, sub-regional, regional and national frames, should start this process from a standstill.

Keywords Reindustrialization strategy • Generic growth poles • Endogenous growth • Knowledge based development

JEL Classification Codes L51 • O14 • O38

1 Introduction

The subject of this paper is the analysis of the role of the public regulations in implementing the project of reindustrialization in Republic of Serbia in line with the European concept of the endogenous, auto-propulsive, self-sustainable and inclusive development, characterised in three paradigms—*sustainable*

S. Adžić (✉) • D. Stojić
Faculty of Economics, University of Novi Sad, Subotica, Republic of Serbia
e-mail: sofija.adzic@gmail.com; stojicd@ef.uns.ac.rs

A. Karasavvoglou et al. (eds.), *The First Decade of Living with the Global Crisis*, Contributions to Economics, DOI 10.1007/978-3-319-24267-5_2

development—creative society—innovative economy. In line with this concept, basic sources of development are generated by technological and business innovations resulting in the development of new, and the improvement of the performances of all existing actors, activities and procedures within the production-organizational, business and institutional system.

The main motivation for the investigation lies in the fact that process of industrialization in communist era was state monitored and not profit oriented. Hence it is of great importance to focus on current state in Serbia's agribusiness and to compare with the previous states from communist times.

On the global level, there are numerous ideas and public policies for the realisation of the strategy of (national) reindustrialization based on the concept of the generation and implementation of technological and business innovations. Without tackling their further analysis here, there is no doubt that only these strategies harmonised with the needs and possibilities of the ruling and the coming social-economic environment have been successfully realised (within which the parts of the production-organizational, business and institutional system are active). All attempts of imitating or consistent use of a universal theoretical model have literally failed. Explicit dealing with the theoretical and practical aspects of reindustrialization in Republic of Serbia is not instantaneous in the first plan. This is especially odd in consideration of the fact that the commitment of key political and professional actors for higher role of new technology within the social-economical development has been present for more than three decades. Nevertheless, economic analyses are inexorable and they show that Republic of Serbia undergoes, without exaggeration, in phase of stagflatory depression, indicating that they are (now) at permanent basis faced with a kind of development crisis—which could be designated as *paradox of institutional and technological changes without (real) changes*. Faced with this paradox, we will try to explain the origin and (too long) retention of factors that block the reindustrialization, as well as ways to overcome them. Since something can be explored and understood only in the context of regular behaviour, in the paper we will use, on the one hand, the ideas and concepts which have their stronghold in one of the general theory of dynamics of complex systems, and on the other hand, the results of our search for answers to the question: *What are the consequences of three basic generic developmental alternatives: (1) completing the process of fordistic industrialization, (2) radical modernization of large production systems, and, (3) development of a creative society and innovative economy based on sub regional and local initiatives and broad as well as interactive cooperation, on conception and realization of the strategy of reindustrialization of Republic of Serbia*? In an effort to elaborate these issues and propose appropriate solutions, the processed material in this paper is structured in two parts.

The first part exposes the synthetic results of researches of the current characteristics of national production-organizational, business and institutional system in the context of their historical development and implications for the structuring of the concept of strategy of reindustrialization according to the European concept of endogenous, auto-propulsive, self-sustainable and inclusive development. A key conclusion is that, due to collapse of old export industries and the disappearance of reproduction unities by disintegration of (former) Socialist Federal Republic of Yugoslavia, no matter what will be produced, on condition that the productions and activities related to the appropriate enterprises can survive in open competition.

The second part deals with three generic development alternatives and policies of their realization with emphasis on phenomena that encourage or block the generating and implementation of technological and business innovations in the process of realization of the strategy of reindustrialization in the Republic of Serbia. Emphasis is on more precise determination of their implications for public regulation of two projects of creating conditions for the sustainability of the reindustrialization project. The first is networking and clusterization, the second is the development of poles of generic growth as centres of social-institutional experiments that lead together to the changing of perceptions of work, production and development and direct the population to commitment, creation, quality and cooperation in the function of achieving excellence in education, exploration and production.

2 Dynamics and Characteristics of Production-Organizational, Business, and Institutional System and Their Implications to the Structuring of Strategy of Reindustrialization

2.1 Development Dynamics of Production-Organizational and Business System from 1947 to 1989

The industrialization of Republic of Serbia in the period from 1947 to 1989, when the production-organization system was finished, with which the country came into the phase of capitalism restoration and (post) socialist transition, was developed according to the mode of industrial districts. The author's research (Adzic 2013, pp. 311–312) shows that, by the end of 1980, 24 industrial districts were formed, where there were four industrial medium-sized centres (with more than 10,000 employees) and 138 small industrial centres (under 10,000 employees). Establishing industrial districts, besides logically encircled structure of production capacities, was followed by development of appropriated logistical capacities (roads, railways, river and canal transportation, ports, warehouses, large commercial enterprises and foreign trade enterprises) and educational capacities (mostly, secondary vocational education for professions in accordance with the features of production structure of a concrete industrial district).

The basic characteristic of the industrialization within the observed period is that the regional production-organizational and business system was developed within the frameworks of mass energy, material and work intensive production based on the imitation of foreign technologies (above all, by importing equipment and buying licenses) and predominant role of political elite within their structural development. The consequences of such approach that can be felt up to date include: (1) poorly accumulated experiences *from the best industrial practice*, mostly because of tolerating high irrationality in using the resources, (2) well rooted habit (especially within business structures) regarding high protection and non-competitive efficiency, and, (3) value system and social relations blocking in cite generation and implementation of technological and business innovation. The goods market was not transmitting the signal indicating the production and business system actors: *What and under which conditions should be produced to be competitive*? The basic signals were coming from the offer side, and then mostly the already present things, without searching for some new ones, were offered. Therefore, the key actors of the production-organizational and business system behaved as the typical groups of special interest (distribution oriented coalitions). And where such groups rule, there are no technological and business innovations, but all the efforts are concentrated to maintain the position (Matejić 2002, pp. 705–709; Adžić and Popović 2005, pp. 179–184).

2.2 *Transition, Deindustrialization and Socio-economical Crisis*

The Republic of Serbia, after the restoration of capitalism, and transfer to the development of market social-economic system are covered by a specific form of long-term (social-economic) crisis. To designate this type of (long-term) social-economic crisis, the notion of *transitionism* is used in the national economic literature (Đuričin 2008, p. 22). Without dealing with the explanations in detail here, transitionism is a complex and multidimensional phenomenon which, besides economic, also covers geopolitical, historical, anthropological and cultural aspects. The economic aspects are marked by the problems resulting from the failure to complete four characteristic processes of the (post) socialist transition: (1) privatisation, (2) macroeconomic stabilisation, (3) institutional reforms and (4) reindustrialization. It appears as the post-transitional stagflation, characterised by the disharmony between the real and financial sector (dominated by the banking system oriented to credit retail, and current business activities, primarily within the sector of non-exchangeable), impotent (in developmental sense—the author's note) real sector, vulnerable macroeconomic stability, lack of institution development, and high regulatory risk, synthetically designated, as stated in the introduction, as the paradox of institutional and technical changes without (real) changes.

2.2.1 Lessons from Poland and Other Ex-communistic Countries

Wojtyna and Hausner (1993) notice that privatization offers the best solution to the efficiency problems of state-owned enterprises. However, many observers believe that some form of industrial policy is unavoidable during the transition period in order to stimulate restructuring before privatization has been completed. They analysed the compatibility and complementarity between privatization and industrial policy in the context of the systemic transformation in Poland. Other ex-communist European countries are observed in Rachwał (2011). The author analyse changes in industry in Poland with respect to changes in other European Union member states. The research problems include: the changing role of industry in the Polish economy in the era of economic transformation, European integration based on globalization and its share of the employment structure and gross value added, changes in the branch structure of Polish industry as well as exports as an expression of restructuring processes, influence of foreign capital on the functioning of industrial enterprises and its role in the re-structuring of the industry.

The most visible result of the transitionism is devastated industry. Many old, especially (which used to be) export industries have disappeared, and none new one has been created. After the first wave of global financial and economic crisis, the process of deindustrialization from 1990 to 2008 in Republic of Serbia has been survived by only each fourth industrial system and from 4 out of 5 employees at large industrial enterprises have lost their job (Jakopin and Bajec 2009, pp. 87–88). The volume of production and employment in national industry in 2013 was only about 40 % of the pre-transition maximum in 1986/1987. Therefore, the national industry practically reduced to three branches—the energy industry, food industry, and industry for production of building materials, on which a basis for the inclusion of Republic of Serbia in the process of European integration cannot be built. There are various views of the basic causes of the occurrence of the transitionism in Republic of Serbia (Đuričin 2008, pp. 22–30; Madžar 2008, pp. 255–265). There is the predominant position that its causes should be sought in the geopolitical cataclysm caused by the disintegration of the SFR Yugoslavia and the incapability of Serbia to, in this context, be included in the process of integration with European Union (Đuričin 2008, p. 22). Not denying the impact and importance of this factor, in the opinion of the authors, the main cause of transition stagflation is the fact that neither the restoration of capitalism (1990/1991) nor the transit to democratic political system (at the end of 2000) fixed the key socio-economic barriers that immobilize the production entrepreneurs and block the generation, implementation and economic valorisation of technological and business innovation. From this point (reindustrialization according to European concept of endogenous and sustainable development), the key is to restructure the national economy, after the restoring of capitalism, in the first stage of transition (from 1990 to the end of 2000), took place in the frame of—"shadow" economy and "brotherly" privatization. After the political changes in late 2000, their key protagonists legalized their own business and property—which resulted in the closure of markets for other participants in market competition. That is why the overflow of effects of global financial and economic crisis, among other things, showed that amnestied protagonists of the "shadow" economy, "brotherly" privatization and culture of small economic freedoms are unable to fulfil the mission of business class—moving the horizons of personal progress, move it for the society, too. The main effects are the low level of institutional capacity and investment myopia. The result is a very slow and uneven infrastructure increase and efficiency of real economy and weakening of human capital performances.

2.3 *Basic Characterisation of Production-Organizational, Business and Institutional System*

In this part we will proceed to the key determinants of regional production-organizational, business and institutional system that are important for the strategy of national reindustrialization, whether they act as motivating, or as limiting factors on the implementation according to European concept of endogenous and sustainable development.

First, industrial districts and sub regional clusters and their relationships within the reproduction unit (former) SFR of Yugoslavia has gone in the period of stagflation transition and deindustrialization. The newly formed production-organisational patterns in the national industry have been structured from what has remained and from the relatively thin layer of new micro, small, and medium enterprises, and they may be formally treated as certain micro-cluster variants (Jovetić and Stanišić 2006, pp. 134–136; Kastratović and Marinković 2008, pp. 228–232). Nevertheless, relevant analytical and expert elaboration does not support this statement, which results in the low level of social-economic coordination and poor support to individual and group development projects, above all in sense of creating conditions for the privatisation development of the real sector and the improvement of authentic (regional) production entrepreneurship and innovation system in line with the European concept of the endogenous and sustainable development, creative society and innovative economy.

Second, the spirit of entrepreneurship is missing both at the group and individual level, as well as the whole social-economic system. The majority of the demonstrated entrepreneurship initiatives have ended in the sphere of non-exchangeable goods (retail, real estate, construction) and very few within the real sector and export industry. This is especially distinctive within the domain of high tech industries where there are only few successful entrepreneurial attempts (Adžić 2008, pp. 207–210; Matejić 2008, pp. 38–40). It is crucial that the overall state of the entrepreneurial spirit in Republic of Serbia is characterized by very little interest in the export business.

Third, strategic coordinating mechanisms are very underdeveloped even besides numerous attempts of the reforms of market infrastructure and infrastructure for public regulation of economy and economic development (Adžić 2006b, pp. 65–66). This is reflected in the following: (1) very short time horizon of decision making (short term authority), (2) very high subjective discount rate (tactics prevails over strategy), (3) market incentives do not stimulate collaboration, co-operation, confidence, dedication, and cautiousness, and, (4) the public intervention is not encouraging the bottom-up cooperation and collaboration, because the use of its mechanisms is based on unconditional cooperation with dominant political feature.

Fourth, STIEOT (*S*cience—*T*echnology—*I*nformation—*E*ducation—*O*rganization—*T*elecommunication) infrastructure (system) is in decent situation and it of more quality than in many regions of similar development level. However, the structure of the STIEOT infrastructure is non-effective in production sense (Adžić 2006b, pp. 199–204). All performed STIEOT infrastructure reconstructions (privatisation, rationalisation, applying European standards in education and science, modernisation, association and programming) the task of which was to change the relation to economic innovation evaluation and its contribution to the social-economic development, have failed. The key issue is that the internal relations among the participants of the STIEOT infrastructure are very poor, thus, there is no capacity to exert higher technological pressure to the real economy by actual offer of relevant human resources and new technology.

3 Three Generic Development Alternatives and Their Implications to Strategy of Reindustrialization on Republic of Serbia

3.1 General Implications of Generic Development Strategies on Reindustrialization

In case of Republic of Serbia, three possible competitive alternatives for the realisation of the strategy of reindustrialization may be identified. Those are: (1) the finalisation of the process of fordistic industrialization, (2) radical modernization of large production systems, and (3) development of creative society and innovative economy based on the sub regional and local initiative, and wide collaboration and interactive co-operation.

The first alternative is deeply built into the existing regional production-organizational, business and institutional system, and it is, in implicit form, built in the current national and regional economical and development policy (Study 2010, 2011). Its realisation is based on the policy of low wages and low prices of basic (national and regional) inputs (aimed at achieving some kind of internal and external competitiveness), and acquiring capital and technologies from external sources, above all by legal entities' borrowing abroad. Since its implementation does not require any major regional effort (in sense of higher renunciation of consumption in favour of higher investment), this alternative is in line with the existing key parameters of political or business culture and economic interests—built in the existing production-organizational and business systems. Major restrictions for its further implementation include two factors.

The first and long-term one is the existing human resources capital, and the new one created by relatively developed university education system—which has already been surplus within the existing production system. The surplus of the university educated (currently, over 80,000 persons with the university degree are unemployed) and creative persons is directed to two options—foreign immigration or finding the position within a framework of an interest (political) group (popular national slogan is *that political parties are key employment institution*), of course, at the expense of obsolete knowledge, and professional and productive entrepreneurial dormancy.

The other, not less significant, problem includes the reflexes of the internal, and external (global) economic crisis reflected in the target segments of global labour market—for the time being, with unforeseeable development, economic and social consequences. In any case, it may be expected that the third option will appear, through which the university educated and creative persons will endeavour to focus their frustrations to the active participation directed to the abandonment of the first alternative, and transfer to the implementation of the second and/or third alternative.

The second alternative is achieved when major regional production systems enter the transnational business systems aimed at ensuring the competitive approach to the global market, and fast technological and business modernisation. This alternative ensures to activate what has remained from the inherited resources (on short-term basis) and available human resources (on mid-term basis), as well as that the major (regional) production systems (on mid-term basis) become focal points of the development, and modernisation of micro, small, and medium enterprises.

On the other hand, their occurrence in higher volume would have an integrating effect to currently very separate and closed sectors of production, education, research, public administration, etc. In this way, (new) development structures are created, prompter transfer of new technology is ensured and (partial) externalisation of development risks. Indeed, from the aspect of the strategy of reindustrialization efficiency increase, the implementation of this alternative is (even besides certain risks) desirable, above all, as the transition mechanism from the existing situation to the third alternative. Two basic restrictive factors have effect here. The first is that the basic condition for its implementation is to ensure investment and ownership attractive, stable, and guaranteed business conditions. The second, not less important factor is the fact that this alternative has been accepted (as the predominant reindustrialization option) by more or less similar countries. Within this context, the existing economic interests (which prefer maintenance to radical change of the existing situation), the prevailing political and ideological orientation to the fordistic concept of the (re)industrialization, cultural parameters (which strongly oppose the new production values, such as quality, accuracy, co-operation, productive interaction, and the like), and general macroeconomic and social instability and uncertainty do not have a stimulating effect to its implementation. The results are in line with this.

To achieve the third (scientifically desirable) alternative, the following is necessary: (1) consistent understanding of the issue of contemporary development, (2) new, active and responsible role of regional executive government, and local authorities in public regulations of economy and economic development, (3) developed STIEOT infrastructure oriented to the needs of real economy, (4) harmonised activity of market, strategic-cooperative and hierarchical mechanisms of economic life regulation, (5) neutralisation of the activity of the distribution oriented coalitions, (6) wider risk acceptance, (7) creating conditions for the balance between individual and common interests, and, (8) higher motivation of employees and other population for life-long learning, especially at the position of work. Finally, its implementation is conditioned by social and political innovations in sense of constituting democratic, but, above all, responsible society, to environment and next generations, non-parasitic institution system, freedom of choice of any kind while observing basic ethic and spiritual values. In this context, development (in sense development of strategy the reindustrialization—the author's note) in this alternative is based on the regional, sub regional and local specifics, supported by STIEOT infrastructure, initiated by entrepreneurial and strategic cooperative initiative, and, formed by the competition and co-operation excluding the protection of monopolistic interests of any kind. Basic inputs within this alternative development include quality human resources, and innovative social and especially political institutions. The best route leading to it is through the second alternative.

From the technical point of view, the key goal of national reindustrialization is the implementation of the concept of the global commercialization based on the dynamic creation and development: (1) economic self-sustainable industrial enterprises and agricultural farms by exogenous standards of the global economy, (2) appropriate market infrastructures and specialized circles of commercial and financial capital oriented toward exports as the main source of profit, (3) appropriate non-productive infrastructures, and, (4) infrastructure for public regulation of business and development—which will, through public and private educational, developmental-research, production, traffic and financial activities provide relatively stable and stimulating conditions for the smooth functioning of the process of its expanded reproduction.

In compliance with this thesis, the analysis of the relationship between economy, and other activity strategies of national reindustrialization are treated as a complex set of inter-dependence between economic, technological and social phenomena (Fig. 1). From the methodological aspect, the (national) strategy of reindustrialization makes a socially organised and institutionally arranged process of cooperative co-ordination of decision making at a macro-level, on one hand, and at mezzo and micro-levels, on the other hand, in order to provide internationally competitive level of quality and process of final products of processing, and trade in industries through the development and implementation of business and technological innovations, and, new forms of social and economic organisation and division of labour.

In this context, the public regulation has two key tasks. The first is to create conditions for increasing the business efficiency of enterprises and agricultural farms, and the other, to create the socio-economic frame for improving

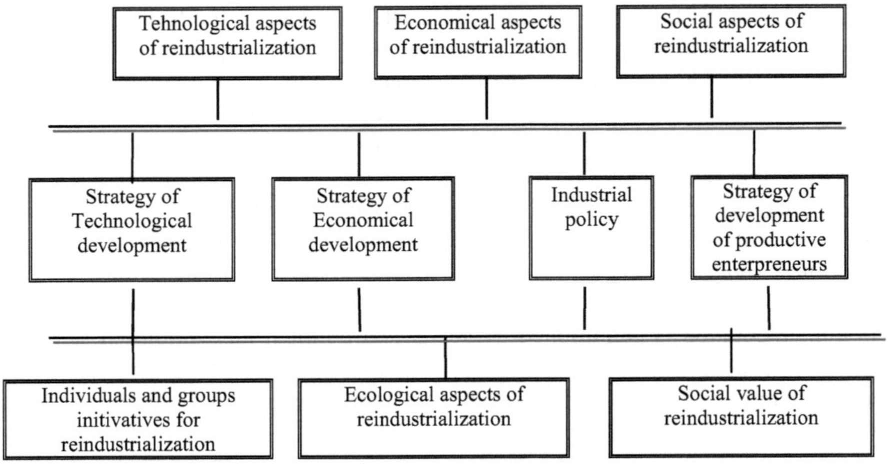

Fig. 1 Strategy of reindustrialization of the Republic of Serbia

performances of human capital and in cite generating and, especially, implementation and economic valorisation of innovations. The first is based on a project of networking and clusterization of both enterprises and agricultural farms, and the other on the development of poles of generic growth based on the development of strong and internationally competent research and educational institutions.

3.2 Networking and Clusterization Strategies as Determinants of the Strategy of Reindustrialization

In accordance with the basic thesis that no matter which product will be produced in Republic of Serbia, under the condition of self-reproduction in terms of open market economy, the basic condition for reindustrialization is that the structure of industry enterprises and agricultural farms has: (1) macro, mezzo and micro organizational structure and management system capable of efficient production and distribution of quality industrial products in sharp and unequal international competition, (2) adequate physical resources and personnel, (3) healthy financial structure, and (4) flexibility, which allows fast and efficient response to changes in natural, internal and external socio-economic environment. Provision of the abovementioned performances is the product of the total social-economic efforts to integrate each industrial enterprise and agricultural farm into a complex, and hierarchically arranged net-system with four levels (Adžić 2006a, pp. 118–121).

The first level should include industrial enterprises and agricultural farms gathered in export macro-clusters organised according to the main production lines in the way that they provide economically and technologically efficient business activities in circumstances of global competition, and other rigidities imposed by protectionist oriented commercial policy of the developed market economies.

The second level should include industrial enterprises and agricultural farms gathered in mezzo-reproduction units the core of which is located within the Republic of Serbia that would be provided the optimum regional or national division of labour and supply with physical inputs (in particular of sources of energy, basic reproduction, and raw materials, intermediary products, machinery, and equipment), and services (business services, services of transport, storing, and cross border transfer) under most favourable economic and technical conditions. In a wider sense, these mezzo-reproduction units should also include large trade companies, both on the side of supply with entrance inputs, and even more on the side of marketing, storing, transport, cross border transfer and placement on target segment of the global market.

The third level should include industrial enterprises and agricultural farms in institutionally arranged frameworks of national social-economical environment. Its basic task is the supply with human and financial capital, public goods, and, services of public administration in the way that would act as a stimulus on their behaviour in the sense of satisfying wider social-economic objectives—based on the criteria of enhancing product competitiveness, processes, economic entities, business and macro-reproduction units.

The fourth level should include industrial enterprises and agricultural farms in macro-reproduction units—in each (selected) segment of the global market. Its task is to provide each industrial enterprise and agricultural farm with economy of scale, and enhancing of development of such forms of production that can reach the level of efficiency, and competitiveness in terms of prices, and quality in the conditions of severe, and unequal international competition based on the available production factors, and those that will develop in future.

3.3 Development of Poles of Generic Growth as a Determinant of Strategy of Reindustrialization

In the exposed context, the implementation of poles of generic growth is, according to the authors, the second key active means of public regulation for the realization of the strategy of reindustrialization. Their main function is to connect researches and educations with the project of reindustrialization in accordance with the need to create conditions for wider application of the third development alternative. The poles of generic growth are set up to: (1) improve the research which has got a direct impact to education, especially in the function of improving the productive entrepreneurship, and application of modern technologies and organisational innovations in production, (2) increase the efficiency and effectiveness of obtaining, and, applying research results, (3) ensure necessary business and scientific support in contemporary knowledge and technology exchange, (4) ensure competence for international co-operation in research, application of its results and advancement during work, and, (5) orient the entrepreneurship to the export industries. These five basic objectives define their mission, which could be most specifically determined as *excellence in research, education and production*. In this context, the poles of generic growth are needed, which will operate for a long time, in difficult manner, and perhaps, hopelessly in spreading the idea of the excellence of all around us, primarily, in research, education, development of new activities and enterprises within the export industries, and the improvement of the performances of the existing enterprises and agricultural farms by introducing new technology and organisational innovations.

From the presented objective structure, the basic principles of the institutional public regulations structure may be determined by four factors.

First, the development of poles of generic growth must be based on the (regional) Programme. The basic objective of the Programme is to, on the non-addressed basis, stimulate the sub regional and local initiatives, and ensure support for all candidates for the set up of the poles of generic growth—by integrating the existing ones, research, educational and production potentials checked by operation and results, which may be ensured from the region or through interregional trans-border co-operation for quite clear, accurate, and specifically based needs of actual producers.

Second, in order for the Programme for development of the poles of generic growth to be successful in promotion and support, the idea on excellence as the basic motto of their existence must be applied, and no interests and intentions must result in decreasing the standard for their measurement. Therefore, the authorities, bodies and individuals having impact to the determining of the excellence level in the process of the evaluation of the generic growth poles must not have the conflict of interest. The objectivity and competence of each evaluation and decision of the Programme are the one of the key conditions for the success of the public regulation.

Third, the innovation of the project content and mechanisms of the Programme must not be made only in the direction of institutional adjustment to the total social-economic context, but without any decreasing of the standards for excellence determination.

Fourth, since the Programme itself is the institutional innovation, introduced in the systems that already include high inertia, and delay in achieving the results, the Programme has got sense only if it is consistently implemented on the long-term basis, i.e. once the decisions are made, they must be implemented in a patient, consistent, and long-term manner.

In line with the conditions of the resources in the Republic of Serbia, the basic constitutive elements the poles of generic growth include are: (1) industrial enterprises, (2) public universities, i.e. faculties, (3) research institutions in public or mixed ownership, and (4) executive government (regional, local). Their role in this context is as follows.

First, the industrial enterprises introduce: (1) demand for research results, (2) demand for university educated personnel, and advancement of their employees,

(3) a part of the assets for the purpose of financing external researches, and, (4) human, and other resources for the support, and co-operation in research, and their implementation to their business, production, and development needs.

Second, public universities i.e. faculties introduce: (1) part of the work time of scientific-research potential satisfying rigorous international standards, (2) part of physical resources (facility, equipment) which may be applied for actual researches, (3) part of IT support in research and education, and (4) part of their offer for post-graduate education, and advancement at work.

Third, research institutions introduce: (1) scientific-research potential satisfying rigorous international standards, (2) part of all physical resources (facility, equipment), (3) available IT support in research, and; (4) specialised administrative and technical support.

Fourth, executive government introduces: (1) administrative resources necessary for the support, and co-operation in research, and their implementation into products, and technologies, (2) part of the funds for the finance of researches and advancements, and only exceptional subsidising of the costs of the evaluation of the research results into technology and products, and (3) the system of accurate and transparent operating quality evaluation within the segments of research, education, and economic evaluation of the research results using various forms of public support.

4 Conclusion

Starting from the findings that the successful completion of (post) socialist transition and of process of preparation for European integration, it is necessary to realize the strategy of reindustrialization based on changes in the structure of production-organizational, business and institutional system with respect to national, regional, sub regional and local specificities. From the point of view of this necessity, clusterization and poles of generic growth are very promising mechanisms to start this process from a standstill, through the integration of research, university education and production within local, sub-regional, regional and national frameworks. To realise this, it is necessary that the public support and backing are concentrated on the aid which has already been the coordinated efforts of the research sector, university education, and production to achieve the excellence which promptly and directly results in technological improvement, competitiveness and production development within the real sector in the Republic of Serbia. The predominant significance is, to a low extent, of material i.e. economic nature, and to a high extent, of cultural nature (confidence, accuracy, giving high significance to the future), and they are determined mostly by the institutional system (in the function of restricting the power of distribution oriented coalitions, and neutralisation of corruption mechanisms within public regulations), and the situation of the knowledge of the national population.

References

Adžić S (2006a) Kako poboljšati izvozne performanse preduzeća u institucionalno neuređenom okruženju? In: Institucionalne promene kao determinanta privrednog razvoja Srbije. Ekonomski fakultet, Kragujevac, pp 118–131
Adžić S (2006b) Privredni sistem i ekonomska politika. Ekonomski fakultet, Subotica
Adžić S (2008) Reindustrijalizacija i konkurentnost: Kako iz postojećeg stanja? In: Kuda ide Srbija: Ostvarenja i dometi reformi. Naučno društvo ekonomista sa Akademijom ekonomskih nauka i Ekonomski fakultet Univerziteta u Beogradu, Beograd, pp 221–240
Adžić S (2013) The influence structuring production-organizational system on regional development – case of Serbia. In: Proceedings of second international scientific conference: regional development, spatial planning and strategic governance – RESPAG 2013. Belgrade, 22–25 May 2013. Institute of Architecture and Urban & Spatial Planning of Serbia, Belgrade, pp 309–322
Adžić S, Popović D (2005) Fiskalni sistem i fiskalna politika – njihov doprinos unapređenju konkurentnosti privrede: Slučaj Srbije. Ekonomija/Economics 1:173–200
Đuričin D (2008) Srbija na raskršću: Dostizanje EU ili tranzicionizam. In: Kopaonik biznis forum 2008 – Tranzicija, dostizanje EU i povezane teme. SES i Udruženje korporativnih direktora Srbije, Beograd, pp 9–38
Jakopin E, Bajec J (2009) Izazovi industrijskog razvoja Srbije: Makroekonomski kontekst. In: Kopaonik biznis forum 2009 – Rast u uslovima globalne recesije i finansijske krize; (Ne) konvencionalne inicijative. SES i Udruženje korporativnih direktora Srbije, Beograd, pp 77–98
Jovetić S, Stanišić N (2006) Poslovni klasteri u industriji kao savremeni model privrednog organizovanja u cilju povećanja nacionalnog inovacionog kapaciteta. In: Tehnologija, kultura i razvoj: Srbija i Crna Gora na putu prema Evropskoj Uniji. Udruženje "Tehnologija i društvo", Ekonomski fakultet Subotica i Institut "Mihajlo Pupin", Beograd, pp 127–138
Kastratović E, Marinković V (2008) Inovacije, klasteri, inovacioni klasteri. Ekonomski vidici 1:223–232
Madžar L (2008) Nedostajuće dimenzije u evaluaciji makroekonomskih performansi Republike Srbije. Ministarstvo finansija Republike Srbije, Beograd
Matejić V (2002) Prilozi istraživanju naučnog i tehnološkog razvoja. Savezni sekretarijat za nauku i razvoj, Beograd
Matejić V (2008) Razvoj Srbije zasnovan na znanju: Pomodna priča ili stvarnost. In: Zbornik radova: Tehnologija, kultura i razvoj 15. Udruženje "Tehnologija i društvo", Ekonomski fakultet Subotica i Institut "Mihajlo Pupin", Beograd, pp 32–40
Rachwał T (2011) Industrial restructuring in Poland and other European Union states in the era of economic globalization. Proced Soc Behav Sci 19:1–10
Study (2010) Postkrizni model ekonomskog rasta i razvoja Srbije 2011-2020 (Postcrisis model of economic growth and development in Serbia 2011-2020). www.fren.org.rs
Study (2011) Strategija i politika razvoja industrije Republike Srbije (Strategy and policy of industry development in Republic Serbia 2010-2020). Republički zavod za razvoj, Beograd
Wojtyna A, Hausner J (1993) Privatization as a restructuring device: can it substitute for industrial policy in the transforming economics? Some lessons from Poland. J Socioecon 22(4):417–443

Investigating Farmer's Perceptions of Adopting Alternative Farming Systems

Sotirios Papadopoulos, Eleni Zafeiriou, Christos Karelakis, and Theodoros Koutroumanidis

Abstract Organic and integrated agriculture are recently developed alternative farming systems aimed at controlling environmental impacts and assuring the quality of agricultural products. Here we aim to: (1) describe the characteristics of certified of organic and integrated farms; and (2) analyze the factors affecting the farmers' decision to implement either organic, integrated or conventional farming. The survey was based on a multinomial analysis applied to data obtained from a survey of farmers (structured questionnaire) in Greece. The findings confirmed that the decision to opt for one of three forms of agriculture was based on both the farms' characteristics and the farmer's attitudes.

Keywords Sustainable • Organic • Conventional agriculture • Farmers • Perceptions • Common agricultural policy

JEL Classification Codes Q10 • Q15 • Q18

1 Introduction

Conventional (intensive) agriculture, which has been predominant during the previous decades, has contributed to increased agricultural productivity and improved farmers' living standards (Tracy 1989). However, tendencies towards environment sustainability, socio-political pressures, market liberalization and repeated nutritional scandals are forcing modern agriculture to adjust its practices towards the production of safer and higher quality produce using environmentally friendly approaches (Reganold et al. 2001), including alternative production solutions, novel cultivating techniques and sustainable management (Parra López et al. 2007). Organic and integrated agricultural practices have been at the forefront of such efforts.

S. Papadopoulos (✉) • E. Zafeiriou • C. Karelakis • T. Koutroumanidis
Department of Agricultural Development, Democritus University of Thrace, Pantazidou 193, 68200 Orestiada, Greece
e-mail: sotpap23@gmail.com; ezafeir@agro.duth.gr; chkarel@agro.duth.gr; tkoutrou@agro.duth.gr

A. Karasavvoglou et al. (eds.), *The First Decade of Living with the Global Crisis*, Contributions to Economics, DOI 10.1007/978-3-319-24267-5_3

Although organic agriculture has been widely applied for several decades, its development has hastened since the 1980s; largely due to the negative consequences of conventional agriculture (e.g., poor product quality and environmental protection) (MacDonald et al. 2000; Stolton 2002). Today, organic agriculture is a viable system of agriculture that meets all of the criteria for sustainable environmental management (Padel et al. 2002).

However, the inability of organic agriculture to be successfully applied in all cultivations (without reducing yield or increasing production cost) has led to the development of integrated agriculture, an intermediate between conventional and organic agriculture (IOBC 2004). Thus, during the last 20 years, under pressure from large retail chains and finally with the support of the Common Agricultural Policy (CAP), the development and rapid evolution of integrated agriculture has begun (Wibberley 1995; Morris and Winter 1999).

Today, integrated agriculture is based on a combination of various management protocols that combine farm sustainability and realistic and financially effective approaches. These management approaches are principally orientated towards environmental protection and the production of quality agricultural products that satisfy market needs (IOBC 2004). From this broad range of existing protocols, most are recognized only in their country of origin, while few are recognized at European or international level. This diversity of standards/protocols often leads to commercial skirmish, during which farmers are asked to apply multiple certifications, resulting in increased production cost (Buzby and Mitchell 2006).

Although the European Union enforces a complete legislative framework and common logo for organic agriculture, no such official definition or integrated regulation yet exists for integrated agriculture. In addition, there is no single common European statistical database for integrated agriculture that is available to researchers and agricultural policy makers.

Here we Bearing in mind the aforementioned, the present paper aim to describe the characteristics of organic and integrated agriculture farmers and investigate the factors affecting their intention to apply these forms of agriculture. The next section describes the materials and methods used, while the third section describes the results of the employed analysis and the last section concludes.

2 Materials and Methods

2.1 Sample Selection

Primary data were gathered from six prefectures (Serres, Drama, Kavala, Xanthi, Rodopi and Evros) of the Makedonia and Thraki region of Greece. The research was conducted in 2012 and included farm leaders belonging to each of the three different forms of agriculture (conventional, organic and integrated) for the year in question.

According to the statistical data from the Ministry of Development and Food, the Payment and Control Agency for Guidance and Guarantee Community Aid

(OPEKEPE) and the Hellenic Agricultural Organization "Demeter" (formerly the National Agricultural Research Foundation), the selected geographical region includes a complete set of cultivation types under organic and conventional agriculture and covers a fifth of the total relevant farms in Greece. The studied regions include a total of 871 organic agriculture farms (totaling 6494 ha) and 27,234 integrated agriculture farms (totaling 97,035 ha). In total, the study includes 162,684 cultivation units encompassing 340,000 ha. Within this geographical unit we identified 8, 9 and 13 cultivated types under organic, integrated and cultivated management respectively. All of the organic and integrated cultivated types were represented within the conventional group.

For selection of the sample in each type of agriculture, a stratified random sampling for distribution (according to Neyman method) was applied (Yamane 1967; Siardos 2009). Simple random sampling was applied within each stratum; therefore, the final sample size was the sum of the samples of the partial strata. In this way, the required information from each stratum of the target population was ensured. Since stratification should be based on those variables that are expected to be directly connected to the basic variables of the research (Daoutopoulos 2011), a "stratum" was defined as the type of cultivation of each form of agriculture. Therefore, the sample size was defined by the relation:

$$n = \frac{\left(\sum N_h s_h\right)^2}{N^2 D^2 + \sum N_h s_h^2}$$

and its distribution in strata by the relation:

$$n_h = \frac{N_h s_h}{\sum N_h s_h} \cdot n$$

where D = the desired standard error given by $D = d/z$ [where d = the desired accuracy (equal to half of the confidence interval or subjects specified) and z = the reliability coefficient corresponding to a probability level]; s_h = the typical values deviation of farms size in each stratum, calculated according to data in farm population; N_h = the population of each stratum; and N = the total sample population.

2.2 Qualitative Research

A qualitative phase preceded the quantitative phase of research, during which the issue under examination was initially inspected (Creswell 1998). During the qualitative phase farmers were interviewed using a semi-structured questionnaire of 14 thematic units. A directed-sampling method was used to ensure richer information of high significance could be collected (Patton 1990). Thus, 42 farmers were chosen (equal to the 10 % of the quantitative analysis sample) and accepted to be interviewed by the researcher. These interviews were recorded.

2.3 Quantitative Research

During the subsequent quantitative phase a survey was conducted using a uniform questionnaire. The questionnaire was structured into three units and was based on internationally approved procedures and the relevant literature (Siardos 2009). The first unit included questions concerning both demographic and personal data of farm leaders (e.g., sex, age, family status, origin, schooling and education), as well as the farmers' relationships with organized groups and incorporation into subsidized programs. The second unit included the general characteristics of farms (e.g., form of exercised agriculture, disposal, certification type and subsidy type), its business gains, as well as issues concerning the methods and farmers' satisfaction with CAP updating. The third unit concerned questions that elicited opinions and positions of farmers towards the CAP and in particular towards those factors that affect the application of organic, integrated and conventional agriculture. Finally, information was collected regarding the farmers' intentions to be incorporated into a type of agriculture and to retain or abandon this approach.

2.4 Methodological Approach

2.4.1 Descriptive Analysis

We first applied a descriptive analysis (Siardos 2009) of the basic research variables to describe the most important characteristics of the farmers and each of the farms types. The aim was to score the frequencies in each category, producing frequency tables. For each x_i value of the X independent variable, this table presents the frequency of f_i appearance (i.e., how many times each discrete value appears in the sample). This approach was also used to calculate the relative frequency, namely the p_i percentage that is determined by the ratio of appearance frequency (f_i) of an x_i value to the total of n observations of the sample.

The examination of the relation among categorical variables was made through the Pearson's Chi-square (X^2) test, which is based on the comparison of frequencies observed in each category (observed frequencies) with frequencies theoretically expected to exist in these categories, asserted by the null hypothesis (expected frequencies).

$$X^2 = \sum_i \sum_j \frac{\left(\text{observed}_{ij} - \text{model}_{ij}\right)^2}{\text{model}_{ij}}$$

Where model_{ij} represents the expected frequencies provided by the relation:

$$\text{Model}_{ij} = \frac{\text{Row total}_i \times \text{column total}_j}{n}$$

and observed_{ij} represents the observed frequencies that actually appeared. In addition, the degrees of freedom are represented by the relation: $df = (\text{rows} - 1)\,(\text{columns} - 1)$

n = total observations (total counts)

The value for X^2 can then compared to a critical value for the X^2 distribution and the relative degrees of freedom. If the X^2 value is higher than the critical value then the relation among the variables is statistically significant. In addition, a Monte Carlo simulation technique was also applied to the descriptive data because of its greater accuracy and to confirm the Chi-square findings. The Monte Carlo simulation technique is advantageous because it does not require a large sample size to work efficiently (Dafermos 2011).

2.4.2 Multinomial Logistic Regression

Next, a multinomial analysis was applied to the sets of comparisons between of two categories. In the case of multinomial logistic regression, one category must be selected as the reference category. In the current project, conventional agriculture was selected as the reference category and compared to each of the alternative (organic and integrated) agricultures.

The general model of the multinomial regression is presented by the relation (1) (Agresti 2013)

$$\log \frac{\pi_j(x)}{\pi_k(x)} = \beta_0 + \beta_{1j}X_{1i} + \beta_{2j}X_{2i} + \ldots + \beta_{nj}X_{ni} \tag{1}$$

where $\pi_j(x)$ is the possibility $P(Y = j|x)$, that is the possibility for someone to select category j of the dependent variable ($j = 1, 2, \ldots, k$) with k being the category of reference. $X_{1i}, X_{2i}, \ldots, X_{ni}$ are the independent variables, which in this case can be both quantitative and qualitative.

3 Results

3.1 Personal Data Description

The majority (86.9 %) of the farmers were male. Among the 150 conventional agriculture farmers surveyed, 133 were male (88.7 %) and 17 were female (11.3 %). Of the 122 organic farmers questioned, 104 were male (85.2 %) and 18 were female (14.8 %). Among the 149 integrated agriculture farmers included in the study, 129 (86.6 %) were male and 20 (13.4 %) were women. Most of the farmers were aged between 35 and 55. A similar proportion of integrated and organic agriculture farmers fell within this age range (50 % and 51 % respectively), whereas this value was significantly higher (63.3 %) for conventional agriculture farmers. These findings are in line with previous research indicating that the majority of farmers are middle-aged (Theocharopoulos 2009).

Seventy-five percent of the farmers were married. Fourteen percent of conventional and integrated agriculture farmers were single, while this value was 19.7 % for organic farmers. Fifty-six percent of conventional agriculture farmers had two children, while this value was 45 % for organic and integrated agriculture farmers. Organic agriculture farmers had the largest percentage of children aged <18 years (35.2 %). Thirty-two percent of conventional agriculture farmers had both adult children and children below 18 years-old, while 34.9 % of integrated agriculture farmers had adult children.

Almost all farmers in the sample gained some form of secondary education. Most conventional agriculture farmers (50.7 %) were high school graduates. Twenty percent of integrated agriculture farmers were elementary school graduates, with farmers being equally distributed across education levels within this farming type. Three (2.4 %) of the organic farmers were graduates of higher education. None of the conventional agriculture farmers had attended a relevant training seminar, whereas almost a third of the farmers applying either integrated or organic agriculture had attended a relevant training seminar.

Almost all conventional agriculture farmers were from a rural family, while 13 % of the farmers practicing an alternative agriculture approach (organic or integrated) did not come from a rural family. Twice as many organic farmers were new farmers (i.e., <5 years of agriculture experience) than for conventional agriculture farmers, which is consistent with our finding that organic farmers tended to be younger than the other types of farmers. However, most farmers (regardless of agriculture type) had between 11 and 25 years of agricultural experience. A relatively high percentage of integrated agriculture farmers (28.9 %) had >25 years of experience.

The majority of conventional and organic agriculture farmers (92 %) declared farming as their main profession, while this percentage drops to 82.6 % for integrated agriculture farmers. Almost 90 % of the organic and integrated agriculture farmers had an additional income outside of farming that accounted for ≤35 % of their total earnings, indicating that agriculture represents their main source of income. Whereas a third of integrated agriculture farmers declared an income outside of agricultural activities that accounted for >35 % of their total income, which likely indicates that agriculture was not their primary occupation.

Half of the conventional agriculture farmers declared that they took up the family agricultural business. In addition, 30 % of conventional agriculture farmers concluded that agriculture was their only available career option. While this value is 45 % and 39.3 % for integrated and organic agriculture farmers respectively. It is noteworthy that 18 % of organic agriculture farmers declared that organic agriculture represented their *way of live*, which was significantly higher than for the other farming types, especially from integrated agriculture farmers where only 3.4 % belonged to this category.

Interestingly, all organic agriculture farmers were individual farmers that did not participate in farmers' groups. This finding is a direct result of the management of the Organic Agriculture Project by the Ministry of Agricultural Development and Food, in which all farmers must be incorporated as individuals (rather than as groups). The opposite was observed for integrated agriculture farmers, where 100 % of the participants were part of an organized farmers' group. This is because of the availability of a financial support program for integrated agriculture farmers that enables the application of integrated management systems to members' farms. Sixty-four percent of conventional agriculture farmers reported currently belonging to a farmers group, while the remaining 37 % had previously belonged to a farmers group.

Almost half of the conventional agriculture farmers that were previously practicing integrated management were unaware of the fact that their certification played an important part in their incorporation into a subsidy program (e.g., Measure 1.2.1-Modernisation of Farms) and thus had not been taking full advantage of their certificate. A quarter of the integrated agriculture farmers declared ignorance on the same subject. In contrast, all organic agriculture farmers knew that certification of organic products was a prerequisite for their admission into subsidy programs (e.g., the "quality retention" granted to organic or integrated olive oil farmers on the island of Thasos).

We found that all conventional and organic agriculture farmers were distributing their products individually (since they did not belong to any farmers group). Whereas half of the integrated agriculture farmers distributed their products through the farmers groups; those integrated farmers that did not belong to the farmers groups were distributing their products individually.

3.2 Description of Typical Farms

We first analyzed the type of agriculture applied to farms immediately prior to their current status. We found that 84 % of the sample farms were exclusively applying conventional agriculture. The remaining 16 % has mostly abandoned conventional agriculture for either organic or integrated agriculture (Fig. 1).

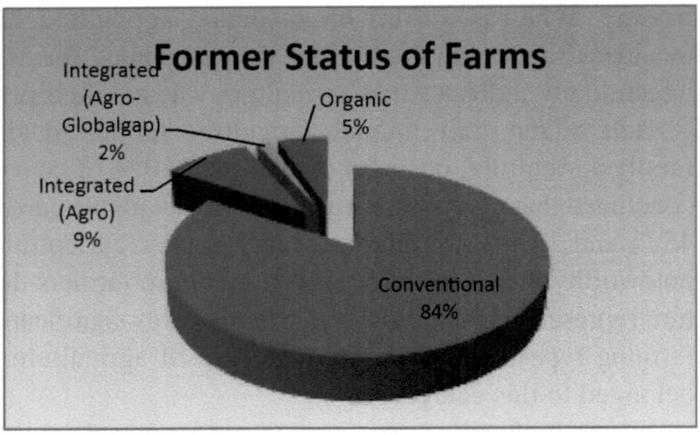

Fig. 1 Former status of form of agriculture for farms

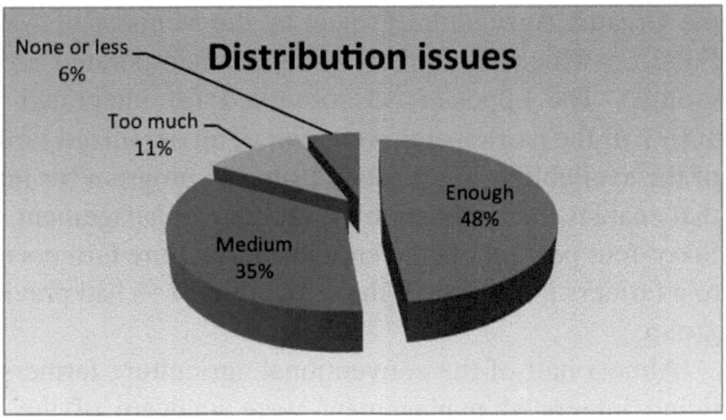

Fig. 2 Agricultural product distribution issues

Regarding the product distribution issues facing the farmers, we found that more than half of the questioned farmers indicated that that they had either moderate or severe issues concerning the distribution of their products. Only 6 % replied that they had no issues concerning the distribution of their products. The remaining 35 % indicated that they had mild issues on the distribution of their products. Conventional and integrated agriculture farmers typically experience moderate to severe issues with distribution, whereas distribution was typically less problematic for organic farmers (Fig. 2).

It is noteworthy that most of the certified organic and integrated agriculture farmers sold their products as conventional, while a negligible proportion of conventional products were distributed as certified. This raises the question of why farmers would go to the trouble of certifying their products if they did not intend to distribute them as certified.

The requirement to pay for certification of agricultural products separates the alternative and conventional forms of agriculture. In the current sample, all integrated agriculture farmers declared that only the farmers' group to which they belonged was subsidized (i.e., not the farmers themselves). Whereas the opposite was true for organic farmers. One third of the conventional agriculture farmers had been previously subsidized through an integrated certification scheme. For these farmers the withdrawal reasons from integrated management included non-satisfactory subsidy, completion of the program and non-announcement of a new incorporation program. Failure to achievement the desired selling price and the certification not being recognized by the European markets were also cited as important withdrawal factors.

The majority of conventional agriculture farmers were either not satisfied or only a little satisfied by the amount of subsidy they had previously received for certifying their products. The majority of integrated agriculture farmers were either a little and moderately satisfied by the amount of subsidy they received, while most of the organic farmers were a little or not at all satisfied. The subsidies covered almost all of the certification cost for integrated agriculture, while in organic agriculture the subsidy was inferior to the cost, since organic agriculture farmers also included a reduced efficiency per 1000 m^2. In all three forms of agriculture, most of the farmers believed that the subsidy did not affect or only slightly affected the final price of their certified products.

3.3 Factors Affecting Application of Every Form of Agriculture

A multinomial analysis was performed to identify those factors affecting the farmers' choice of agriculture-type (i.e., conventional, organic or, integrated) and the results are shown in Table 1. In the first half of Table 1 a comparison is made between integrated and conventional agriculture. The lower half of the table compares organic and conventional agriculture. The following variables were found to significantly affect the application of either organic or integrated agriculture.

3.3.1 Integrated Versus Conventional Agriculture

The farmers' opinion regarding the future of agriculture contributes to their selection of either integrated or conventional agriculture. In particular, those who believe that organic agriculture will be most applied in the future are more likely to select integrated (rather than conventional) agriculture. Those who believe that integrated agriculture will be the dominant future agriculture were more likely to select integrated (over conventional) agriculture.

Furthermore, the income percentage outside rural activities of individuals was also identified as an important contributor to the selection of integrated (over conventional) agriculture. In particular, farmers whose income percentage from non-rural activities was <25 % were less likely to select integrated (over conventional) agriculture. On the contrary, when agriculture was not the main source of income, the farmers were more likely to select integrated (over conventional)

Table 1 Factors affecting farmers' choice of agriculture-type—multinomial analysis results

Type of agriculture		B	(SE)	Exp(B)	95 % CI for Exp(B)	
					Lower bound	Upper bound
Integrated	Intercept	−1.461	(1.440)			
	[80 = Organic]	2.395	(0.686)**	10.973	2.860	42.093
	[80 = Integrated]	3.095	(0.540)**	22.092	7.661	63.707
	[13 = <25 %]	−3.403	(1.292)**	0.033	0.003	0.419
	[9 = YES]	1.766	(0.665)**	5.849	1.588	21.546
	[2 = <35]	−0.707	(0.683)	0.493	0.129	1.882
	[2 = 36–55]	−1.237	(0.575)*	0.290	0.094	0.897
	[4 = Town-Small town]	−1.424	(0.511)**	0.241	0.088	0.655
	[12 = YES]	2.410	(1.410)	11.137	0.702	176.660
	[40 = Not at all-A little satisfied]	0.792	(1.022)	2.208	0.298	16.356
	[40 = Average satisfaction]	0.490	(0.942)	1.633	0.258	10.349
	[40 = Enough]	2.255	(0.875)*	9.538	1.716	53.024
Organic	Intercept	−28.203	(2667.79)			
	[13 = <25 %]	0.946	(1.759)	2.576	0.082	81.013
	[9 = YES]	3.288	(1.205)**	26.793	2.526	284.168
	[2 = <35]	3.646	(1.555)*	38.338	1.820	807.397
	[2 = 36–55]	−0.223	(0.976)	0.800	0.118	5.414
	[4 = Town-Small town]	0.409	(0.663)	1.506	0.410	5.525
	[12 = YES]	−0.608	(1.995)	0.545	0.011	27.166
	[40 = Not at all-A little satisfied]	5.772	(1.677)**	321.092	11.989	8599.750
	[40 = Average satisfaction]	6.464	(1.751)**	641.489	20.734	19,846.894
	[40 = Enough]	5.263	(1.518)**	193.052	9.845	3785.557

agriculture. In addition, farmers that had attended a training seminar were more likely to select integrated (over conventional) agriculture.

Farmer age was also identified as an important contributing factor. Farmers between 36 and 55 years-old were less likely to select integrated (over conventional) agriculture, compared to an individual >55 years-old. Whereas the farmers aged >55 years preferred integrated agriculture. Place of residence also contributed to the farmers' selection; those farmers residing in a town or a small town were more likely to be involved in conventional agriculture than integrated agriculture. Whereas those farmers residing in the village preferred integrated to conventional agriculture. Finally, the farmers' satisfaction with the CAP updates also contributes to their agriculture-type selection; farmers that were quite satisfied about their awareness of CAP were more likely to select integrated than conventional agriculture, compared to those farmer that were very satisfied.

3.3.2 Organic Versus Conventional Agriculture

Attendance at a training seminar was found to contribute to the farmers' selection of organic versus conventional agriculture; farmers that had attended a training seminar were more likely to be involved in organic (rather than conventional) agriculture. Also, farmers <35 years-old were more likely to choose organic (versus conventional) agriculture, as compared to farmers >55 years-old. Finally, the farmers' satisfaction about their awareness of CAP contributes to their selection of organic versus conventional agriculture; farmers that were quite satisfied about their awareness of CAP were more likely to selects organic agriculture. Whereas the farmers that were not at all or only a little satisfied about their awareness of CAP were more likely to select organic agriculture.

4 Discussion

Our data indicate that organic agriculture is mostly limited to non-demanding cultivations (e.g., Lucerne, wheat and olives) of low inputs. The yearly fluctuations observed in the proportion of organic agriculture were due to the increase/decrease of the hectares available for these cultivations. Therefore, the amount of organic agriculture subsidy is not capable of attracting demanding cultivations of greater potential and high inputs. On the contrary, integrated agriculture is capable of including more types of agriculture without limitations, according to types of cultivation managed by the farmers' organization to which the farmers belong. Therefore, the form of agriculture applied by a farmer seems to be fully dependent upon his/her participation in a recognized farmers' organization. Although the sampled farmers are mostly middle-aged, we found that organic farmers tended to be younger than integrated and conventional farmers. This finding suggests a potential for age renewal in organic farming and is therefore an encouraging sign for the future of organic agriculture.

Given that ~60 % of the integrated and organic certified farmers in our sample had never attended a relevant training seminar, this suggests that the CAP is ineffective at affecting the application of alternative forms of agriculture; according to Ferto and Forgacs (2009), education is a principal variable of CAP for affecting these forms of agriculture.

The majority of the participating farmers were professionally involved in agriculture, with the exception of the ones involved in integrated agriculture, in which a significant percentage was involved in integrated management as a secondary source of income, which is in contrast with the findings of Theocharopoulos (2009). A partial abandonment of integrated agriculture (according to Agro

2.1–2.2) and return to conventional agriculture was also observed, demonstrating that the current subsidy policy is insufficient for encouraging farmers to maintain their involvement in the certification scheme. Interestingly, almost half of the integrated agriculture farmers were unaware of (and therefore failed to take advantage of) the financial benefits provided by agricultural policy.

Based on our findings, we conclude that integrated agriculture farmers believe that the future of agriculture should be primarily integrated, with a secondary contribution from organic farming. In addition, those farmers that are involved in rural activities as a second source of income tend towards integrated agriculture. Furthermore, we found that education (as a purely non-financial factor) is capable of leading farmers to take up alternative forms of agriculture. Logistic regression analysis indicated that young organic farmers (<35 years-old) indirectly pointing out that the interest of the young people about food safety and environmental protection is in accordance with organic agriculture. Whereas the farmers aged >55 had a preference for integrated agriculture, which was purely based on the level of subsidy available.

5 Conclusion

Here we aimed to describe the characteristics of Greek organic and integrated agricultural farmers and to identify the factors affecting their intention to apply these forms of agriculture. We found that farmers' opinions about the future of agriculture play an important role in selecting a specific form of agriculture. Additional factors influencing the farmers' choice of agriculture type include age, education and training, level of subsidy and whether farming is a premium or secondary source of income. To our knowledge, no other study has addressed the impact of the CAP on the implementation of alternative agriculture forms. As such, our findings should be useful for both agricultural policy makers and researchers.

References

Agresti A (2013) Categorical data analysis, 3rd edn. Wiley, New York

Buzby JC, Mitchell L (2006) Private, national and international food-safety standards. USDA Economic Research Service, Washington, DC

Creswell JW (1998) Qualitative inquiry and research design: choosing among five traditions. Sage, London

Dafermos B (2011) Social statistics and research methods with SPSS. Ziti Publications, Thessaloniki

Daoutopoulos GA (2011) Methods of social research, ΣΤ' Έκδοση. Zigos Publishing, Thessaloniki

IOBC (2004) Integrated production: principles and technical guidelines, 3rd edn. Commission "IP_Guidelines and Endorsement". IOBC-WPRS Bull 16(1). Διαθέσιμο στο http://www.iobc-wprs.org/ip_ipm/

Ferto I, Forgacs C (2009) The choice between conventional and organic farming—a Hungarian example. In: 113th EAAE seminar. Belgrade, Republic of Serbia, 9–11 December 2009

MacDonald D, Crabtree JR, Wiesinger G, Dax T, Stamou N, Fleury P, Gutierrez Lazpita J, Gibon A (2000) Agricultural abandonment in mountain areas of Europe: environmental consequences and policy response. J Environ Manag 59:47–69

Morris C, Winter M (1999) Integrated farming systems: the third way for European agriculture? Land Use Policy 16(4):193–205

Padel S, Lampkin N, Dabbert S, Foster C (2002) Organic farming policy in the European Union. Adv Econ Environ Resour 4:169–194

Parra López C, De Haro Giménez T, Calatrava Requena J (2007) Diffusion and adoption of organic farming in the southern Spanish olive groves. J Sustain Agric 30(1):105–151

Patton MQ (1990) Qualitative evaluation methods, 2nd edn. Sage, Thousand Oaks, CA

Reganold JP, Glover JD, Andrews PK, Hinman HR (2001) Sustainability of three apple production systems. Nature 410:929–930

Siardos GK (2009) Μεθοδολογία Κοινωνιολογικής Έρευνας. Εκδόσεις Ζήτη

Stolton S (2002) Organic agriculture and biodiversity. Approved by the IFOAM World Board. Dossier 2, IFOAM-Growing Organic Programme, Netherlands. Διαθέσιμο http://www.ifoam.org

Theocharopoulos A (2009) Economic and environmental analysis of alternative forms of agriculture. PhD Thesis, Department of Agricultural Economics, School of Agriculture, Aristotle University of Thessaloniki

Tracy M (1989) Government and agriculture in Europe 1880–1988 in Western Europe. Harvester Wheatsheaf, London, 382 pp

Wibberley J (1995) Cropping intensity and farming systems: integrity and intensity in international perspective. J R Agric Soc Engl 156:43–55

Yamane T (1967) Statistics: an introductory analysis, 2nd edn. Harper and Row, New York, NY

The Impact of Migration on Albanian Agriculture: A Snapshot

Matteo Belletti and Elvira Leksinaj

Abstract This study aims to identify the relation between migration and agriculture in Albania. After more than 20 years of free trade, migrant worker remittances remain a vital voice in Albanian national economic wealth. At the same time, the agricultural sector seems to have remained frozen in time: a farming system derived from the land reform of 1991 that is still characterized by smallholdings oriented to auto-consumption with some very informal trade connections to the local food markets. Moreover, a substantial proportion of the Albanian population still lives in rural areas and still works in agriculture. On this premise, it is not surprising that the majority of remittances from abroad go to the rural population and it is acceptable to assume that the remittances absorbed by the rural population may have been partly used to overcome the lack of policy support and to provide agriculture with the minimum input of capital needed to fund some connection to the market.

However, with regard to this assumption, recent studies suggest that this is not the case. These studies claim that the increase in the total rural income in Albania from the transition to the first decade in the twenty-first century is probably due to the direct effect of the remittances instead of to any investment of remittances in agricultural productivity. Moreover, these studies infer that remittances directed to the rural population in many cases are used by the households "to escape" from agriculture rather than to improve agricultural income. Hence, with respect to these papers, the present is a confirmatory study designed to further explore the relation between remittances from abroad and agricultural income generation in Albania. We rely on an up-to-date review of the most recent research conclusions on the impact of international migration on Albanian farming system to better comprehend the lack of progress in the post-transition Albanian agricultural economy, the migration process being a potential shock element to a labor-intensive rural economy as a whole. Qualitatively, the present study guaranties greater statistical power with respect to the previously mentioned research. This improvement can be attributed to the use of a highly disaggregated and a more recent probability

---

M. Belletti (✉)
The Polytechnic University of Marche, Ancona, Italy
e-mail: m.belletti@univpm.it

E. Leksinaj
The Agricultural University of Tirana, Tirana, Albania
e-mail: eli_leksinaj@yahoo.com

A. Karasavvoglou et al. (eds.), *The First Decade of Living with the Global Crisis*,
Contributions to Economics, DOI 10.1007/978-3-319-24267-5_4

sample that is representative of the Albanian farm population. The inferential analysis is carried out in R.

Keywords Agricultural economy • Farm household • Incentives • Migration • Rural culture • Trans-locality

JEL Classification Codes Q12 • Q13 • R23

1 Introduction

In analysing the relationship between migration remittances and the agricultural economy, in contrast to what was affirmed by previous studies, this paper suggests that migration remittances are not necessarily used by rural households in Albania as part of a strategy to move out of agriculture, but rather rural migration influences the Albanian agricultural economy, not in general as a consequence of some kind of cause and effect at a motivational level, but rather according to the economic dimension of the farm households. The migration process is a determining factor of workforce decline at farm level, regardless of the presence-absence and magnitude of migrant worker remittances.

Furthermore, this paper will clarify how the verified dual economic behavior referring to the presence-absence of migrants at farm household level can be used as a hidden indicator of the main structural pattern characterizing agriculture in Albania: peasant farms oriented to auto-consumption where technical and economic efficiency is achieved through labor-intensive farming rather than the substitution of labor with capital in a time saving fashion (Ellis 2003).

Two papers (McCarthy et al. 2006; Miluka et al. 2010) perhaps constitute the only background on the topic in Albania and consequently the central comparative basis to which we refer. Our main criticisms of these works are:

- **At the database level**: the probability data samplings utilised are random but they were not extracted from the Albanian farm population. As a consequence, referring to the relation between migration and agriculture, we claim that they are biased and not representative of Albanian agriculture;
- **At the approach level**: we claim that the methodology used—applied migration instruments—creates an additional bias relative to the farm household sampling distribution. Moreover the necessity to rely on instruments highlights problems such as variable omission, endogeneity and the inadequacy to describe such a complex socioeconomic scenario using a linear regression model;
- **At the interpretation level**: these studies maybe wrongly attribute a general effect on farm behaviour to migration, without any reference to the structure and the stratified economic dimension of the farm sampled, thereby confounding causal factors, which results in contradictory, unclear, stereotyped conclusions on the matter.

Additionally, we report here below the main conclusions of these two papers constituting our reference point in the study. In bold type, a synthetic comment to these conclusions, as anticipation on our findings, is proposed:

- Migration of one or more household members is being used by rural households in Albania as part of a strategy to move out of agriculture. **False**;
- The impact of family labor is *unequivocal*: members of households with migrants abroad work significantly fewer hours in agricultural production, both in total and on a per capita-basis. **Partly true**;
- Expansion of leisure hours by remaining members as a result of migration abroad by household members, as a consequence of remittances. **False**;
- Women in migrant households work proportionately more than men, when compared with their counterparts in non-migrant households. **False**;
- Migration has no impact on the farm's technical efficiency and migrant households actually appear to invest less in productivity-enhancing and time-saving farm technologies in crop production. **We verified that this is not the case**;
- Credit and insurance markets are either underdeveloped or entirely absent. **Our previous studies on microcredit suggest that this is not true** (Belletti and Leksinaj 2012);
- Migrant households are shifting their on farm investment from crop to livestock production. These findings, together with the reduction in work effort in agriculture, particularly by males, can be interpreted as evidence of divestment behaviour by migrant households out of agriculture and into livestock. **In the present study, the opposite scenario seems to emerge**.

2 Materials and Methods

To develop the analysis we utilized an Area Probability Sample of 909 observations—farms—representative of the Albanian farm population. The data sample is deliverable of the cooperation between the Albanian Ministry of Agriculture, Food and Consumer Protection (MAFCP) and the National Agricultural Statistical Services (NASS) of The United States of America (Cela and Volk 2009). The sample is a snapshot of Albanian agriculture in 2009 and it is the most recent and complete picture available on the structure and economy of the primary sector in Albania. In this paper, all monetary values are expressed not in Lek—the Albanian national currency—but in Euro in order to simplify the understanding of the results. The exchange rate considered is rounded to the average in 2009:

$$Lek/Eur = 140$$

The key variable considered in the study is the agricultural income at farm level (FI), derived as total revenue (TR) minus total costs (TC):

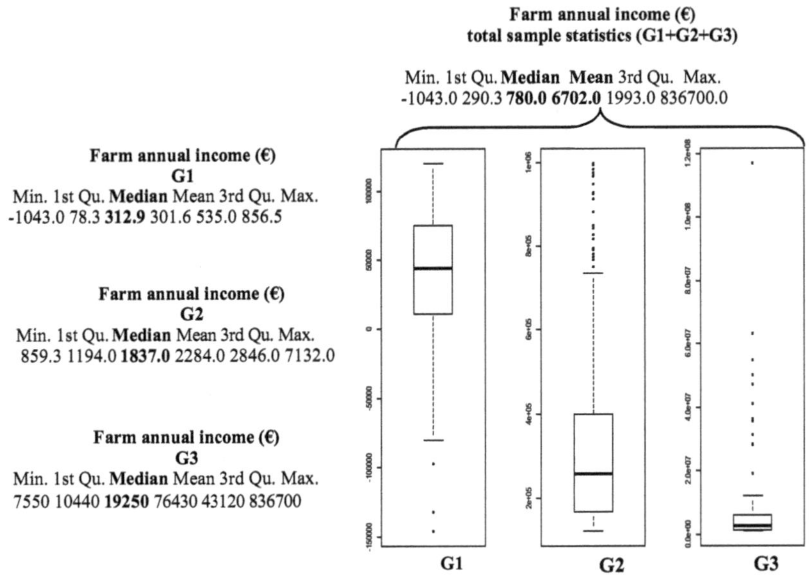

Fig. 1 Summary of the sample statistics. *Source*: Elaboration on MAFCP database, R output

$$FI = TR - TC$$

The FI total sample distribution was particularly right skewed—note in Fig. 1, median 780 €, mean 6702 €—so **in the first stage** we decided to subset the sample population with respect to FI to reduce the skewedness without losing information. In this regard, Fig. 1 summarises the sample statistics highlighting the skewedness of farm income distribution and illustrating the FI distribution level within G1-G2-G3. Note the IQR refers to the whole sample as an indicator of the population condensation around a very small income level.

Within the subsets obtained, the FI distribution skewedness has been reduced but it persists (Fig. 1) so **in the second stage** we decided to confront medians instead of means. Here is the result of the key analytical stage, the partition on the data sample referring to FI in three subsets: group1 (G1), group2 (G2) and group3 (G3). Two farm income thresholds—a lower bound (LBT) and an upper bound threshold (UBT)—represent the two subsetting reference points (Fig. 2). As reference points on the value of money in Albania, consider that the Albanian monthly minimum wage is around 150 € and the Albanian GDP per capita in 2009 was around 2750 € (Gjeci et al. 2013). In addition, based on the information reported by Germenji and Swinnen (2007), consider that the Albanian monthly wage in the rural areas is hypothesised to be in the range of 30–70 €.

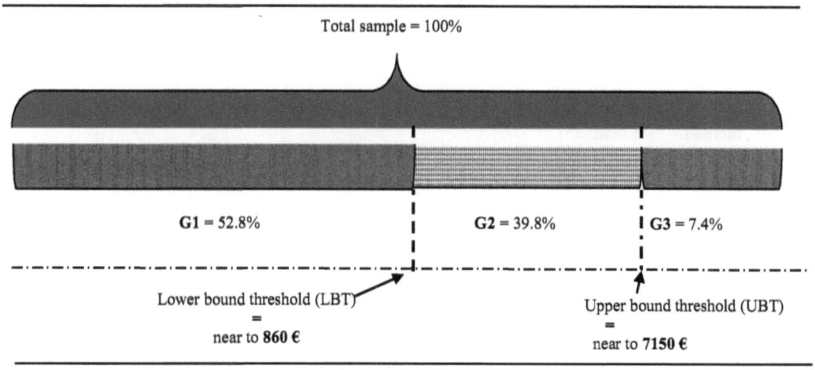

Fig. 2 The key partition on the data sample referring to FI. *Source*: Inference on MAFCP database

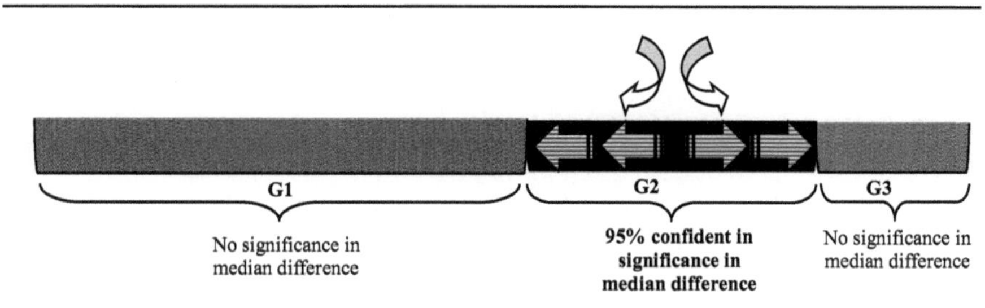

Fig. 3 Subset identification method. *Source*: Inference on MAFCP database

However, how was this partition identified? Why was the sample divided exactly in these three subsets identifying these specific farm income thresholds? This specific partition was defined by exploring our main research question, which is:

- Is the FI—both at a statistical and at practical level—significantly different in the presence-absence of migrants and consequently with respect to the presence-absence of a flow of remittances directed from abroad toward the Albanian rural society?

The answer to this, key, question is represented in Fig. 3. G2 has been obtained by stretching the fascia to the left and to the right as much as possible without sacrificing the 95 % significance in the median difference in farm income generation with and without migrants at a household level. Therefore, with respect to G2 we are 95 % confident in rejecting the hypothesis of no difference in median (bootstrap) between farm household with and without migrants.

In Fig. 4, the output in R on the median difference in G2 is represented; recall that G2 includes nearly 40 % of the farms in the whole sample. The simulation test verifies that the FI is greater in those farm households that do not have family members living and working abroad. Specifically, within G2, the annual FI median

inference(y = fromsixtonine$CM/140, x = fromsixtonine$emigrants, est = "median", type = "ht", null = 0, alternative = "twosided", method = "simulation")

Response variable: numerical, Explanatory variable: categorical

Difference between two medians

Summary statistics:

n_no = 238, median_no = 1935.857, n_yes = 124, median_yes = 1637.571, Observed difference between medians (no-yes) = 298.2857

H0: median_no - median_yes = 0

HA: median_no - median_yes != 0

p-value = 0.052

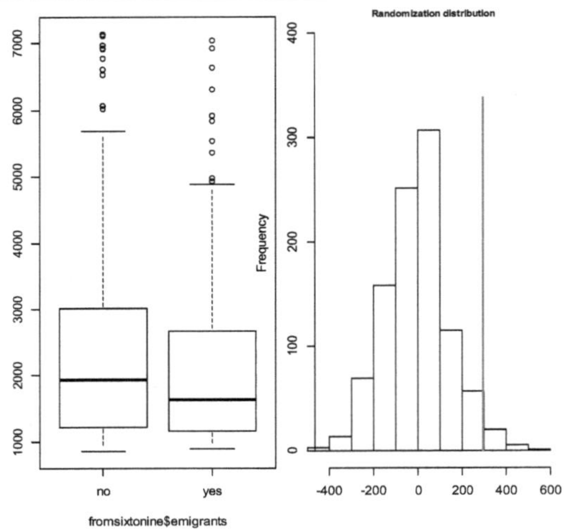

Fig. 4 FI bootstrap median difference in G2 with respect to the presence/absence (yes/no) of migrants. *Source*: Inference on MAFCP database, R output

in those households without migrants is around 1900 € versus a FI around 1600 € in those families experiencing migration. Thus, with a significance of 95 % we can reject the null hypothesis; i.e. the FI median is around 300 € greater—in this respect remember that the Albanian monthly minimum wage is around 150 €, so we could assert that the difference is both statistically and practically significant—in those farms that are not experiencing a concrete loss of workforce due to migration at family level. Hence, in contrast to the previous studies, the empirical evidence suggests that the impact of migrant worker remittances cannot be generalized, but rather considering a specific farm income partition is needed.

Now, having explained the dependent variable—FI, quantitative—as a function of the explanatory variable—presence-absence migrants, categorical—**in the third stage** of the analysis we tested other variables of interest with respect to the same explanatory variable, taking into account the sub setting previously performed with respect to FI, the latter being a key component to the interpretation of the full picture.

Thereafter, we executed a comparison in the bootstrap median distribution—again we decided to simulate with respect to the median because of the skewedness of the sample distribution with respect to the variables considered—distribution referring to the variables of interest—workforce, labor productivity, decision making in production, incentives, motivations and gender concerns—with the aim of answering the following questions:

- Is the per capita, at a family level, labor supply significantly different in the presence-absence of migrants?
- Does migration have an impact on the Albanian farm's technical efficiency?

- Do migrant households actually appear to invest less in productivity-enhancing and time-saving farm technologies in crop production (Rozelle et al. 1999)?
- Are migrant households shifting their on farm investment from crop to livestock production?
- Is the expansion of leisure hours by the remaining members in households with migrants a consequence of remittances?
- Do women in migrant households work proportionately more than men, when compared with their counterparts in non-migrant households (Mendola 2012)?

The overall picture on the relation between migration and agriculture in Albania, emerging from the synthesis of the three research stages previously described, is presented in the next section.

3 Results

At an *income generation* level, in contrast to the previous studies (McCarthy et al. 2006; Miluka et al. 2010), the relationship between emigration and the faming economy has been verified and the empirical evidence suggests that the impact of migrant worker remittances cannot be generalized, but rather consideration of a definite farm income partition is needed. Indeed, two income thresholds have been identified. A LBT and a UBT which cover two different farm economic behaviors related to the presence-absence of migration. Within this space, the total farm income level increases from left to right.

In the first partition, G1, starting from the farthest left up to the lower bound threshold, around 52.8 % of the data sample farms are identified. Within this group there is no a difference on average in the income generation between farms households with and without migrants.

Between the lower and the upper bound thresholds, G2, around 39.8 % of the data sample farms are identified. In this fascia, the income generation is statistically significantly higher on average in farms without emigrants than in farms with emigrants.

Beyond the upper bound threshold, G3, around 7.4 % of the data sample farms are identified. As in the case of G1, within this group there is no difference on average in the income generation between farms households with and without migrants.

G1 represents those farms that we define as strictly oriented to auto-consumption due to their very small economic dimension. Within this group the average income between farms with and without migration is not significant. And, the fact that migration—a net loss in the work force from the point of view of the production unit—does not influence the income generation is attributed to the presence of hidden unemployment (Carletto et al. 2004) that works as a compensation force with respect to the loss of workers.

In G2, the "bulk" of hidden unemployment at farm household level is assumed to no longer exist. And, consistently with this hypothesis, we observe the capacity to create a higher income, on average, on the farms without migrants.

In the third farm group, we identify the greatest, and probably most capitalized and market oriented, farms in Albania. In this scenario the same concept of remittances from abroad could be challenged as not appropriate to this specific empirical contest, because we are no longer speaking about *peasant households* (Ellis 2003).

At a *farm family labor* level, up to the upper bound threshold (G1 + G2) there is a significant difference (95 %) in labor use, both in total and on a per hectare basis, as a function of the presence-absence of migration from the farm households. This is obviously the consequence of the family member's departure. Nevertheless, no differences in labor use on per family member basis have been revealed. The per capita labor effort does not decrease in the presence of migration. In addition, beyond the upper bound threshold (in G3) no difference in labor utilization is reveled between with and without migrant presence. This is straightforward because G3 identifies the greater and probably most capitalized and market oriented farms—the typical industrial farm—in Albania. In G3 production is not labor-intensive and consequently the impact of workforce loss disappears.

At a *production orientation* level, there is no empirical evidence of the prevalence of livestock on those farms experiencing migration. On the contrary, the farms with emigrants up to the upper bound threshold produce and auto-consume cereals almost twice as much—99 % significance—as those without emigrants. The relocation of production from the cultivation of cereals towards livestock is not a peculiarity of emigrant households but rather it represents a general change in agriculture in Albania occurring over the transition period. The period of transformation toward livestock could be explained if one considers that livestock provides greater food availability to the peasant farm household, oriented towards self-consumption, due to its short cycles compared to the longer cycles of cereal production (Macours and Swinnen 2008; Belletti and Leksinaj 2011), rather than any relevance to migration.

At a *gender* level, we did not detect empirical evidence in support of the prevalence of female work effort on those farm households affected by migration (Katz 2003).

At a *technical* level, the significance of labor substitution (0.42 vs. 0.20 ha) with mechanized tillage in families affected by emigration in comparison with farms households without migration was verified. This is true up to the upper bound income threshold (G1 + G2, 99 % significance). Moreover, the median farm size—referring to the agricultural utilized area (AUA)—is significantly greater (1.38 vs. 0.83 ha) in the case of households with migration (G1 + G2, 99 % significance). These statistics suggest that remittances might attribute to the increase in land size and mechanization rather than fleeing the countryside.

Nevertheless, as previously pointed out, within G1 no significant difference at income level was determined, while in G2 the farms without emigrants generate a higher income on average, both in total and per family member basis, although they are significantly smaller and less mechanized than those with emigrant members, indicating improved technical and economic efficiency with respect to the "greater" and "more mechanized" farms experiencing migration. This statement might seem equivocal but it is not. In fact, given the very limited farm size in absolute terms, the relative gain in mechanization and farm size experienced in G2 by the farms with emigrants cannot necessarily offset their loss in family labor force in terms of productivity. This is because of the lack of a "critical mass" sufficient to trigger a return to scale dynamics.

Nevertheless, in this regard it is important to highlight how the division between productive and non-productive use of remittances is increasingly viewed as a false dichotomy (Gedeshi et al. 2003; Nicholson 2004). A tractor or a piece of land, for instance, can be considered both as a form of productive investment and as a form of capital investment. However, what really matters—from the point of view of the *trans-national families*—is maintaining the household as a whole. Moreover, it would be naive to discriminate, and therefore lucidly compare, given the many hidden *opportunity costs* considering the complexity of the family dynamics. In this regard, Vargas-Lundius et al. (2008) effectively define the concept of *Transnationalism* in relation to migration as follows:

> Constant and increasing movements of people across the globe are creating new forms of social arrangements and organizations and socially constructed self-identities. *Transnationalism* is a concept that is increasingly used to capture the nature of today's cross-border movements and their outcomes.

Beyond the upper bound threshold (G3), we identify the greatest and probably most capitalized and market oriented—the typical industrial farm—farms of Albania. The same concept of remittances from abroad could be challenged as inappropriate to the specific empirical contest, because we are no longer speaking of poor households.

4 Conclusions

In the post-transition Albanian rural dimension, the smallholding structure oriented to auto-consumption has been consolidated, relying on non-farm incomes rather than being weakened by the contribution of non-agricultural wages. We have to think about Albania as a *trans-local* society of excellence. In the realm of *trans-locality*, the dichotomy between "here" and "there", between rural and urban, between "at home" and "abroad" is systematically overloaded (Greiner and Sakdaporlak 2013).

In Albania, the main farming pattern is the orientation to auto-consumption due to the very small economic dimension of the production units. In this context, migration—a net loss in the workforce from the point of view of the production unit—does not influence the farm income generation due to the presence of hidden unemployment that works as a force compensation with respect to the loss of hands.

Beyond a determined threshold in the farm economic dimension, the "bulk" of hidden unemployment at farm household level is assumed to no longer exist and, consequently, we observe the capacity to create a higher income on the farms without migrants. To clarify this assumption we have to recall the main structural pattern characterizing agriculture in Albania: peasant farms oriented to auto-consumption where technical and economic efficiency is achieved through labor-intensive farming rather than the substitution of labor with capital in a time saving fashion.

Agriculture is embedded in the Albanian society. Imagining people eager to escape at the first opportunity, from a non-well identified condition of existential depression induced by agriculture, is wrong. Assuming a predisposition to laziness as soon as there is an opportunity, suggests a lack of knowledge of the Albanian lifestyle and their "*habit loop*" (Duhigg 2012) founded on trans-locality.

At a farm family labor level, the presence of migrants does not induce a growth in leisure time for the remaining members as a consequence of remittances. The statistical significance on differences in farm performance relating to the presence-absence of migrants at a household level is due to the impact of migration on the family workforce availability rather than to a hypothetically remittance driven decline in work motivation at household farm level. Furthermore, it is assumed that the lower the starting income, the smaller the *marginal opportunity cost* of spending 1 hour working will be. This is indirectly supported by Germenji and Swinnen (2007). Indeed, these authors affirm that, despite the fact that migrants do not come from the poorest rural households, the farm households with migrants are generally poorer than compared to those without relatives abroad. More specifically, the households with migrants are more likely to be involved only in agriculture (80.5 % vs. 65.4 % for non-migrant households), have less wage labor (11.9 % vs. 22.7 %) and fewer non-farming businesses (9.9 % vs. 15.8 %).

More generally, within a *trans-local approach* to issues such as migration (external or internal) and remittances, it is not surprising to note that the contribution of migrants to their own household income does not create any form of *moral hazard* at a *family habit* level. In the framework of trans-locality, migration does not mean dependency and subsidy but rather participating in the family wellbeing in a deterritorialised socio-spatial manner. King et al. (2006) report, in a suggestive style, on the meaning of family as a basic value in rural Albania. Here a quote from the above mentioned article, is an extract from an interview of a middle-aged man from a village near Kukes in the northeast highlands:

> Look, you have to understand something. The mentality here is very different from the one in the developed world you live in, because an immigrant, even if he earns money with great sacrifice, has to look back to his family and its most important needs... which are, firstly, the house, the living conditions... then marriages, funerals and stuff like that. Not only the members of a family must take responsibility, but all relatives are responsible and must help each other, uncles, cousins, grandmothers, grandfathers, small children, they all are part of the same picture. Nobody helps you but your family.

Rural migration does not influence the Albanian agricultural economy generically and adversely, but rather according to the economic dimension of the farm households involved in the migration process as a determining factor of workforce decline at farm level, regardless of the presence-absence and the magnitude of migrant worker remittances.

The tendency to have greater and more mechanized farms in those families with emigrants suggests a systemic attempt to cooperate with the family of origin with a special consideration to, not against, the agricultural heritage. Nevertheless, the auto-consumption oriented Albanian farming seems to suffer the loss of hands relatively (Mendola 2012), despite the attempt to compensate with more land and mechanization. Therefore, once again, this is as a result of a technical and not a motivational reason.

Heuristic is critical in reasoning. We can imagine the family as a group made up of simple rational agents competing among themselves, or choose to see an empathetic and cooperative household committed to improving a shared future rather than to fruitlessly erasing a common past.

References

Belletti M, Leksinaj E (2011) The perspective of rural development in Albania, evidence of microfinance in agriculture. In: Karasavvoglou A (ed) Economies of Balkan and Eastern Europe countries in the changed world. Cambridge Scholars Publishing, Newcastle, pp 294–305

Belletti M, Leksinaj E (2012) Constrains and strengths of microfinance in agriculture: a comparison between Albania and Honduras. In: 3rd conference on Economies of Balkan and Eastern Europe countries in the changed world, University of National and World Economy, Sofia, 11–13 May 2012, pp 283–291. http://ebeec.teikav.edu.gr/ebeec2012/documents/EBEEC_2012_Proceedings.pdf. Accessed 29 Mar 2014

Carletto G et al (2004) Internal mobility and international migration in Albania. ESA Working Paper 06-13. ftp://ftp.fao.org/docrep/fao/007/ae068e/ae068e00.pdf. Accessed 16 Apr 2014

Cela R, Volk T (2009) Agricultural statistics database: survey on data and methodology in Albania. Available via INSTAT. www.instat.gov.al. Accessed 17 July 2014

Duhigg C (2012) The power of habit. Random House Trade Paperbacks, New York, NY

Ellis F (2003) Peasant economics. Cambridge University Press, Cambridge, MA

Gedeshi I, Mara H, Preni X (2003) The encouragement of social-economic development in relation to the growth of the role of remittances. Center of Economic and Social Studies (CESS), Tirana

Germenji E, Swinnen J (2007) Human capital, market imperfections, poverty, and migration: evidence from rural Albania. Available via Econstor. http://hdl.handle.net/10419/74905. Accessed 26 Nov 2014

Gjeci G et al (2013) Streamlining of agriculture and rural development policies of SEE countries for UE accession. Available via Agricultural Policy Plus. www.app.seerural.org. Accessed 22 Dec 2013

Greiner C, Sakdaporlak P (2013) Translocality: concepts, applications and emerging research perspectives. Geogr Compass 7:373–384. doi:10.1111/gec3.12048

Katz E (2003) The changing role of women in the rural economies in Latin America. In: Davis B (ed) Food, agriculture and rural development: current and emerging issues for economic analysis and policy research. FAO, Rome, pp 31–66. ftp://ftp.fao.org/docrep/fao/006/y4940e/y4940e00.pdf. Accessed 06 Jan 2013

King R, Dalipaj M, Mai N (2006) Gendering migration and remittances: evidence from London and Northern Albania. Popul Space Place 12:409–434. doi:10.1002/psp.439

Macours K, Swinnen J (2008) Rural-Urban poverty differences in transition countries. World Dev 36(11):2170–2187. doi:10.1016/j.worlddev.2007.11.003

McCarthy N et al (2006) Assessing the impact of massive out-migration on agriculture. ESA Working Paper 06-14. ftp://ftp.fao.org/docrep/fao/009/ah631e/ah631e00.pdf. Accessed 16 Nov 2013

Mendola M (2012) Rural out-migration and economic development at origin: a review of the evidence. J Int Dev 24:102–122. doi:10.1002/jid.1684

Miluka J et al (2010) The vanishing farms? The impact of international migration on Albanian family farming. J Dev Stud 46(1):140–161. doi:10.1080/00220380903197978

Nicholson B (2004) The tractor, the shop and the filling station: work migration and the self-help development in Albania. Eur Asia Stud 56:877–890. doi:10.1080/0966813042000258088

Rozelle S, Taylor E, de Brauw A (1999) Migration, remittances and agricultural productivity in China. Am Econ Rev 89(2):287–291. doi:10.1257/aer.89.2.287

Vargas-Lundius R et al (2008) International migration, remittances and rural development. IFAD-FAO. http://www.global-mechanism.org/specials/paul/.cups/.java/.jpi_cache/file/1/jar/1/.Trash/layout_1.pdf. Accessed 28 Feb 2014

Part II
Social Capital in Balkan Societies

Crisis and Social Capital in Greece: A Comparative Study Between Rural and Urban Communities

Anna Tokalaki, Anastasios Michailidis, Maria Partalidou, and Georgios Theodossiou

Abstract Greece is facing a severe economic crisis that has also been perceived as a crisis of human values, ideology and on parallel a crisis of trust in people and institutions. The role of trust (both individual and institutional) has been highlighted within the social capital literature as a factor of growth and prosperity of societies; especially in terms of adaptability to volatile conditions where the need for cooperation in order to achieve common goals is of great importance. At the same time, much has been written about the existence of higher levels of social capital in closed societies such as rural ones when compared to urban. The main aim of this paper is to investigate the relation of trust and solidarity, between urban and rural areas in Northern Greece, using empirical research to a large sample of 503 residents. Research results lead to the segmentation need of the population into three distinct clusters with respect to different levels of social capital within different rural–urban context. The main policy implication would be whether the increase in social capital could be a tool for "survival" in the current economic crisis in Greece and at the European level.

Keywords Community • Crisis • Rural • Social capital • Trust • Urban

JEL Classification Codes C38 • 131 • 138

A. Tokalaki • A. Michailidis (✉) • M. Partalidou
Department of Agricultural Economics, Aristotle University of Thessaloniki, P.O. Box 225, 54124 Thessaloniki, Greece
e-mail: tassosm@auth.gr

G. Theodossiou
Department of Business Administration, Technological Educational Institute of Larissa, Larissa, Greece
e-mail: geortheo@yahoo.gr

A. Karasavvoglou et al. (eds.), *The First Decade of Living with the Global Crisis*, Contributions to Economics, DOI 10.1007/978-3-319-24267-5_5

1 Introduction

Within the contemporary discussion on societal challenges and community resilience, research on social capital may contribute to a comprehensive analysis of local development and the implementation of new forms of governance and policies towards social innovation and social cohesion at the local level. The main supported idea claims that economic variables are not enough to ensure sustainable development by themselves, particularly in relation to social and environmental dimensions of this fact. Specifically, it is argued that economic growth does not necessarily produce immediate local development. The latter requires the presence of social, cultural and political factors, which are not governed solely by the system and market mechanisms. While it is important that local development must be seen as a development project, built and dictated by the function and mechanisms of the market, it is not only that; it is a product of social relations that arise through conflict, competition, cooperation and reciprocity. And the conditions under which a community develops and flourishes are not fully understood.

Various researchers, such as Hemenway et al. (2001), Putnam (2004), Helliwell and Putnam (2004), Lim and Putnam (2010), highlight the role of social capital as fundamental factor for local development. A crucial conceptual tool for strengthening the concept of civic involvement and the building of civil society, social capital refers to "fundamental social virtues, such as trust, norms of reciprocity and networks of spontaneous participation of citizens who contribute to improving the efficiency of society by facilitating the achievement of collective action" (Putnam et al. 1993). Social capital refers to the existence of networks in society active citizenship and participation, access to institutional or informal information networks and information returns and trust between individuals (Kritsotakis et al. 2009).

The importance of social capital for economic development, social inclusion and well-being of people is increasingly recognized (Coleman 1990). And amidst the current economic crisis social capital is seen as a tool for adapting to volatile conditions that both rural and urban areas are facing.

The current severe economic crisis and state guardianship of Greece, on the one hand dissolves confidence in the medium—and especially the social macro-level, but on the other hand as an external threat is a factor of strengthening cohesion and driving social innovation and new forms of local governance in micro-social level of families and closely related social groups. It has been also articulated in the literature that rural areas are embedded within trustworthy relationships (bonding social capital in closed groups such as family) in comparison to urban areas, and although in Greece the contribution of social capital to local development is not yet fully elaborated, a handful of papers reveals low levels of trust towards institutions on the one hand and strong family ties on the other (Koutsou et al. 2014).

The aim of this paper is to study the relations of trust and solidarity in different areas (both urban and rural ones) in Northern Greece. Within this research we try to identify the similarities and differences between the permanent population in terms of a set of variables related to social capital (volunteering, trust, networking etc.) and the construction of rurality and solidarity amidst the current economic crisis. The primary data come from stratified random sampling procedure of 503 residents of the prefecture of Thessaloniki in the region of Central Macedonia.

2 The Conceptual Approach to Social Capital and Trust

The concept of social capital has been introduced into different academic discourses and disciplines, within different interpretations, considerations and conceptions, following mostly the work of Coleman (1988), Putnam et al. (1993), Portes (1998) and Fukuyama (2001). Bourdieu (1986) for example defined social capital as "the sum of current or potential resources associated with having a network of permanent inter-relations of acquaintance and peer recognition, which is more or less institutionalized, or, in other words, by joining a group as a whole [people] institutions [action], which is not only endowed with common properties, but are also united by ties permanent and useful". In this definition Bourdieu emphasizes in the economic nature of social capital and how it can contribute to the transfer of resources and power within social groups or from a social group to another (Defilippis 2001). According to the World Bank (2012), there is measurable evidence that micro-level migration, trade, economic reforms, economic development, security, and even effect of new technologies are affected by the interaction between people, and briefly concludes that while social capital belongs to microeconomics it also affects macroeconomic factors.

Putnam (1993) refers to features of social organizations, where trust, norms and networks can improve the efficiency of society by facilitating coordinated actions of individuals/members of their mutual benefit. Specifically, the concept refers to the stock of trust, reciprocity and rules in social networks that exist among people so as to enable a coordinated and effective collective action. The latter has the effect of improving the quality of public life, efficiency of social and representative institutions as well as economic development (Putnam 2004). Moreover, Putnam argues that social capital is a resource that individuals or groups of people hold or fail to hold. According to Putnam, "working together is easier in a community which has been inherited a substantial stock of social capital". Thus, it is clear that for Putnam «*communities as a whole and not individuals are those who hold stocks of social capital and thus how social capital can be both a 'private good' and a 'public good'*». Social capital is the consistent "glue" that holds societies tied. It is a matter of socialization, trust and cooperation at the local level.

According to Sztompka (1993), trust operates in an "as if" basis, e.g. as if actors know how other actors will act. Accordingly, confidence 'is a bet in relation to the future contingent actions of others'. Moreover, for Sztompka (1995) "trust refers to the absolute faith that we either have in favour of individuals or institutions." Moreover, according to Putnam et al. (1993), trust is the belief that the word or promise of a party is reliable and that a party will fulfill its obligations in a relation of transaction. Finally, trust is the belief that an entity behaves in a specific way (Weber 1978).

3 Methodology

3.1 Study Area

As the research interest of this study focuses on relations of trust and solidarity in different areas (urban and rural), the Prefecture of Thessaloniki was chosen as the study area. Due to the complex nature of the concept of social capital and to increase the explanatory power and reliability of the information collected, we decided to carry out the fieldwork in locations around the Prefecture of Thessaloniki (14 municipalities), which share many common characteristics, while at the same time greatly vary, composing a representative sample. The area hosts the second largest city in Greece, while it is composed of a plurality of rural areas. The very different context of socio-economic development and different development experiences allows the identification of the relationship of social capital and the level of socio—economic development of the region. The study area has been selected as it is one of the most characteristic Greek prefectures comprised of both rural and urban areas while it also includes a very large urban centre located in the centre of its map. In this sense, the prefecture of Thessaloniki is a very good case study of rural–urban continuum.

3.2 Data Collection

To achieve the main objectives of this study, we used primary data, which were collected by using properly designed questionnaires. The completion of the questionnaires was conducted from February 2013 until April 2013. The sampling was done in such a way that the results will facilitate generalization to the whole Greek population. The population of the study is defined as all residents over 18 years old from all municipalities of Greece and as a sampling frame we used voter rolls. The sample was selected with the technique/method of stratified sampling and the final sample was composed of 503 individuals. From a technical-architectural point of view, the design process of the questionnaire is divided into four levels of functionality. These levels consist of: (a) the section that provides information about personal or demographic characteristics of the respondents, (b) the section that provides information on social capital characteristics including variables about trust, (c) the section that provides information about the definition of some important terms (social capital, economic crisis, city and village) and (d) the section that provides information about the ranking of several determinative characteristics of social capital. In order to encourage participation and minimise the cognitive burden on respondents, most questions were framed in *Likert* scale intervals (Michailidis et al. 2010; Loizou et al. 2013, 2014).

3.3 Data Analysis

Prior to all that respondents were asked to give the definition of few concepts (e.g. social capital, economic crisis, village and city) which are then illustrated in word clouds through the methodology of Discourse Analysis (Liltsi et al. 2014) showing the manner in which people perceive simple but great words with conceptual importance for the present investigation. According to this analysis, depending on the frequency of responses in each category the relative size of the letters was defined. Besides a two-step cluster analysis was used to classify the respondents in discernible clusters in order to explore the different levels of social capital and trust (Michailidis et al. 2011b, 2012).

4 Results and Discussion

Onwards, four "word clouds" have been designed, using statistical frequencies and content analysis out of the respondents' answers. More specifically, concerning the construction of the word "social capital", the largest percentage of the sample answered that they do not know what that means and they followed the responses "values", "solidarity", "money" and "people". Similarly, referring to the question about the "economic crisis", 23.1 % of the sample gave answers that describe what we have been experiencing in the last 4 years in Greece, while in a smaller margin followed the responses that analyze the psychological impact and the aftermath of the economic crisis (debt, hike). Finally, for the questions about the "village" and the "city", we observed that respondents described the village with positive concepts like "nature", "peace", "family" and the city as negative concepts like "bustle", "traffic", "exhaust" and "anxiety".

Using summary statistics through the SPSS v. 20.0 (SPSS 2011), resulted the mean value of the stock of social capital in rural, suburban and urban areas of Thessaloniki. There is a statistically significance difference in the distribution of social capital between rural areas and the rest of the study area. More specifically, the rural areas have the largest stock of social capital in average 5.33, followed by the suburban areas with average 4.85, and finally the urban areas with an average of 4.81 (Fig. 1).

The sample of the research was sectioned based almost on all variables of the questionnaire as distinguished in Table 2. Using the data which were gathered from the answers of the respondents of the study area and the implementation of the two-step analysis in clusters through the SPSS v. 20.0 (SPSS 2011), the optimal

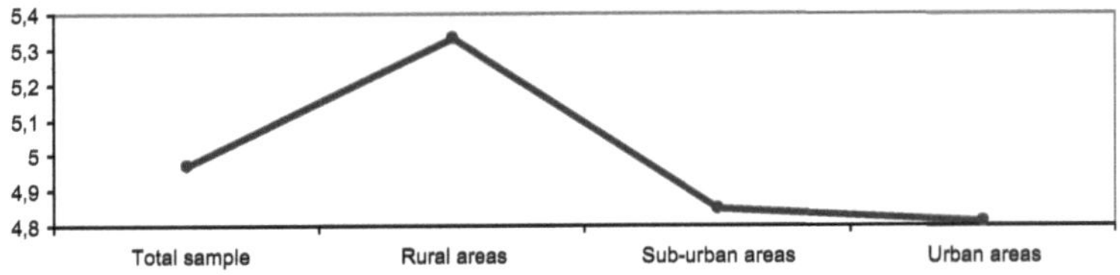

Fig. 1 Rural-Urban continuum of social capital

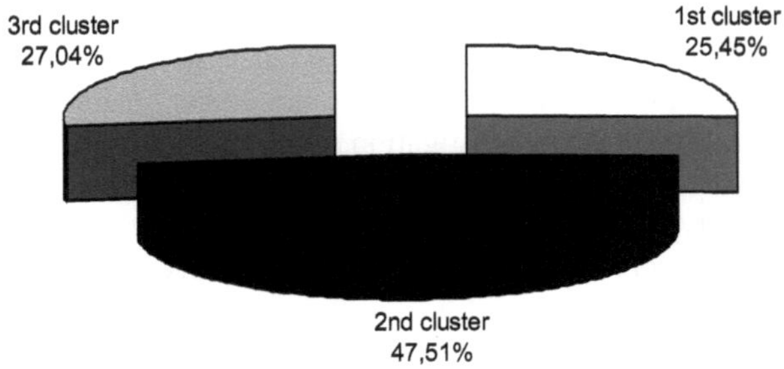

Fig. 2 Distribution in clusters

solution of the three clusters showed. In Fig. 2, the distribution of observations in each cluster is graphically distinguished, while Fig. 3 demonstrates the relative importance of the estimators of model (predictors importance). More specifically, according to Fig. 2, result. The first cluster is the 25.45 % of the observations, the second cluster—which is the largest—is the 47.51 % and the third cluster is the 27.04 % of the total observations.

In Fig. 3 we observe the relative importance of the ten variables, namely the importance of their participation in the formation of three clusters emerged. Thus, we see that social capital has a greater relative importance among ten variables, and personality follows. Age, gender and finally education have the least relative importance.

More specifically, the clusters are presented in Table 2, and are described as follows: the first cluster is composed of 128 persons (or 25.4 %) who believe that the social capital of the region of residence is rather large. They feel distinguished in society and are generally satisfied with their lives while they are ready to take risks in the future. The cultural and educational level is high, as most of them are degree holders: University Education/Higher Technical Education or Master's/doctorate. Moreover, they are interested in art, history and being informed by the constantly updated media (press/newspapers/internet). In this cluster, we mostly find middle-aged females (44 years). The principal occupation is in the public sector, which explains—at least in part—the relatively high risk they have taken or are willing to take both in the past and in future, because they feel the "safety" of the public sector. Finally, the respondents of this cluster have high monthly income (2000 euros and above).

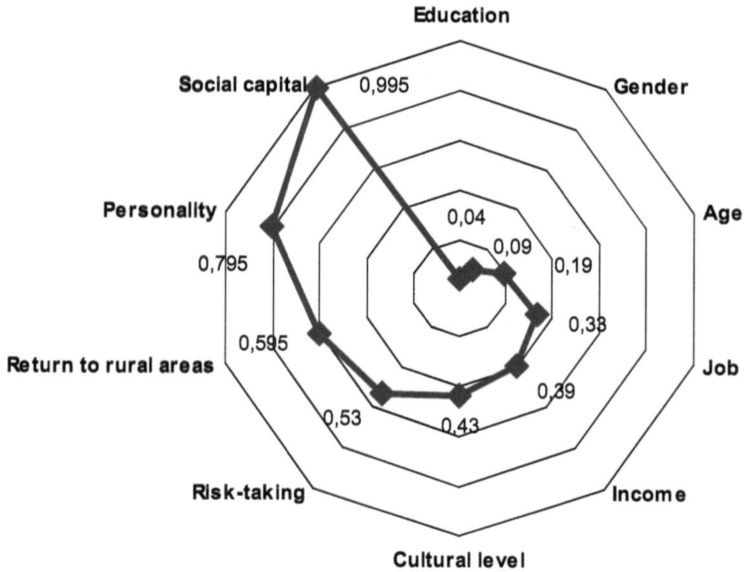

Fig. 3 Relative importance estimators

The second cluster consists of 239 persons (47.5 %) who feel that the social capital of the region of residence is rather small. People of this cluster feel satisfied with their lives but not well—established in society, while the risk-taking possibility is low. The main employment is in the private sector and perhaps this explains the slight mood for taking a risk. Namely it is "the uncertainty" which is caused by the private sector as opposed to the public that we have seen in the above cluster. Also, these people are less educated (high school/technical school diploma holders) and their cultural level is relatively low, while their average monthly family income is 1000–2000 euros. All this, perhaps, is the cause that people of this cluster do not feel well—established. Finally, in this cluster most of participants are women around 30 (32 years old).

The third and last cluster includes 136 individuals (27.1 %) and is a very special category, as reported primarily in people returned from the city to the countryside or rural areas. People in this cluster, consider that the social capital of the region of residence is small. One possible explanation for this is maybe the fact that they recently moved to an area (last 4 years) and still do not feel completely a single and stable piece of the new district of residence. At the same time, it is people who do not feel well-established in society, who are not satisfied with their lives. However, they want to take some risk and this is reflected in the decision to move to another area. The level of education is high (degree holders: University Degree/Higher Technical Institution Degree or students) and their cultural level is high. The cluster includes mostly men, average aged with low monthly family income. Finally, most of these are students or unemployed with low income, and this probably explains the fact that they do not feel satisfied, but marginalized.

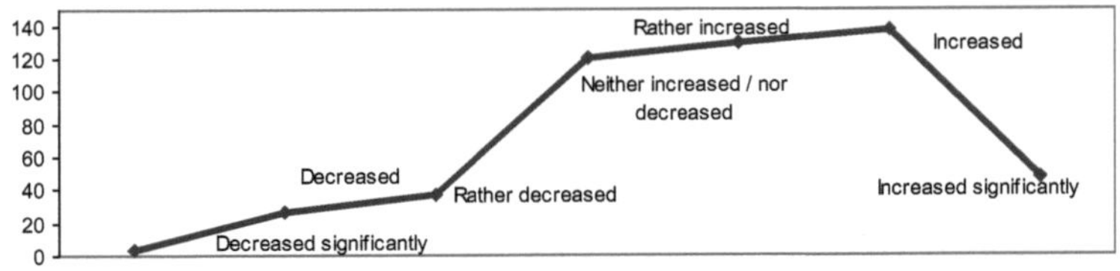

Fig. 4 Comparison of social capital in times of economic crisis

According to Fig. 4, we observe that social capital over the last 4 years (economic crisis) has an increasing trend as most of the respondents argue that social capital/solidarity between people is greater in the recent years. In this question participants have been asked to compare the present value of social capital with the one few years ago.

5 Conclusions

Social capital is an important factor to achieve high levels of local development because of the influence on the availability or unavailability to the implementation and results of local development policies. High levels of social capital function in favor of a more qualitative local governance and an active local community, thus leading to a balanced socio-economic development locally.

In the present study the relationships of trust and solidarity are examined in different areas (rural, suburban and urban) and through a series of variables (volunteering, trust, networking, etc.) associated with social capital resulting segmentation of the population into three distinct clusters, each of which has its own characteristics. The first cluster includes individuals who have high perception of the social capital of the region of residence and people who feel well-established in society satisfied with their lives. On the other hand, the second cluster consists of individuals who perceived the social capital of the region of residence as a minor element, people who feel satisfied with their lives but not well-established in the society. Whilst, the third cluster consists mainly of people who returned from the city to "nature" and realize the social capital of the region of residence as low. Also, these people do not feel well-established and are not satisfied with their lives.

Furthermore, through the examination/measurement of social capital in rural areas and city, we end to the conclusion that rural areas have a higher stock of social capital, followed by semi-urban urban areas (Table 1). It is worth mentioning that the third cluster in partitioning of the total sample demonstrates a paradox. That is, while the perceived social capital of rural area is high compared to other areas, residents who moved there perceived it as lower. An explanation for this might be their recent removal in a relatively unknown place for them and their difficulty to acclimatize and adapt to their new life.

Table 1 Mean value of social capital

Area	Social capital
Rural areas (117 respondents)	5.33
Suburban areas (130 respondents)	4.85
Urban areas (256 respondents)	4.81
Total sample (503 respondents)	4.97

Table 2 Percentage of the defining characteristics of the analysis in clusters

Variables	First cluster (128 cases)	Second cluster (239 cases)	Third cluster (136 cases)
Social Capital *(multidisciplinary variable/16 statements)*	Rather high (78.2 %)	Rather low (66.4 %)	Low (52.1 %)
Personality *(multidisciplinary variable/3 statements)*	Acclaimed and satisfied (75.3 %)	Only satisfied (50.8 %)	Neither acclaimed nor satisfied (64.1 %)
Return to the country *(bilateral variable)*	No (100.0 %)	No (100.0 %)	Yes (64.7 %)
Risk-taking *(multidisciplinary variable/12 statements)*	Relatively high (67.3 %)	Low (58.2 %)	Very high (48.9 %)
Cultural Level *(multidisciplinary variable/12 statements)*	High (74.2 %)	Relatively low (55.5 %)	Relatively high (60.4 %)
Education *(regular variable)*	University/Higher Techn. Institution (61.2 %)	High School/ Techn. School (54.1 %)	Third level education/student (61.2 %)
Gender *(nominal variable)*	Female (67.5 %)	Female (58.3 %)	Male (59.4 %)
Age *(numeric variable)*	Average age 44.2 years	Average age 31.5 years	Average age 38.6 years
Job *(nominal variable)*	Public employee (61.3 %)	Private sector employee (55.8 %)	Student or unemployed (66.2 %)
Income *(regular variable)*	High (53.1 %)	Average (88.6 %)	Low (77.2 %)

Then, observing Table 2 we realize that individuals with high educational attainment and high cultural level, perceive social capital in the region of residence rather high in contrast with those who have lower educational and cultural level. There is a positive correlation between social capital and educational/cultural level. As far as the relationship between social capital and risk-taking is concerned, these figures prove a positive correlation. It is remarkable again the opposition at the third cluster of the first segmentation. This cluster includes people with high educational and cultural level. However, the perceived social capital of the area is low, probably for the same reason as explained above.

Regarding the relationship between social capital and economic situation, highly paid people have rather high level of perceived social capital, middle-income people have rather low perceived social capital and low-income people have even less perceived social capital. Thus it is confirmed that the economically disadvantaged have less social capital stock because of insecurity and uncertainty, regarding the outlook of their lives while trying to respond to the daily struggle of survival.

Finally, as demonstrated through the literature, the stock of social capital in Greece was small, but through this paper we result in the idea that the stock of social capital between relatives, friends and even colleagues the last 4 years has increased significantly. Jalan and Ravallion (1999), argue that local communities can and proceed to mutual guarantee against any income fluctuations. Therefore, it appears that social capital is largely determined locally, in socio-economic conditions, and there exists only among households that share similar socio-economic identities.

In summary, due to the economic crisis, Greece experiences a continuous decline in many sectors, so it becomes imperative that new measures for its development to be taken. Therefore, it is of high necessity for the leaders of our country to implement policy measures that contribute initially to the development of each local society in general, and lead to the "rebirth" of society. According to the analytical results described above, the responsible individuals could implement various policy measures for each of the above categories according to its characteristics and needs. Arguably, the application of three different policy measures would be more effective, in contradiction to the application of a single action. One measure will not satisfy the needs of all citizens and it will also be concise and simpler than applying different policy measures for each of us individually.

From a methodological point of view the contribution of this paper consisted in the application of modern multivariate methodologies in the field of social capital. In particular, although several articles have been conducted to examine and evaluate the social capital our study presents a first application of clustering methodologies in the field of social capital. The main benefit of employing the above methodologies is that they can handle optimally both continuous and categorical variables as well as attributes (Michailidis and Papadaki-Klavdianou 2008; Krikeli et al. 2010; Koutsouris et al. 2014) and thus, a two-step clustering model can be very useful, in the examination of social capital, as the several categorical variables of Table 2 can be better accommodated (Michailidis et al. 2006, 2011a; Charatsari et al. 2011, 2013).

References

Bourdieu P (1986) The forms of capital. In: Richardson J (ed) Handbook of theory and research for the sociology of education. Greenwood Press, New York, NY

Charatsari C et al (2011) Farmers as consumers of agricultural education services: willingness to pay and spend time. J Agric Educ Ext 17(3):253–266

Charatsari C et al (2013) Great expectations? Antecedents of women farmers' willingness to participate in agricultural education programmes. Outlook Agric 42(3):193–199

Coleman JS (1988) Social capital in the creation of human capital. Am J Sociol 94:95–120

Coleman JS (1990) Foundations of social theory. Harvard University Press, Cambridge, MA

Defilippis J (2001) The myth of social capital in community development. Hous Policy Debate 11(4):781–806

Fukuyama F (2001) Social capital, civil society and development. Third World Q 22:7–20
Helliwell JF, Putnam RD (2004) The social context of well-being. Philos Trans R Soc B Biol Sci 359(1449):1435–1446
Hemenway D et al (2001) Firearm prevalence and social capital. Ann Epidemiol 11(7):484–490
Jalan J, Ravallion M (1999) Are the poor less well insured? Evidence on vulnerability to income risk in rural China. J Dev Econ 58:61–81
Koutsou S et al (2014) Young farmers' social capital in Greece: trust levels and collective actions. J Rural Stud 34:204–211
Koutsouris A et al (2014) The phantom of (agri)tourism and agriculture symbiosis? A Greek case study. Tour Manag Perspect 12:94–103
Krikeli V et al (2010) Communication improvement through music: the case of children with developmental disabilities. Int J Spec Educ 25(1):1–9
Kritsotakis G et al (2009) Individual and contextual influences of social variables in health outcomes: the impact of social capital. Arch Hell Med 26:523–535 (in Greek)
Liltsi P et al (2014) Mapping perceived happiness alongside the rural-urban continuum. Proc Econ Finance 9:288–301
Lim C, Putnam RD (2010) Religion, social networks, and life satisfaction. Am Sociol Rev 75(6): 914–933
Loizou E et al (2013) Investigating the drivers that influence the adoption of differentiated food products: the case of a Greek urban area. Br Food J 115(7):917–935
Loizou E et al (2014) Return migration: evidence from a reception country with a short migration history. Eur Urban Reg Stud 21(2):161–174
Michailidis A, Papadaki-Klavdianou A (2008) The contribution of agricultural extension services to the productivity and socioeconomic profile of dairy cattle farmers. Outlook Agric 37(2): 119–124
Michailidis A et al (2006) Understanding participation constraints of potential skiers. Tour Econ 12(3):421–435
Michailidis A et al (2010) Information and communication technologies as agricultural extension tools: a survey among farmers in West Macedonia, Greece. J Agric Educ Ext 16(3):249–263
Michailidis A et al (2011a) Adoption of sustainable irrigation practices in water scarce areas. Bulgarian J Agric Sc 17(5):579–591
Michailidis A et al (2011b) Who goes online? Evidence of internet use patterns from rural Greece. Telecommun Policy 35(4):333–343
Michailidis A et al (2012) Mobile communications technology in rural societies of developing countries. J Rural Dev 31(3):319–334
Portes A (1998) Social capital: its origins and applications in modern sociology. Annu Rev Sociol 24:1–24
Putnam RD (1993) The prosperous community: social capital and public life. Am Prospect 13: 35–42
Putnam RD (2004) Commentary: 'health by association': some comments. Int J Epidemiol 33(4): 667–671
Putnam RD et al (1993) Making democracy work. Civic traditions in modern Italy. Princeton University Press, Princeton, NJ
SPSS (2011) IBM SPSS statistics base 20. SPSS, Chicago, IL
Sztompka P (1993) Civilizational incompetence: the trap of post-communist societies. Z Soziol 22(2):85–95
Sztompka P (1995) Trust: the missing resource of post-communist society, mimeo. Institute of Sociology, Jagiellonian University, Krakow
Weber M (1978) Economy and society. In: Roth G, Wiittich C (eds). University of California Press, Berkeley
World Bank Group (2012) World development indicators 2012. World Bank Publications, Washington, DC

Social Dialogue in the Era of Memoranda: The Consequences of Austerity and Deregulation Measures on the Greek Social Partnership Process

Theodore Koutroukis and Spyros Roukanas

Abstract The aim of this paper is to contribute to the current debate on the consequences of joint EC-ECB-IMF Programmes that directly impact on the Greek industrial relation system via an analysis of the changes in the institutional framework of the labour market and the social partnership process. Moreover, it will test the hypothesis that the Memoranda have had a negative impact on the quality of social dialogue in Greece.

The paper examines immense transformations in the Greek industrial relations system and evaluates the direction of change in the field of social dialogue. Furthermore, it analyses how the radical changes introduced since 2010, which have amended essential features of the Greek labour legislation, have promoted significant implications for the role of social partners.

Finally, using a comparative assessment, it examines the impact of EC-ECB-IMF Programmes on the reshape of the national industrial relations system towards highly decentralized collective bargaining, and the abandonment of social dialogue as an essential means to influence economic and social policy.

Keywords Social dialogue • Crisis • Greece • Industrial relations

JEL Classification Codes J5 • M5

1 Introduction

During the past 4 years Greece has faced an enormous change in the fields of employment relations, social dialogue and labour market. Current debate on the consequences of joint EU-ECB-IMF programs has found that exists directly impact on the Greek industrial relation system and especially on social partnership process.

T. Koutroukis (✉)
University of Aegean, Chios, Greece
e-mail: t.koutroukis@fme.aegean.gr

S. Roukanas
University of Piraeus, Piraeus, Greece

A. Karasavvoglou et al. (eds.), *The First Decade of Living with the Global Crisis*, Contributions to Economics, DOI 10.1007/978-3-319-24267-5_6

Over the past 20 years the social partners' role in the Greek industrial relations system has enriched. Thus, the notion of SD has been broaden to mean (Aranitou and Yannakourou 2004):

- The bi-partite social dialogue, specifically between employer and employee organizations
- The tri-partite dialogue at the national level among government, social partners and stakeholders' representatives, as well as any social partner's participation in several boards of directors.
- Certain atypical SD schemes such as pertinent SD procedures among social partners.

This paper will test the hypothesis that the Memoranda have had a negative impact on the quality of social dialogue in Greece and assess the impact of EC-ECB-IMF Programmes on the current industrial relations landscape in Greece in comparison with the previous situation.

2 Theoretical Background

It is widely accepted that social partnership/social dialogue (SP/SD) procedures have been a vital precondition for the success of economic and social policies. Several studies have found that when a decision-making organization wishes to assure that the continuous involvement of the parties concerned is maintained, it has to convince those parties that its policies have taken into account their interests and opinions (Koutroukis and Kretsos 2004, 2008; Koutroukis 1997).

Social Partnership—in a modern view—is, as defined by the Copenhagen Centre (1999):

> people and organisations from some combination of public, business and civil constituencies who engage in voluntary, mutually beneficial innovative relationships to address common social aims through combining their resources and competencies.

From another point of view the Greek Economic and Social Committee has defined Social Dialogue as the:

> Attempts that aim to touch differing opinions and interests in order to solve common problems or efforts to explore and appoint common targets regarding related issues or simply procedures that help distinct social groups to exchange ideas (OKE 1999).

SP/SD has taken many forms in the European Union such as information, consultation, negotiation, bipartite, tripartite or multipartite collective bargaining and agreement, and co-decision (Ishikawa 2003). Moreover, social dialogue can take part at the plant/company level, and/or the region, sector, inter-professional, national, European or international levels. SD has already been evaluated as an effective tool at the local level, as plenty of good practices have been developed in Europe and other parts of the world (Degryse 2000).

Table 1 Prerequisites for tripartism

Clear goals	Tripartism requires targets, aims and objectives e.g. economic stability, competitiveness, security at work, income policy
Visible results	Delivery of measurable results is necessary for the agendas of the social partners, e.g. safety and health at work, vocational training, employment creation, income guarantees
Bipartism	Well-functioning bipartism is seen as essential for building tripartite structures
Multi-level approach	The diffusion of national models down to regional, local, municipal and enterprise levels is important
Civil society	Further discussion is needed on where the involvement of civil society is necessary and desirable, and on the representativeness of civil society organizations
Monitoring	Institutions and models need constant review and must develop the ability to adapt, change and be flexible
Responsibility	It is important to adopt a problem-solving approach, accept compromises and trade-offs and create a shared understanding of each other's difficulties

Source: European Foundation for the Improvement of Living and Working Conditions (2002)

According to many researchers the main benefits and advantages (added value) of continuous and stable partnership schemes are a shared understanding, a mutual trust and flexibility of approaches. Another point that has been mentioned by the participants of an international conference is that

> "social partnership and tripartism work best when there is an open agenda to the partnership system, balancing the interests of employers and unions with a perspective on the overall interests of society and particularly where there is a degree of mutual trust between the participants" (European Foundation for the Improvement of Living and Working Conditions 2002).

It is generally accepted that some prerequisites are essential for the promotion of tripartite co-operation and partnership. A conference that has been organized by the European Foundation for the Improvement of Living and Working Conditions has concluded that the most important of them are (Table 1).

3 Current Trends of Social Dialogue in Greece

The concept of SD/SP in Greece means a variety of institutionalised and non-institutionalised procedures of dialogue among social partners. A national process of SD has begun in the 1990s, as the government committed itself in consultations with social partners before legislating on economic and social issues (OKE 2002).

Thus, the social partners' role has been differentiated and included in a new context that was characterized by a more limited role of the state in industrial relations. Furthermore, several developments towards a system of free collective

Table 2 Main austerity measures implemented in Greece

Public sector	Private sector
– Employment reduction – Pay cuts or freeze – Pensions cut or freeze – Increase in retirement age – Increase in working hours without simultaneous or respective increase in pay – Privatizations	– Easier/cheaper dismissals – Pay cuts or freeze – Pensions cut or freeze – Atypical contracts – Bargaining decentralization – Greater working time flexibility – Lower minimum wage

Source: Koukiadaki and Kretsos (2012)

bargaining and voluntary labour disputes settlement have been promoted (Lavdas 2007). However, a central-level bargaining system regarding wage setting at sectoral, firm or territorial level continued to exist (Lavdas 2007).

Nevertheless, the activation of SD institutions has been delayed in Greece in comparison to other EU countries due to a lack of a long-lasting SD tradition (Aranitou and Yannakourou 2004).

The implementation of Memoranda I and II includes economic and labour market reforms in wages, collective bargaining, pensions and employment in the public sector. The adjustment of Greek labour market took place in a quick way and labour market flexibility has become widespread. The main austerity measures taken in Greece are shown in Table 2 (Koukiadaki and Kretsos 2012).

Before the adoption of measures of economic and social policy, the government organized quick bilateral consultation with the social partners (trade unions and employer organizations), as the situation was characterized as urgent. Due to the same reason, OKE (the Greek Economic and Social Committee) did not activate any SD process on the reform of collective employment relations in 2010 (Patra 2012).

On July 15, 2010, national employer and employee organizations concluded a modest "National general collective agreement for years 2010–2012" (EGSSE)—(Patra 2012).

In the Updated Memorandum (6 August 2010), the Greek Government, was asked to follow SD in order to adopt legislation and reform the collective bargaining system in the private sector (Patra 2012). A second update of the "Memorandum of Understanding on Specific Economic Policy Conditionality". It confirmed the will to reform the system of collective bargaining "at the firm level in close cooperation with social partners".

Certain scholars have assessed the situation of SD in Greece. Lavdas (2007) has noticed that "attempts at tripartite policy consultation and policymaking are affected not just by the politics of disjointed corporatism but by the particular historical-ideological legacies as well" and claims that "the most persistent influence on economic policy in Greece has been the inherited asymmetry in the social content of disjointed corporatism" (2007).

The main obstacle of SD was its difficulty to extend negotiations to issues beyond pay and remuneration. Another problem concerns the occasions when the process broke down, as a result of strong conflicting forces from the unions or employers (Lavdas 2007).

According to Lavdas "this implies the reproduction of a pattern of power relations relying on a weak and asymmetrically penetrated state apparatus" and, furthermore, he pointed out that "the politics of stalled social dialogue reflect the combined difficulties of building less porous political institutions and extending the Europeanising strategy to further areas" (Lavdas 2007).

According to Aranitou and Yannakourou (2004), "SD in Greece nowadays yields substantial results on a national level mainly in milieus that foster positive preconditions for a culture of debate". Moreover, they claim that the establishment of institutions and instruments by legislation favouring such SD had not practically managed so far to create the necessary potential.

According to Kioukias (2003), the Greek case shows that "the traditional statist or pseudo-participatory methods of policy formation and implementation are no longer particularly useful and/or acceptable" (Kioukias 2003, p. 130).

Tsarouhas claims that "the evidence points to limited change in the Greek social partnership stemming from the EES process, a rhetorical shift and a new institutional amendments notwithstanding" (2008, p. 361).

SD in Greece has faced many obstacles during the 1990s due to the long tradition of state intervention in implementing economic and social policies. Nonetheless, SD has been strengthened through the constitution of pertinent institutions (i.e. Economic and Social Committee, Organisation for Mediation and Arbitration etc.) (Aranitou and Yannakourou 2004).

4 Social Partnership in the Era of Memoranda

Social partnership procedures in Greece have been affected by the policies adopted under the pressures of Memoranda. More specifically, the main legislative initiatives that have been undertaken by the Government are the following:

Memorandum I (3 May 2010)

Law 3833/2010 (15 March 2010) titled "Protection of the national economy-Emergency measures for coping with fiscal crisis", which included the reduction of pay and benefit levels and affected the industrial relations in both public and private sectors. That law included certain measures for the reduction of financial debts and the income policy of year 2010, and (a) prohibited any salary increases and (b) provided for a 12 % reduction of pay and benefits for public sector employees for 2010.

Law 3845/2010 (6 May 2010) titled "Measures for the application of the support mechanism for the Greek economy by the euro area Member States and the International Monetary Fund". The "Memorandum of Economic and Financial Policies" of 3 May 2010, signed by the Greek Government and the representatives of EU-ECB-IMF (Patra 2012).

Law 3863/2010 (15 July 2010) titled "New Public Insurance System and other provisions, arrangements in labour relations". That law has regulated issues on pensions and social security and provided certain crucial changes in employee relations (Patra 2012):

The "Updated Memorandum" (6 August 2010)

Law 3871/2010 titled "Fiscal management and responsibility", prohibited any salary increases for 2010 and the first half of 2011. For the second half of 2011 and for 2012, the only increases allowed were the ones provided by the National General Collective Agreement (EGSSE 2010-2011-2012).

Second Update of the "Memorandum" (22 November 2010)

Law 3899/2010 titled "Urgent measures for the application of the program of support of the Greek economy" reformed the framework of collective bargaining and the arbitration procedures (Patra 2012).

Medium Term Fiscal Strategy Framework (June 2011)

The "Medium-term Fiscal Strategy Framework", adopted by the Greek Parliament, included important changes in the areas of labour law and social security. After Memorandum I, the government accepted to introduce several issues of social and labour policy in social dialogue procedure but GSEE refused to participate.

Memorandum II

Law 4046/2012, included the plans for the "Financial Assistance Facility Agreement" and the Memorandum of Understanding II, and has promoted several structural reforms including labour flexibility, protection of employment and increase of competitiveness. The reforms of Memoranda I and II that impact industrial relations and social dialogue are included in Table 3 (Patra 2012).

5 Conclusion

Due to a huge public debt Greek Government has been obliged to ask for external financing by the EU, ECB and IMF and was committed to implement measures of reform that are described in two Memoranda of Understanding (Koukiadaki and Kretsos 2012; Patra 2012).

The reduced role of social dialogue in the planning and implementation of the austerity measures seems to be combined with several concerns of the abandonment to the European model of social partnership. To justify itself, the government claimed that the strong pressure by the lenders left no time for SD/SP consultations concerning the bail-out agreement. In other words, international or European institutions (EU, ECB, and IMF)—as represented by the Troika—as well as the

Table 3 Measures affecting industrial relations and social dialogue

Memorandum I	Memorandum II
– Provision that the terms of occupational and company level agreements may deviate from the respective terms of sectoral collective agreements and national general collective agreements and the terms of EGSSE – Amendments in the procedure of appeal to the organization for mediation and arbitration – Raise of layoff limits, in cases of mass layoffs- – New determination of the level and method of payment of severance compensation – Measures for prevention of layoffs of older employees in the phase before retirement, regardless of mass or individual layoffs – Alternative determination of terms of employment and the minimum wage of young people below 25 years who are entry levels in the labour market – New determination of the overall terms of employment and social security of those employed in apprenticeship positions, which may not be more than 1 year – New determination of the highest duration of specific-term employment contracts – Reduction of allowances and all kinds of remuneration of public sector employees by 8 % – Reduction of the earnings, severance pay, allowances and all kinds of remuneration of personnel employed by state-owned organizations by 3 % – Re-adjustment of the Christmas, Easter and holiday bonuses (Christmas bonus 500 €, Easter bonus 250 €, Holiday bonus 250 €) – Increase of the limit of collective dismissals [(i) Up to six employees for enterprises or branches of enterprises employing 20–150 people, and (ii) 5 % per cent of the workforce and up to 30 employees for enterprises or branches of enterprises, employing more than 150 people] – Amendment of the level and method of payment of severance compensation, with much more strict terms for the employees than in the past i.e. reduced amount of severance compensation and/or expanded period of layoff notification – Amended rights of older employees (55–65 years) in layoffs were amended – New terms of employment and compensation of entry level workers in the labour market, aged below 25 years	– Changes in the length of collective agreements – Removal of 'tenure' in all existing legacy contracts – Freeze of 'maturity' salary increases based on time at work until unemployment falls below 10 % – Changes in the way to recourse to arbitration, allowing requests for arbitration only if both parties consent and the ability of arbitrators to rule only on the basic wages and not the benefits – Adjustments on the basic salary level, i.e. the wage floors, by reducing the minimum of the EGSSE by 22 %, and a freeze in that salary until the end of the program period, while the reduction for youth, under the age of 25, to be 32 % of the basic salary – Adjustments to non-wage labour costs, by reducing the social security contributions from the part of the employers by 5 % – Closing of the Organization of Labour Housing and Organization of Labour Home – Staffing plans should be consistent with the target of reducing public employment by 150,000 by the end of 2015 – Transfer of 15,000 redundant staff to the labour reserve in the course of 2012 – The Government commissions an expert assessment of the new wage grid – The Government sets up an electronic automated system linking the census data base with the single payment authority (SPA) – Government will promote smooth wage bargaining at the various levels and fight undeclared work – Exceptional legislative measures on wage setting – The minimum wages established by the EGSSE were reduced by 22 % compared to the level of 1 January 2012 and—for the ages below 25—the wages established by the national collective agreement will be reduced by 32 % without restrictive conditions – Reforms in the wage-setting system – Measures to foster the re-negotiation of collective contracts – Legislation on collective agreements is amended with a view to promoting the adaptation of collectively bargained wage and non-wage cost to changing economic conditions on a regular and frequent basis

(continued)

Table 3 (continued)

Memorandum I	Memorandum II
– Provision for an apprenticeship contract, which should last up to 1 year and be remunerated with a 70 % of the minimum wage – Reduction in the percentage of overtime pay – Prohibition of any salary increases for 2010 and the first half of 2011. For the second half of 2011 and for 2012 the only increases allowed were the ones provided by the EGSSE 2010-2011-2012 – Provision for a right to appeal to a three-member arbitration board, to those arbitration decisions issued after 6 May 2010 – Provision for a *special enterprise collective agreement*, in which pay and terms of employment may deviate from those of sectoral agreements – Amendment in the composition of the bi-partite board of directors of OMED – The maximum duration of short-term work based on an employer's unilateral decision by the employer was set at 9 months per calendar year – Abolishment of part-time workers' higher hourly rate – Worker's duration of employment to 36 months for the same indirect employer – Further reduction of all kinds of remuneration of public sector employees, up to 25 % of the salary – Provision for a ratio of 1–10 recruitments during 2011 and 1–5 for the period 2012–2015 in the public sector – Increase of working time from 37.5 to 40 h in the public sector – Reduction of fixed-term employees by 50 % in 2011 and by 10 % each following year – Reduction of lump sum payments during retirement – Adjustment of supplementary pensions – Imposition of a special levy of 8 % to pensioners under 60-years old, who receive pension above 1700 € – Reduction of spending on farmers' pensions – Assessment and rationalization of social benefits – Tightening of the criteria applicable in the case of disability pensions	– Collective agreements regarding wage and non-wage conditions can only be concluded for a maximum duration of 3 years – Agreements that have been already in place for 24 months or more shall have a residual duration of 1 year – Collective agreements which have expired will remain in force for a period of maximum 3 months. If a new agreement is not reached, after this period, remuneration will revert to the base wage and allowances for seniority, child, education, and hazardous professions will continue to apply, until replaced by those in a new collective agreement or in new or amended individual contracts – Revision of the pertinent legislation so that arbitration takes place when agreed by both employees and employers. The government will clarify that arbitration only applies to the base wage and not on other remuneration, and that economic and financial considerations are taken into account alongside legal considerations – An independent assessment of the function of arbitration and mediation shall be prepared, with a view to improve the arbitration and mediation services in order to guarantee that arbitration awards adequately reflect the needs of wage adjustment – Clauses on tenure contained in law or in labour contracts are abolished. – The Government reduces social contributions for these companies in a fiscally-neutral manner – The Government enact legislation to reduce social contributions to IKA by 5 % and implement measures to ensure that this is budget neutral – An independent assessment on the effectiveness of the labour inspectorate structure and activities – Quantitative targets on the number of controls of undeclared work to be executed will be set for the labour inspectorate – The labour card is progressively introduced and every firm in specific sectors will be obliged to use it by end-2012

(continued)

Table 3 (continued)

Memorandum I	Memorandum II
	– Creation of a single payment authority for the payment of wages in the public sector – Adoption of legislation/decrees for a simplified remuneration system bargaining

Source: Koukiadaki and Kretsos (2012), Patra (2012)

Greek government shaped the agenda of reforms without social partners' participation.

More specifically, Troika has been the strong partner as its role in the management of the crisis and the reforms in the Greek system of industrial relations is crucial. Thus, monetary forces and fiscal constraints put tripartism aside and Greek government in collaboration with the Troika undertook some policies of reform in labour market (wages, labour market, social and employment protection) Patra 2012).

The new measures regarding employment relations had a direct impact on the national industrial relations system. Due to the Memoranda, social partnership has been set aside, in preference to Troika's monologue and several direct legislative initiatives in circumstances of urgency. In some cases the Troika did not accept social partners' joint opinions. The strategy and policies pursued by the Government fits more fully the preferences of the troika than the social partners' ones (Patra 2012).

The Government's initiatives have created a new flexible landscape in the labour market that affects the distribution of power and the role of the professional organisations involved in the Greek industrial relations system.

Probably, the IMF representatives dominated in Troika, and thus the European culture of institutional SD has been put aside and SP was collapsed.

According to Koukiadaki and Kretsos the employment and industrial relations landscape in Greece after the memoranda resembles that of a laissez-faire environment, in which the negotiation capacity of social partners has been reduced (2012).

In the new industrial relations landscape there is no incentive for the enterprises to engage in a regulated labour market. Thanks to the new legislative framework, employers may undermine the provisions of a collective agreement and regulate the terms and conditions of the employment relation [that is limited only by the National General Collective Agreement (GSEE)]. As the negotiation of workplace regulations will no longer result in arbitration, it is likely that the future employment relations will be introduced by employers through signing individual agreements than collective ones (Koukiadaki and Kretsos 2012).

In the era of Memoranda, Troika's monologue has replaced the SP/SD procedures. The future of SD procedures in Greece will depend on the new balance between capital and labour. The latter will be affected by the industrial relations climate, the durability of SP/SD institutions, the social partners' willingness to participate in SD and the influence of the European social partnership model.

References

Aranitou V, Yannakourou M (2004) The social dialogue in Greece. Athens

Degryse C (2000) European social dialogue: a mixed picture. ETUI, Discussion Working Papers, Brussels

European Foundation for the Improvement of Living and Working Conditions (2002) Challenges and opportunities for social dialogue and tripartism. European Union Presidency conference, Elsinore, 29–30 October 2002

Ishikawa J (2003) Key features on national social dialogue: a social dialogue resource book. ILO, Geneva

Kioukias D (2003) Reorganising social policies through social partnerships: Greece in European perspective. Soc Policy Adm 37(2):121–132

Koukiadaki A, Kretsos L (2012) Opening Pandora's box: the sovereign debt crisis and labour market regulation. Ind Law J 41(3):276–304

Koutroukis T (1997) Social dialogue: the European and the Greek dimension. Manag Inf 8 (in Greek)

Koutroukis T, Kretsos L (2004) Social dialogue in Greece: the national and the local dimension, in labour. Institute for Urban Environment and Human Resources, Athens, pp 57–70

Koutroukis T, Kretsos L (2008) Social dialogue in areas and times of depression: evidence from social Greece. Afr J Bus Manag 2(3):77–84

Lavdas K (2007) Interest groups in disjointed corporatism: social dialogue in Greece and European 'Competitive Corporatism'. West Eur Polit 28(2):297–316

OKE (1999) Social dialogue in Southeastern Europe. Opinion No 29, Athens

OKE (2002) Social dialogue in Greece: assessment-trends-prospects (opinion). Athens

Patra E (2012) Social dialogue and collective bargaining in the time of crisis: the case of Greece. Working paper No 38, ILO, Geneva

The Copenhagen Centre (1999) New employment partnerships in Europe: innovative local employment strategies. Copenhagen

Tsarouhas D (2008) Social partnership in Greece: is there a Europeanization effect? Eur J Ind Relat 14(3):347–365

Social Capital and Corruption: Evidence from Western Balkan Countries

Marija Džunić and Nataša Golubović

Abstract Throughout the last decade, empirical evidence from transition countries has confirmed low levels of social capital, a resource often regarded as a determinant of the speed of reforms, economic growth and social development in these countries. On the other hand, corruption is considered to be closely related to social capital, whereas high levels of corruption reflect institutional weakness, which impedes contract enforcement. Such environment prevents building trust relations between economic actors. There are opinions that certain types of social capital are likely to increase corruption, which brings into question the causal direction of their relationship. The aim of the paper is to measure and compare the levels of social capital and corruption in Western Balkan countries. In addition, relations between social capital, corruption and GDP *per capita* levels will be explored in order to establish whether higher corrupt countries report lower levels of trust and civic participation and therefore lower GDP *per capita*.

Keywords Corruption • Social capital • Trust • GDP • Western Balkans

JEL Classification Codes Z13—Social Norms, Social Capital and Social Networks • D73—Corruption

1 Introduction

The concept that is receiving growing attention in the literature about corruption is social capital. Exploring the relationship between corruption and social capital is particularly relevant for the former socialist economies (Rose-Ackerman 1999). These countries have undergone a process of systemic transformation. Abrupt political and economic changes in early 1990s created a kind of institutional vacuum, which is characterized by fast destruction of existing institutional infrastructure and slow development of the new one. It contributed to social disintegration process, disruption of social ties, crisis of the existing system of values and norms. In such conditions, many phenomena which characterize transition period—

M. Džunić (✉) • N. Golubović
Faculty of Economics, University of Niš, Niš, Serbia
e-mail: marija_dzunic@ni.ac.rs; natasa.golubovic@eknfak.ni.ac.rs

A. Karasavvoglou et al. (eds.), *The First Decade of Living with the Global Crisis*, Contributions to Economics, DOI 10.1007/978-3-319-24267-5_7

grey economy, irregular transactions, smuggling, bribery and corruption have become common behavioral patterns.

Empirical studies that attempted to establish potential relation between social capital and corruption were mainly focused on investigating the influence of generalized trust and civic engagement on the level of perceived corruption within a society. These studies confirmed that societies with higher level of generalized trust and civic engagement tend to have lower level of corruption (Bjornskov 2004; La Porta et al. 1997; Uslaner 2004). Although civic engagement on the whole is connected to lower corruption, high levels of certain types of civic engagement are actually linked to higher, rather than lower, corruption (Harris 2007; Lipset and Lenz 2000).

The aim of the paper is to explore the relationship between social capital and corruption in Western Balkan countries. In addition, we will try to establish whether higher corrupt countries report lower levels of trust and civic participation and therefore lower GDP *per capita* levels. For that purpose, we will analyze the relationship between selected indicators of corruption, social capital and GDP *per capita*. The paper is organized as follows: Sect. 1 contains introductory remarks and outlines expected contributions of the study. Section 2 reviews studies on social capital and corruption, explains conceptual framework and empirical strategy. Section 3 describes the data and sampling issues. Section 4 discusses the main findings. Section 5 presents conclusions, along with the recommendations for further research.

2 Corruption and Social Capital

Corruption as a social phenomenon has a long history (Brioschi 2004). Although many authors attempted to define corruption and identify factors that may lead to it (Mauro 1995; Paldam 2002; Rose-Ackerman 1999; Schleifer and Vishny 1993), there is a lot of ambiguity about causes and forms of corruption (Advig and Fjeldstad 2000; Lambsdorff 2007).

Andrei Schleifer and Robert Vishny focus their attention only on corruption in public sector. They define corruption as "the sale by government officials of government property for personal gain" (Schleifer and Vishny 1993, p. 599). The most commonly used definition of corruption is that it represents the abuse of public power for a private gain. This definition points out that the source of corruption is in public authorities. Because of its operativity, this definition has been accepted by the World Bank and Transparency International. Perhaps the most comprehensive definition of corruption is given by Vito Tanzi (1995), who emphasizes that corruption is associated with a deliberate violation of impartiality in decision making process, for the purpose of appropriating benefits for oneself or for related individuals from this behavior. This definition is wider than the former, since it includes corruption both in public and private sector. It represents a solid analytical framework for the study of corruption. However, using this definition as a criterion for evaluating whether certain transaction can be labeled as corruption or not, causes certain problems. The point is that it is quite difficult to operationally define bias in decision making and violations of the impartiality principle (especially in the cases when there are no formal rules and decision-making is left to the discretion of state officials—for example granting the import license). In addition, temporal separation of service provision by the corrupted individual and the counter service provided by the corrupter creates analytical problems in establishing the existence of private benefits for the corrupted. As in some cases we have counter service for the organization where corrupted is a member (for example a political party), it is difficult to identify personal benefits.

Definition accepted by the World Bank is focused on corruption in the public sector, which is, by its size and consequences, a far more significant phenomenon than corruption in the private sector. State institutions represent fertile ground for the emergence and spread of corruption (Treisman 2000).

As far as the causes of corruption are concerned, the concept that is receiving growing attention in the literature is social capital. Social capital refers to those features of social organization that support coordination and cooperation within society (Putnam 1993). Trust, social networks and social norms are considered as parameters of social capital (Putnam 1995; Raiser 1999). It is often emphasized as a source of economic development and progress. Empirical research confirmed that there is a positive correlation between social capital and economic development (Raiser 1999; Putnam 1993).

Numerous empirical studies flourished in an attempt to address the potential relation between those features of social organization such as trust, norms and networks (social capital) and corruption. Empirical studies confirmed that societies with higher level of generalized trust and civic engagement tend to have lower level of corruption. Higher level of trust encourages cooperation beyond one's narrow social network. Trusting societies tend to have efficient governments, less corruption, which lead to higher level of economic development (Bjornskov 2004; La Porta et al. 1997; Uslaner 2004). However, we can ascribe this effect to generalized and not particularized trust. Strong ties, family orientations and particularized trust, according to Harris (2007), are associated with higher corruption. There are some ambiguities about causal direction of this relationship. Higher level of trust leads to lower corruption, but corruption increase could also lead to lower level of trust because individuals receive signals that honesty may not pay off (Bjornskov 2004).

Social capital, however, does not always produce positive externalities (Fukuyama 1995; Putnam 2000). In order to understand the relationship between social capital and corruption it is therefore necessary to distinguish between different kinds of social capital: bonding and bridging. Bonding social capital refers to social relations between members of the group who share similar interests. Bridging social capital is associated with the cross-cutting ties between different groups. The absence of cross-cutting ties hinders the circulation of ideas, information and resources between groups, which negatively affects growth. Bonding social capital creates high level of trust and trustworthiness and specific reciprocity inside the group, excluding those individuals outside the group. This characteristic is particularly important regarding corruption, because exclusiveness is necessary in order to hide corrupt practices. There are few empirical studies dealing with the extent to which bonding social capital affects the level of corruption. One such study was conducted by Lipset and Lenz (2000), who found that countries with high level of familism tend to be among the more corrupt. A more comprehensive study, performed by Donna Harris (2007), revealed that bonding social capital affects corruption both directly and indirectly, because it makes corruption more predictable, especially when it discourages trust and cooperation between members of the group and outsiders.

3 Methodological Framework of the Research

As the aim of the paper is to measure and compare the level of social capital and corruption in a specific group of Western Balkan countries (Albania, Bosnia and Herzegovina, Croatia, FYR Macedonia, Montenegro and Serbia), relevant databases concerning these social phenomena will be used for this purpose. The main criterion for selecting empirical databases was the availability of data and their comparability in different periods.

There are many obstacles in the attempt to measure the level of corruption, which are caused by the lack of universally accepted definition and existence of many types and forms of corruption. It is not possible to measure corruption directly, as corrupt activities take place in secrecy so that the time, actors and the amount of appropriated benefits in corrupt activities cannot be officially determined. None of the parties in such transactions want to leave evidence that could later be used against them. In such conditions, the only effective way of measuring corruption examines the perceptions of corruption. This refers to the examination of individuals that may be or have been participants or observers of corruption activities. This kind of measurement is conducted by using survey method, where the respondents answer the questions verbally or in writing, in the presence or absence of interviewer. This method of measuring corruption also faces certain problems that, above all, refer to the credibility of collected data. In an effort to conceal involvement in illegal activities, individuals can give false information, which distorts the picture of the level of corruption. One of the most frequently used indicators of corruption—Corruption Perception Index (CPI) is based on this method of measuring corruption (Transparency International 2010). CPI is an aggregate index which measures perception of corruption in the public sector (the corruption of government officials and public servants). The index is composed on the basis of 13 different sources, which comprise the opinions of experts, institution representatives and business leaders. The objects of measurement are the perceptions of corruption, instead of real facts (for example, number of convictions or newspaper articles). Regardless of the methodological problems in calculating the index, the CPI is a widely used indicator of corruption.

Concerning the measurement of social capital, following the example of previous empirical studies, two databases have been selected: World Values Survey (WVS 2009) and European Values Study (EVS 2011), as the most comprehensive databases, comprising data on attitudes of individuals and their social activities in different areas of human interest—religion, politics, economic and social life. For the purpose of collecting data, both studies apply systematized and standardized approach based on interviewing a representative sample of respondents in each of the countries covered by the survey. It is important to note that the formulation of the questions in different surveys is the same, which allows the comparison of data obtained. The use of identical questionnaires and data collection methodology allows us to use the data of the World Values Survey for the third and fourth wave of research (published in 2000 and 2005), and the fourth wave of European Values Study (completed in 2010), in order to provide full data coverage.

Taking into account the historical and social diversities, the comparative analysis of social capital and corruption in Western Balkan countries will include an overview of CPI values as indicator of corruption and trust and civic participation as components of social capital in the selected sample of countries. The level of perceived corruption and available social capital in the analyzed country group will be compared to indicator values in developed European countries (EU members and Scandinavian countries), in order to fully illustrate the state of social capital and corruption in Western Balkans and their mutual relations. An overview of GDP *per capita* levels in current US dollars, (World Development Indicators, World Bank) should point to possible effects of social capital availability and spread of corruption on economic performance of analyzed countries. Correlation and regression analysis will be used in order to estimate the relations between social capital, corruption and GDP *per capita*, as well as to determine if there are statistically significant effects of social capital and corruption on GDP *per capita*. The analysis of variance will be used to explore mean differences of all listed indicators between Western Balkans and other groups of European countries. The limited availability of data in different periods, as well as problems of the quantification of social capital and corruption, requires caution in the interpretation of the main findings.

4 Results and Discussion

4.1 Perception of Corruption

Measuring corruption at the national level is based on the Corruption Perception Index (CPI), an aggregate indicator of the administrative and political aspects of corruption. The index values enable the ranking of countries based on the perception of respondents about the prevalence of bribery of public officials, misuse of taxpayers' money, irregularities in the implementation of public procurement and the like. CPI value ranges from 0 (high corruption) to 10 (total absence of

Table 1 Corruption perception index in the countries of Western Balkans (2010)

Country	Corruption perception index	Country ranking
Albania	3.3	87
Bosnia and Herzegovina	3.2	91
Croatia	4.1	62
Macedonia FYR	4.1	62
Montenegro	3.7	69
Serbia	3.5	78
Western Balkans Average	*3.65*	

corruption). Table 1 shows the CPI values for the Western Balkan countries in 2010 (Transparency International 2010).

Western Balkan countries occupy positions in the middle of the ranking list of 178 countries surveyed in 2010. The countries with the highest rankings are Croatia and FYROM, both with the rank 62, with respect to the same index value (4.1 out of a possible 10). The highest level of perceived corruption in the public sector is measured in Bosnia and Herzegovina (3.2), which ranks this country 91st in the list. Other Balkan countries are ranked between these positions. The average value of the CPI for the given group of countries of 3.65 indicates a high level of corruption, as measured on the basis of subjective perceptions of respondents about the prevalence of corruption. In order to compare the extent of corruption in the Western Balkans with other countries, Table 2 shows the values of CPI and the rankings of EU and Scandinavian countries.

Index values in Table 2 indicate that the lowest level of corruption is measured in the Scandinavian countries, where CPI is almost three times higher than in the Western Balkans. The level of corruption is relatively low in Western Europe, with an average index of 7.83. The comparison of European countries by the level of perceived corruption reveals a noticeable gap between the Northern and Western Europe and south-European countries, where some countries, such as Italy and Greece have very low values of CPI, similar to the Balkan countries. Finally, the group of Central and Eastern Europe countries, which have relatively recently become members of the EU and belong to the group of transition economies, have the highest level of widespread corruption within the EU. Most developed countries in this group, such as Estonia, Slovenia and Poland, are already approaching Western European countries, while the rest of the countries still cope with relatively high levels of corruption.

The CPI values for the EU and Scandinavian countries imply a very disadvantaged position of the Western Balkans in the field of perceived corruption. Index values indicate that the level of corruption in the Balkan countries is the highest in Europe, even three times higher than the perceived corruption in the Scandinavian countries and two times higher than in Western Europe. Observing the data on the level of corruption at different time periods (Table 3), a positive trend can be noticed, as the level of corruption on average decreased by 0.8 points for a 5 year period (according to the methodology of calculating the CPI, as a significant change

Table 2 Perception corruption index in the EU and Scandinavia (2010)

Country	Corruption perception index	Country ranking
Denmark	9.3	1
Finland	9.2	4
Sweden	9.2	4
Norway	8.6	10
Iceland	8.5	11
Scandinavia	*8.96*	
Netherlands	8.8	7
Luxembourg	8.5	11
Ireland	8.0	14
Germany	7.9	15
Austria	7.9	15
United Kingdom	7.6	20
Belgium	7.1	22
France	6.8	25
Western EU	*7.83*	
Cyprus	6.3	28
Spain	6.1	30
Portugal	6.0	32
Malta	5.6	37
Italy	3.9	67
Greece	3.5	78
Southern EU	*5.23*	
Estonia	6.5	26
Slovenia	6.4	27
Poland	5.3	41
Lithuania	5.0	46
Hungary	4.7	50
Czech Republic	4.6	53
Latvia	4.3	59
Slovakia	4.3	59
Romania	3.7	69
Bulgaria	3.6	73
Central and Eastern Europe	*4.84*	
EU27	*6.30*	

in the level of corruption perception is considered a change in the value of the index by more than 0.3 points). If we take into account the fact that in the year of 2000 the measured value of the CPI in the former state of Yugoslavia (to which belonged five of the observed six Balkan countries) was 1.3, it can be concluded that in the last 10 years the level of corruption has been decreasing, although the index values still indicate widespread corruption.

Table 3 Corruption perception index in Western Balkans (2005, 2010)

Country	Corruption perception index 2005	Corruption perception index 2010
Albania	2.4	3.3
Bosnia and Herzegovina	2.9	3.2
Croatia	3.4	4.1
Macedonia FYR	2.7	4.1
Montenegro	2.8	3.7
Serbia	2.8	3.5
Western Balkans Average	*2.83*	*3.65*

When interpreting these data, it should be noted that the Index is based on the subjective perceptions of individuals in these countries, not in real cases of corruption that have been prosecuted by the relevant institutions. Although data on the perceptions of individuals are highly subjective, their use is justified by the fact that corruption involves hidden actions that are difficult to measure. Also, over time, the perception of corruption has proved to be reliable in assessing the level of corruption.

4.2 Social Capital in Western Balkans

4.2.1 Measuring Trust in Balkan Countries

Most surveys obtain data on the level of trust by asking the standard question: "Generally speaking, would you say that most people can be trusted or that you cannot be too careful in dealing with people?". The measure of trust obtained this way is the percentage of the population in a country that believes that people in general can be trusted. Data on the level of generalized trust in Western Balkan countries for 2010 are presented in Table 4. Empirical data indicate the low average level of trust in Western Balkans.

In order to further illustrate the state of trust in the analyzed countries, the average generalized trust in the Balkans is compared to the average level of trust in the 27 members of EU (33.1 %). The results indicate a large gap in the level of trust between these two country groups. The largest gap is observed by comparing the level of trust in Western Balkan countries with traditionally high trust in the Scandinavian countries, where over 65 % of respondents are willing to trust people (EVS 2011). In developed European countries there is a growing trend of the average level of trust, which is another important difference from the Balkan countries. According to this, the differences between Western Balkans and EU in the level of trust are similar to those in the level of perceived corruption.

Table 4 Generalized trust in Western Balkans (2010)

Country	Generalized trust (%)
Albania	10.6
Bosnia and Herzegovina	26.6
Croatia	19.7
Macedonia FYR	20.1
Montenegro	24.9
Serbia	11.8
Western Balkans Average	*18.9*
EU27	*33.1*

Table 5 Generalized trust in Western Balkans (2000–2010)

Country	2000	2005	2010
Albania	27.0	24.4	10.6
Bosnia and Herzegovina	28.3	15.8	26.6
Croatia	28.4	18.3	19.7
Macedonia FYR	8.2	13.5	20.1
Montenegro	30.4	32.9	24.9
Serbia	25.1	18.4	11.8
Western Balkans Average	*24.6*	*20.6*	*18.9*

Data from different time periods (Table 5) point to a continuous decline of trust. Before the year 2000, a quarter of respondents were willing to trust the people in their environment, while over the next 5 years, only one fifth of the respondents maintained that attitude. In the third period, the average percentage of trusting individuals was less than 20 %. The only exception to this trend is FYROM, as the only country where the level of trust has increased in the last decade. During the past 5 years, a significant increase in trust was recorded in Bosnia and Herzegovina, while trust in Croatia increased for modest 1.3 %. The lowest levels of trust according to the latest measurements are measured in Albania (10.6 %) and Serbia (11.8 %), where the level of trust decreased 2.5 times in a decade's time.

The presented data imply the consistency of the levels of trust within the group of observed countries, indicating similar conditions of social capital accumulation, along with the fact that the level of trust in the Balkan countries lags significantly behind the level of trust in the developed market economies. Given the fact that the Balkan countries belong to the group of post-socialist countries, some theorists (Paldam and Svedsen 2000, 2001; Adam et al. 2004) claim this gap to be caused by the breakdown of social capital in the socialist regime, in which all kinds of social interactions outside the immediate networks of family and friendship relations have been discouraged. However, since more than a decade has passed since the change of the political systems in the surveyed countries and the level of trust has not increased, these theories are called into question.

4.2.2 The Intensity of Civic Participation

Besides measuring the level of trust based on direct questioning of individuals about their readiness to trust people, another method of measuring social capital is by determining the intensity of their participation in different social organizations. It is assumed that an individual will be more inclined to trust the individuals in an organization where he himself is a member, than total strangers. Measuring the degree of formal civic participation is based on the questions about belonging to various voluntary organizations. Table 6 presents the citizen participation in formal social networks in Western Balkans, in the two observed periods, as a percentage of respondents who identified themselves as belonging to these organizations.

The measurement of the intensity of citizens' participation is based on the assumption that not all social organizations are equally significant in terms of the formation of social capital, so various organizations in the table are sorted in specific types of organizations (Putnam, Olson and others). The intensity of social participation in the Balkan countries can be assessed as low, according to a small number of organizations with over 10 % of participants.

Comparing the average citizen participation in two consecutive periods shows that social participation almost invariably decreases in all the countries and all types of organizations. The exception is the increase in participation of Croatian citizens in organizations of Putnam-type, as well as maintaining the same level of participation in other organizations in Serbia and Montenegro (as it is a very low percentage of participation, it cannot be evaluated as an important step in encouraging social participation).

The relatively high level of citizen participation is recorded in sports organizations (average 9.46 %), political parties (8.87 %) and trade unions (7.71 %), while the lowest participation is in human rights organizations (1.8 %). On average, citizens of Western Balkans most intensively participate in organizations of Olson-type (6.98 %) compared to Putnam-type organizations. The highest percentages of participation were measured in Albania, and the lowest in Bosnia and Herzegovina. Bearing in mind that the Balkan countries belong to the post-socialist economies, the participation in community organizations in these countries must be considered with respect to the specifics of social participation in the pre-transition period. In these countries, gradual transformation of forms of social participation has been taking place, from the mandatory memberships in political parties and trade unions, to the voluntary participation in independent organizations with their own autonomy and identity. In most of these countries, political factors have a great impact on all forms of social activity, which explains the high level of citizen involvement in Olson-type organizations.

In addition to the formal participation of individuals in voluntary organizations, an important element of social capital is the intensity of informal social contacts. Social activism in informal networks is divided into bridging and bonding social capital. Bridging social capital is expressed through the frequency of spending time with friends, the importance of friends in life and spending time with different

Table 6 Belonging to voluntary organizations in Western Balkans (2005–2010)

Type		Albania		B and H		Croatia		FYROM		Montenegro		Serbia	
	Period	2005	2010	2005	2010	2005	2010	2005	2010	2005	2010	2005	2010
Putnam	Sports/recreation	10.6	9.7	11.3	4.9	11.9	13.2	12.9	8.4	9.6	4.5	9.6	6.9
	Cultural education	13.5	4.6	4.1	1.9	5.6	8.6	11.7	7.5	5.8	3.0	5.8	4.4
	Youth work	12.3	8.9	2.1	1.1	2.1	4.0	5.1	5.8	1.9	2.6	1.9	2.0
	Average	*12.1*	*7.7*	*5.8*	*2.6*	*6.5*	*8.6*	*9.9*	*7.2*	*5.8*	*3.4*	*5.8*	*4.4*
Olson	Trade unions	9.4	7.7	6.8	2.2	10.6	6.0	6.0	4.1	14.7	4.6	14.7	5.7
	Professional associations	10.8	7.2	2.4	0.9	3.2	2.9	6.7	4.5	4.0	2.6	4.0	3.6
	Political parties	14.5	11.0	7.1	4.4	3.7	6.9	11.5	11.4	12.3	4.6	12.3	6.7
	Average	*11.6*	*8.6*	*5.4*	*2.5*	*5.8*	*5.3*	*8.1*	*6.7*	*10.3*	*3.9*	*10.3*	*5.3*
Other	Religious or church	20.4	12	8.0	3.9	12.9	10.3	10.9	4.0	3.0	3.4	3.0	3.3
	Environment	10.4	6.0	1.9	0.9	2.1	3.1	4.9	4.7	2.5	2.2	2.5	2.4
	Human rights	6.4	5.3	0.2	0.4	0.7	0.7	3.4	0.3	0.8	1.6	0.8	1.1
	Welfare	13.6	8.2	1.5	1.2	2.1	3.0	7.2	2.5	3.6	2.6	3.6	2.3
	Local community	11.6	6.5	1.1	0.6	1.6	1.8	5.6	3.8	0.6	1.4	0.6	2.1
	Women's groups	13.6	7.4	2.7	2.1	2.2	2.9	6.0	2.7	1.8	2.7	1.8	1.8
	Peace movements	7.2	5.1	0.2	0.6	1.1	1.0	5.4	1.0	0.4	1.5	0.4	1.1
	Voluntary health	12.9	6.5	2.5	0.9	3.1	2.6	7.8	2.7	1.8	2.4	1.8	2.8
	Other groups	5.2	5.6	3.1	1.1	4.4	4.3	7.7	4.4	3.9	1.6	3.9	1.4
	Average	*11.3*	*7.0*	*2.4*	*1.3*	*3.4*	*3.3*	*6.5*	*2.9*	*2.0*	*2.2*	*2.0*	*2.0*

Table 7 Bridging social capital—friends important in life (2000–2010)

Country	2000	2005	2010
Albania	19.1	32.0	17.7
B and H	71.6	70.6	39.7
Serbia	48.3	57.5	41.5
FYROM	49.6	49.2	74.8
Montenegro	47.1	42.8	51.9
Croatia	48.4	36.3	34.8

Table 8 Bridging social capital—family important in life (2000–2010)

Country	2000	2005	2010
Albania	96.3	96.1	91.0
B i H	97.2	98.7	76.8
Serbia	88.6	92.0	86.1
FYROM	98.0	98.1	93.6
Montenegro	88.3	92.3	92.0
Croatia	85.3	78.7	77.1

social groups. Bonding social capital refers to relations with close relatives and is measured with the following indicators: the importance of family in life, preparedness to help immediate family and concern for the family. Tables 7 and 8 show the percentages of respondents that consider friends, acquaintances and family members "very important" in their lives.

Based on presented data, it can be concluded that individuals who live in Western Balkans highly value relations with friends and family and rely on their support during life. With the exception of Albania, in all Balkan countries, about half of the respondents highly values relations with friends and acquaintances. In Croatia, the data record decline in the importance of these kind of social relations over time, while in other countries in the latest period, the percentage of respondents who rely on friends is higher than 40 %. The importance of bonding ties in the Balkans is very high, considering that over 90 % of respondents declare that family is very important in life. The intensity of this kind of social relations is constant over time, as in all periods the percentage of respondents who place a great importance on family is high. Only in the last period a decrease of dependence on family ties is observed.

Informal social networks have the character of a safety net and are suitable for building personalized relationships of trust, reciprocity and solidarity. Bridging ties are crucial for obtaining information, discovering new opportunities and advancing in society, while bonding ties strengthen relations within homogeneous groups and provide help and support to overcome problems of material and immaterial character. Our findings reveal that the citizens of Western Balkans in the difficult years of economic and political changes have turned to strengthening informal social ties and personalized trust, seeking safety in social niches composed of close relatives and friends.

4.2.3 Corruption, Social Capital and GDP *Per Capita*

The comparative analysis indicates the inverse relationship between the level of perceived corruption and the availability of social capital. Specifically, countries with low levels of corruption are at the same time countries with continuously high levels of trust (for example, the Scandinavian and Western Europe countries). On the other hand, in the Western Balkans the level of trust is low, while corruption perception indexes show high levels of corruption. Further question is to determine whether this state of corruption and social capital affects GDP *per capita* levels in the analyzed countries. Table 9 shows the values of the corruption perception index, the percentages of generalized trust and GDP *per capita* in current US dollars (World Development Indicators, The World Bank).

The comparative data indicate that low values of social capital indicators and high level of corruption perception in Western Balkans are accompanied by the low levels of GDP *per capita* (the average value of GDP *per capita* in the Western Balkans is 6267 dollars, which is the lowest average value in comparison to all other groups of European countries). At a first glance, it can be assumed that GDP *per capita* levels are proportional to the level of generalized trust, while the relationship between GDP *per capita* and the level of corruption is such that countries with widespread corruption report low levels of GDP *per capita*. In contrast to Western Balkans, the Scandinavian and Western European countries are characterized by the absence of corruption and high levels of trust, followed by high values of GDP *per capita*.

In order to get quantitative estimations of the relationship between presented variables, the first step is to determine correlation coefficients between the indicators of corruption perception, trust, civic participation (sum of participants in welfare, cultural, local community, environment and youth organizations) and GDP

Table 9 Corruption, social capital and GDP *per capita* (2010)

Country	Corruption perception index	Generalized trust (%)	GDP *per capita* (current US dollars)
Albania	3.3	10.6	3764
B and H	3.2	26.6	4362
Croatia	4.1	19.7	13,327
FYROM	4.1	20.1	4442
Montenegro	3.7	24.9	6636
Serbia	3.5	11.8	5073
Balkan average	***3.65***	***18.9***	***6267***
Scandinavia	*8.96*	*67.6*	*55,064*
Western EU	*7.83*	*38.6*	*49,692*
Southern EU	*5.23*	*22.4*	*26,374*
Eastern EU	*4.84*	*23.9*	*13,495*
EU27	***6.30***	***33.1***	***31,126***

Table 10 Correlation coefficients

Variables	CPI	Trust	Civic participation	GDP *per capita*
CPI	1	0.784** (0.000)	0.763** (0.000)	0.877** (0.000)
Trust		1	0.584** (0.000)	0.756** (0.000)
Civic participation			1	0.645** (0.000)
GDP *per capita*				1

**Correlation is significant at the 0.01 level (2-tailed), N = 35

Table 11 Partial correlations

Control variable	Variables	CPI	Trust	Civic participation
GDP *per capita*	CPI	1	0.594** (0.000)	0.424* (0.014)
	Trust		1	396* (0.023)
	Civic participation			1

**Correlation is significant at the 0.01 level
*Correlation is significant at the 0.05 level

Table 12 Model summary

Model	R	R square	Adjusted R square	Std. error of the estimate
1	**.809**[a]	**.654**	0.620	13,924.76

[a]Predictors: (constant), CPI, trust, civic participation

per capita levels for all the listed countries. Table 10 presents the correlation matrix, calculated by Spearman's rho (two-tailed test).

Correlation analysis indicates statistically significant correlations between all the observed variables, implying the strongest positive relation between CPI and GDP *per capita* (0.877). Partial correlation coefficients between CPI, trust and civic participation, controlling for GDP *per capita* are presented in Table 11.

It is important to note that GDP *per capita* levels are strongly correlated with all the social capital and corruption variables, leading to a possibility of creating a representative linear regression model. The proposed model tests the influence of corruption perception, trust and civic participation on GDP *per capita* levels as dependent variable:

$$\text{GDP}\,\textit{per capita} = \beta_0 + \beta_1\,\text{CPI} + \beta_2\,\text{Trust} + \beta_3\,\text{Civic participation}$$

Model summary, ANOVA results and regression coefficients obtained by OLS method are presented in Tables 12, 13 and 14.

The coefficient of multiple correlation R = .809 (Table 12) indicates high level of compliance of all tested variables, while coefficient of determination $R^2 = .654$ confirms the representativeness of the proposed model, since 65.4 % of the fluctuation in GDP *per capita* levels in selected countries is explained by the fluctuations in the chosen independent variables. OLS regression reveals statistical significance of only one predictor—CPI, indicating a strong linear association of perception of

Table 13 ANOVA[b]

Model	Sum of squares	df	Mean square	F	Sig.
Regression	$1.135e^{10}$	3	$3.782e^{9}$	19.507	.000[a]
Residuals	$6.011e^{9}$	32	$1.939e^{8}$		
Total	$1.736e^{10}$	35			

[a]Predictors: (constant), CPI, trust, civic participation
[b]Dependant variable: GDP *per capita*

Table 14 Regression coefficients

	Unstandardized coefficients		Standardized coefficients	
Model	β	Std. error	βeta	t
Constant	−23,368.73 (0.006)	7866.37		−2.971
CPI	**8121.15**[a] (0.000)	2084.035	**0.733**	3.897
Trust	62.559 (0.784)	226.185	0.050	0.277
CP	54.909 (0.703)	142.769	0.053	0.385

[a]Dependant variable: GDP *per capita*

corruption and the level of GDP *per capita* in the selected sample. Standardized β coefficient value points that 73.3 % of the GDP *per capita* variability is explained by the CPI variations, taking into account the variability of all independent variables. Trust and civic participation turn out to be insignificant predictors in the proposed model.

The comparative analysis of data on both corruption perception and social capital has implied an evident gap between the Scandinavia and Western Europe on one side, and the countries of Southern and Eastern Europe and the Western Balkans, on the other. In order to further estimate this gap, we have conducted a one way ANOVA of the differences in mean values of indicators between five respective groups of countries (Scandinavia, Western Europe, Southern Europe, Eastern Europe and Western Balkans). Table 15 shows that there are statistically significant differences between these groups concerning mean values of CPI, trust, civic participation and GDP *per capita*.

For the purpose of further exploration of differences among means, in order to provide specific information on which indicators differ significantly between groups of countries, we have conducted post hoc test, where multiple comparisons of means are estimated by LSD (Least Significant Difference) test. Due to the space limitations, we present only the comparisons of indicator mean values in Western Balkan countries to other country groups (Table 16).

Multiple comparisons show significant mean differences of the CPI indicators between Western Balkan countries and all other country groups, confirming that, among all European countries, the levels of corruption perception are the highest in

Table 15 One way ANOVA—differences between groups of countries

	Sum of squares	df	Mean square	F	Sig.
CPI					
Between groups	120.548	4	30.137	43.636	0.000
Within groups	20.719	30	0.691		
Total	141.267	34			
Trust					
Between groups	8893.260	4	2223.315	30.567	0.000
Within groups	2182.067	30	72.736		
Total	11,075.327	34			
Civic participation					
Between groups	6573.862	4	1643.466	5.001	0.003
Within groups	9858.719	30	328.624		
Total	16,432.582	34			
GDP per capita					
Between groups	$1.236e^{10}$	4	$3.091e^{9}$	18.569	0.000
Within groups	$4.994e^{9}$	30	$1.665e^{8}$		
Total	$1.736e^{10}$	34			

Table 16 Post hoc test (comparisons of Western Balkan countries to other country groups)

				95 % Confidence interval	
	Mean difference	Std. error	Sig.	Lower bound	Upper bound
CPI W. Balkans to:					
Scandinavia	−5.31**	0.50323	0.000	−6.3377	−4.2823
Western Europe	−4.18**	0.44882	0.000	−5.0916	−3.2584
Southern Europe	−1.58**	0.47981	0.002	−2.5632	−0.6034
Eastern Europe	−1.19**	0.42915	0.009	−2.0664	−0.3136
Trust W. Balkans to:					
Scandinavia	−48.63**	5.16427	0.000	−59.1769	−38.0831
Western Europe	−19.6**	4.60592	0.000	−29.0066	−10.1934
Southern Europe	−3.46	4.92394	0.487	−13.5227	6.5894
Eastern Europe	−4.97	4.40411	0.268	−13.9644	4.0244
Civic part. W. Balkans to:					
Scandinavia	−25.52*	10.97704	0.027	−47.9348	−3.0986
Western Europe	−27.55**	9.79023	0.009	−47.5485	−7.5598
Southern Europe	4.07	10.46620	0.700	−17.3082	25.4415
Eastern Europe	0.72	9.36125	0.939	−18.3949	19.8416
GDP W. Balkans to:					
Scandinavia	−48,796.87**	7812.60094	0.000	−64,752.3264	−32,841.4069
Western Europe	−43,424.29**	6967.92272	0.000	−57,654.6883	−29,193.8950
Southern Europe	−20,107.17*	7449.02272	0.011	−35,320.1006	−4894.2327
Eastern Europe	−7228.17	6662.60847	0.287	−20,835.0284	6378.6951

**Correlation is significant at the 0.01 level
*Correlation is significant at the 0.05 level

Western Balkan countries. Significant differences appear also in the mean values of trust and civic participation indicators when comparing Western Balkan countries with Scandinavia and Western Europe. Concerning GDP *per capita* levels, significant mean differences occur when comparing Western Balkan countries with Scandinavia, Western and Southern Europe. According to the level of generalized trust and civic participation, Western Balkans are closest to the countries of Eastern Europe, with which they share a common feature—going through the transition process and transformation of their political and economic systems.

5 Conclusion

The comparative analysis of social capital and corruption in Western Balkan countries has clearly pointed out the adverse relationship between these social phenomena. The analyzed countries are characterized by low levels of generalized trust as well as the poor level of civil society development, but also by highest levels of perceived corruption among the European countries. Strong informal networks of bonding social relations and lack of efficient formal institutions seem to be beneficial for spreading corrupt activities. Also, the analysis shows declining levels of generalized trust over time. Even though a positive trend is noticed in the membership in social organizations, citizens of Balkan countries still do not engage much in this kind of associations. On the other hand, they are intensively relying on informal contacts and ties within primary relationships (family and friends), with an extremely high percentage of those who rely on this type of social networks in everyday life. The fact that the creation of social capital in the Balkan countries was directed towards strengthening the informal networks as an alternative to the generalized trust or formal participation, has contributed to low economic activity and adverse economic results. The analysis clearly indicates that countries with highest levels of corruption are also the countries with low levels of generalized trust, which is followed by slow economic activity and low GDP *per capita* values.

Taking into account the limitations in measuring subjective perceptions of corruption and social values such as trust, the interpretation of the results should be taken with caution. An attempt was made to determine the quantitative relations between social capital and corruption, in order to identify the strength of correlations between them as well as measurable effects on GDP *per capita*. There is a strong correlation between all indicators of social capital in the selected sample of 35 European countries, and furthermore, GDP *per capita* strongly correlates with both social capital (trust and civic participation) and corruption perception indicator values. A regression analysis has pointed out to statistically significant effects of corruption perception index on the GDP *per capita* levels. Concerning the Western Balkan countries, the analysis of variance has indicated the existence of significant differences in mean values of both social capital and corruption perception indicators, leading to conclusion that these countries are experiencing highest levels of corruption perception, while showing lowest levels of trust, civic participation and GDP *per capita*.

Acknowledgements The authors are grateful to the Republic of Serbia Ministry of Education, Science and Technological Development for the funds and support that made this research possible.

References

Adam F, Makarovic M, Roncevic B, Tomsic M (2004) The challenges of sustained development: the role of socio-cultural factors in East Central Europe. Central European University Press, Budapest

Advig JC, Fjeldstad O (2000) Research on corruption: a policy oriented survey. The Norwegian Agency for Development Co-operation (NORAD), December 2000

Bjornskov C (2004) How does social trust affect economic growth. Working paper 06-02, Aarhus School of Business, Department of Economics

Brioschi CA (2004) Breve storia della corruzione: dall'età antica ai giorni nostri. TEA, Milano

EVS (2011) European values study 2008: integrated dataset (EVS 2008). Gesis Datenarchiv, Köln. ZA4800, datafile version 3.0.0. Doi: 10.4232/1.11004

Fukuyama F (1995) Trust: the social virtue and the creation of prosperity. Hamish Hamilton, London

Harris D (2007) Bonding social capital and corruption: a cross-national empirical analysis. Environmental economy and policy research working papers, no 27.2007. University of Cambridge, UK

La Porta R et al (1997) Trust in large organizations. Am Econ Rev Pap Proc 87(2):333–338

Lambsdorff JG (2007) The institutional economics of corruption and reform: theory, evidence and policy. Cambridge University Press, Cambridge

Lipset SM, Lenz GS (2000) Corruption, culture, and market. In: Harrison LE, Huntingdon SP (eds) Culture matters: how values shape human progress. Basic Books, New York, NY

Mauro P (1995) Corruption and growth. Q J Econ 110(3):681–712

Paldam M (2002) The cross-country pattern of corruption: economics, culture and the seesaw dynamics. Eur J Polit Econ 18(2):215–240

Paldam M, Svedsen GT (2000) An essay on social capital: looking for the fire behind the smoke. Eur J Polit Econ 16(2):339–366

Paldam M, Svedsen GT (2001) Missing social capital and the transition in Eastern Europe. J Inst Innov Dev Transit 5:21–33

Putnam RD (1993) Making democracy work: civic traditions in modern Italy. Princeton University Press, Princeton, NJ

Putnam RD (1995) Tuning in, tuning out: the strange disappearance of social capital in America. Polit Sci Polit 28(4):664–683

Putnam RD (2000) Bowling alone: the collapse and revival of American community. Simon & Schuster, New York, NY

Raiser M (1999) Trust in transition. EBRD working paper no. 39. EBRD, London

Rose-Ackerman S (1999) Corruption and government. Causes, consequences and reform. Cambridge University Press, Cambridge

Schleifer A, Vishny R (1993) Corruption. Q J Econ 108(3):599–617

Tanzi V (1995) Corruption: arm's-length relationships and markets. In: Fiorentini G, Pelzman SM (eds) The economics of organised crime. Cambridge University Press, Cambridge

Transparency International (2010) Corruption perceptions index 2010 [Online]. Available: http://www.transparency.org/cpi2010/in_detail [16 Apr 2014]

Treisman D (2000) The causes of corruption: a cross national study. J Public Econ 76(3):399–457

Uslaner EM (2004) Trust and corruption. In: Lambsdorf JG et al (eds) Corruption and the new institutional economics. Routledge, London

World Bank, World Development Indicators [Online]. Available: http://data.worldbank.org/data-catalog/world-development-indicators [16 Apr 2014]
WVS (2009) World values survey 1981–2008 official aggregate v.20090901

Tax Morale and Compliance in Greece: An Approach for the Construction of a Questionnaire Survey

Panagiotis Mitrakos, Aristidis Bitzenis, Ioannis Makedos, and Panagiotis Kontakos

Abstract No comprehensive empirical research has been conducted to assess the qualitative variables that affect tax ethics in Greece. The proposed method of empirical research of this working paper is the use of a questionnaire survey. Accordingly, the steps toward the construction of such a questionnaire survey and the performance of stratified surveys are presented. The aim of the questionnaire survey is, firstly, to estimate the level of tax ethics and, secondly, to identify the factors that influence it. The size and impact of the problem in Greece is discussed based on international transparency indices. The results of the survey are expected to support the structuring of useful proposals and measures for improving the level of tax ethics and tax compliance in Greece.

Keywords Questionnaire survey • Tax ethics • Empirical evidence • Shadow economy • Greece

JEL Classification Codes O17—Formal and informal sectors; shadow economy; institutional arrangements • E26—Informal economy; underground economy • D0—Microeconomics

1 Introduction

The definition, assessment and analysis of tax morale and of the factors that influence it are extremely important in the confrontation of tax evasion and the underground economy. At the same time, no comprehensive empirical research has been conducted to assess the qualitative variables that affect tax ethics in Greece. The proposed method of empirical research of this paper is the use of a questionnaire survey. Accordingly, the steps toward the construction of such a questionnaire survey are presented. The aim of the questionnaire survey is, firstly, to estimate the

P. Mitrakos (✉) • A. Bitzenis • I. Makedos • P. Kontakos
Department of International and European Studies, University of Macedonia, Thessaloniki, Greece
e-mail: john130570@gmail.com

A. Karasavvoglou et al. (eds.), *The First Decade of Living with the Global Crisis*, Contributions to Economics, DOI 10.1007/978-3-319-24267-5_8

level of tax ethics and, secondly, to identify the factors that influence it. The results of the survey are expected to support the structuring of useful proposals and measures for improving the level of tax ethics and tax compliance in Greece.

In the next section of the paper, the significance of the economic impact of shadow economy is discussed based on international transparency indices. In the third section, various possible working assumptions are presented which need to be verified through the questionnaire survey and stratified interviews. This is followed in the fourth section by a presentation of the economic, social and cultural features of Greece. For the construction, use and analysis of the questionnaire other international empirical studies with similar content are considered in the fifth section. Further, to assess the level of tax morale a series of questions are addressed relating to the justification or not of acts of tax evasion in particular issues.

2 Shadow Economy as an Obstacle for Economic Growth

A widely acceptable term of the shadow economy does not exist in the international bibliography. According to Schneider (1986), shadow economy consists of financial activities that create added values and that is why they should be included in the National Income but not in the official counting of units. Moreover, according to the wider definition of the EU, shadow economy includes the financial activities that taxable individuals avoid to declare and are called undeclared employment.

The answer to the question "why does shadow economy exist?" is directly related to the controlling taxation system. Deficient controls and most importantly lack of or limited penalties imposed, in comparison to the benefit from concealing incomes, reinforces shadow economy. Unequal and high taxation in combination with the poor socio-economic living conditions are the basic factors of income concealment, tax evasion and tax avoidance.

The Transparency International organization, which produces the Index CPI, claims that combating corruption is a world-wide movement that shares a common vision; i.e. a vision for a world where the governments, enterprises, the society, its civilians and their daily lives are corruption-free. In 1993, some few people decided to be against corruption and they set up the organization Transparency International. Today this organization is present in more than 1000 countries with the aim to bring out important changes against corruption. The secretarial department of the organization deals with corruption in regional and international level. With its headquarters in Berlin, it undertakes initiatives, coordinates knowledge exchange and conducts relative and numerous surveys to fight corruption.

In parallel, the Index of Perception of Corruption assesses and categorizes countries according to the perception of corruption for the public sector every year since 1995. It is a complex index that combines a series of surveys and assessments that are conducted by the most reliable organizations. In order for a country to enter into the CPI Index, it must first be assessed by three different sources of data that this index uses. When a country is not present in the

Table 1 The damage in Greek economy from shadow economy and corruption

	2003	2004	2005	2006	2007	2008	2009	2010	2011	2012
Damage in bn euros	21	21	21	20.5	20.1	19.7	24.4	26.5	27.3	28.1
CPI index	4.3	4.3	4.3	4.4	4.6	4.7	3.8	3.5	3.4	3.6
Ranking of Greece	50	49	47	54	56	57	71	78	80	94

Source: http://www.transparency.org/

classification, it means that there is not sufficient information about it and not that there is no corruption.

In Table 1 below is presented the damage caused to the Greek economy from the increase in the levels of corruption and shadow economy. Specifically, according to the Transparency Index, Greece was ranked from the 50th position in 2003 to the 94th position in 2012, with the decrease of the transparency index from 4.2 to 3.6. Moreover, the damage in economic terms was serious, from 21.5 billion in 2003 up to 28.1 billion in 2012.

According to Schneider (2013), the prolonged presence of the financial crisis in the level of Greece has decreased shadow economy in 2013, and this happened not only in Greece but also in Spain. In particular, the recession in the economies of Greece and Spain appeared to be very powerful and in combination with the significant decrease of incomes has shrunk the demand for shadow economy to a significant extent, as for instance in the cases of private lessons, housekeeper services and technical services. This means that crisis and shadow economy are in a reverse relationship.

In Greece, shadow economy as a percentage of Gross Domestic Product receded from 24 % in 2012 to 23.6 % of GDP in 2013. In 2007, prior to the financial crisis, shadow economy had ascended to 25.1 %, and in 2003 to 28.2 %. As a result, a material reduction has occurred by 4.6 % in the period 2003–2013. Accordingly, in Spain, for the same time period, shadow economy decreased from 22.2 % in 2003 to 18.6 % of GDP in 2013.

3 Working Assumptions

The underground economy and tax evasion are two of the major problems of the Greek economy. Estimates of the level of the underground economy rank Greece in the higher positions among OECD countries (Schneider and Enste 2000). According to the theory and empirical research, there is a high degree of negative correlation between tax ethics, tax evasion and the underground economy.

Although no comprehensive research and assessment in tax ethics has been performed in Greece, it is estimated that the average Greek citizen has clearly lower tax ethics in relation to the relevant taxpayer in developed countries of the West. Excessive relaxation of tax ethics has also contributed significantly to higher levels of tax evasion and underground economy in comparison with other developed countries.

Based on the economic, social and cultural characteristics of the country, which are discussed in the next section, some possible assumptions which need to be verified by this study are the following:

1. The tax ethics of the average Greek citizen is very low in comparison with citizens in OECD countries and EU. The extent of tax ethics in comparison with other countries has not been scientifically researched. It is required to be tested in Greece, also by comparing the results with surveys that have used similar methods and performed for other countries.
2. For the existence of low tax compliance are not responsible purely economic and tax agents but a combination of social, political and cultural factors. It has been tested in other countries; its validity, or not, will need to be confirmed also in the case of Greece.
3. The modus operandi of the Greek tax system affects negatively the tax consciousness of society, because it does not render justice and is not understood by the majority of citizens because of the complexity in its configuration. The influence of the complexity of the legislation has been tested in a survey conducted in the U.S., where it is found that this variable is not statistically significant. It will be tested whether the same applies in Greece.
4. Lack of confidence in the functioning of key institutions such as the parliament, the judiciary, the government and the administration, adversely affect the tax treatment of its citizens because they contribute to the weakening of ties with the state structures and functions. It has been tested in other countries and has been verified. It will be validated also in Greece.
5. Mismanagement of public revenues negatively affects tax ethics. It has been tested in other countries and has been verified. It will also be tested in Greece.
6. The sense of public opinion that there is widespread tax evasion in the country affects adversely the tax morale. It has been tested in other countries and has been verified. It will be also confirmed in Greece.
7. The structure of the political system and the allocation of powers in a state have a direct influence on the tax treatment of its citizens. In particular, the existence of democratic institutions directly contributes to the development of citizens' sense of responsibility which is expressed through the demonstration of tax consciousness.
8. The high degree of corruption within the administration acts as a disincentive for tax compliance and has contributed to the weakening of tax conscience of citizens; its significance and influence on the tax consciousness, however, has not been estimated. It will be assessed in the case of Greece.

4 Key Characteristics of the Political, Social and Labour System in Greece

To facilitate an understanding of the factors that were considered in the construction of the questionnaire, an outline of the specific features of the businesses, cultural, economic and social and political life of the country is provided in the next paragraphs.

4.1 Key Features of the Greek Tax System

Complexity of the Tax System The Greek tax system can be characterized as excessively complicated and labyrinthine, while changing very often, which results in conditions that discourage new investments. The plethora of tax provisions is characterized by a) lack of internal consistency, b) inability to express the general economic policy and c) fragmentation. A complex tax system, however, is likely to adversely affect the tax consciousness of citizens because it allows its exploitation by individuals who are aware of its operation. The general feeling of non-tax equity impacts negatively on the tax morale of society, affecting its confidence towards the state and its institutions, and ultimately increases the possibility for tax evasion.

Relationship Between Direct and Indirect Taxes The relationship and composition of direct and indirect taxes is the benchmark for the assessment of a tax system. Direct taxes contribute to a fairer distribution of the tax burden, through progressive taxation. Greece is characterized by a tax system that is unduly burdened by indirect taxation, which leads to lack of proper distribution of tax burdens at the expense of lower income taxpayers.

Tax Amnesties Due to tax collection reasons, but also due to the impossibility of efficient tax audits of all businesses, the respective governments tend to pass laws for closing old cases of taxpayers without audit verification. Such tax amnesties which are repeated at regular intervals substantially reward the inconsistent and irregular taxpayers who have the possibility to avoid any tax audit by paying usually relatively small amounts to the tax authorities.

Erosion of the Tax Base In the taxation of personal income there are plenty of deductions from income tax or through the declaration of certain expenses. These usually work to the benefit of taxpayers with higher incomes, contributing in this way to a system of regressive, instead of progressive taxation.

A tax system that is dominated by indirect taxes, concessions/discounts mainly in favour of high-income earners and which rewards the inconsistent taxpayers with frequent tax amnesties, is characterized as unfair, since it cannot achieve neither horizontal nor vertical tax equity. Citizens, who perceive the existence of injustice, are more likely not to fully comply with their tax obligations, i.e. have greater propensity to tax evasion.

4.2 Employment Structure

Fragmentation of Capital The existence of a large number of small businesses and self-employed complicates tax audits. Small businesses often resort to undeclared work and the informal economy to cut costs in order to become more competitive and to survive financially.

High Level of Self-Employed Workers in Family Businesses and Employees in the Primary Sector These occupational categories have the most significant contribution to the overall tax evasion and underground economy of a country. This is not due to some inherent criminality of this class of professionals, but is mainly related to the difficulty to control such activities on the part of the supervisory authorities. Many researches have come to the same conclusion because in most tax systems the most difficult controlled tax categories are the self-employed and the farmers (e.g. Slemrod 2007).

4.3 Growing Counterproductive Attitudes

Benefits policy, protection of closed professions, bureaucracy, lack of productivity assessment in the public sector, salary inequalities, which do not relate to the qualifications or the productivity of employees, all have assisted in the cultivation of a counterproductive culture.

The feeling of injustice suffered by a large portion of citizens when certain groups of occupations are favoured is, in our opinion, one of the main causes of relaxation of tax morale in the country. Furthermore, the common feeling that the public sector is counterproductive creates additional incentive for tax avoidance, since tax revenues in the perception of citizens finance this gloomy situation.

4.4 Override Individualism: Consumer Standards

The primacy of consumption patterns at the expense of other values such as altruism, collective success and national consciousness, push people to try to ensure more and more material goods and personal projection through actions that encourage tax evasion. Inevitably, the consumption pattern and individualism involve people in low tax consciousness or help shape it. In short, there is a negative interaction between atomistic and over-consumption mentality and tax consciousness.

5 Methodology

The method of empirical research in this study is the use of a questionnaire survey. It should be noted that the survey questionnaire has secured funding through the project "Thales Research Programme" for the assessment of the level, causes and impact of shadow economy in Greece. The funding is necessary in order to carry out all the necessary preparatory work to reproduce and fill in the questionnaire on a sample of at least 5000 people.

For the construction, use and analysis of the questionnaire were considered empirical studies with similar content, e.g. Alm (1999), Alm et al. (1992), Bosco and Mittone (1997), Torgler (2007), but adapted to the particularities of the Greek political, social, and tax system and the way of operation of the Greek tax authorities.

To assess the level of tax ethics are used a series of questions relating to the views on the justification or not of acts of tax evasion, and in particular of issues relating to the completion of tax returns. Further questions are posed to ascertain the views on issues such as the functioning of the state, public administration, management of public revenues and on issues related to the experience of respondents from filing tax returns. The purpose of the questionnaire is, first, to assess the level of tax ethics, and secondly, to identify the factors that influence it.

5.1 Construction of the Questionnaire

a. The questionnaire starts with a general question that reveals the public perception of the causes of tax evasion in the country. The results of this question assist to determine whether the causes of public opinion on tax evasion as shaped by the answers, validate or not our estimates of the causes of tax ethics, which will be revealed in the next questions.

   "Why do you think people tax evade?" (you may select up to two of the following reasons considered as important for tax evasion)

   1. Dishonesty
   2. There is no reason to pay taxes.
   3. Lack of punishment in case of tax evasion.
   4. Mismanagement of public revenues.
   5. Very high taxation rates.
   6. Existence of corruption.
   7. Injustice in the tax system.

b. In the next stage the questions for assessing the level of tax ethics are formulated. These questions have a rating depending on how acceptable or reprehensible are the proposals submitted for answers. The total score will reveal the size of the tax morale. In other words, the purpose of these questions is to create a kind of indicator of tax ethics. This index may—under certain circumstances—be used in comparison with other countries. The specific conditions where consideration should be given relate to what is allowed or not under particular jurisdictions. Particular attention is also paid to the proper expression and translation of the questions in the language of the country to be used.

   Indicative questions that reveal the level of tax ethics and employed in the questionnaire include (rated on a scale 1–6, where 1 means: strongly agree and 6 means: strongly disagree):

   1. The trade or exchange of goods and services with a friend or neighbour are not required to be declared to the tax authorities.
   2. Statement of all the basic income in tax return but hiding relatively small but secondary income is not reprehensible.
   3. A taxpayer may seek exemptions using receipts for goods or services not provided to him. People who do not have tax exemption can give these receipts to a person receiving tax breaks.
   4. It is not wrong to declare income of minor importance as it is not usually checked by the tax authorities.
   5. Given the high cost of living, those who evade taxes should be fined but not with very severe penalties.
   6. A person who does not pay taxes cannot be held responsible for this at a moral level, as s/he may have made use of loopholes in the law.

Furthermore, we believe that the use of multiple queries instead of the ones used by WVS (World Value Survey) and EVS (European Value Survey) have the potential to uncover the real beliefs of the respondents. The questions posed by WVS and EVS are general in nature and one can easily resort to a false statement condemning tax evasion, although in practice acts just in the opposite way.

The question used by the organizations WVS and EVS for assessing the amount of tax ethics is as follows:

> State whether you believe that the following act can always be justified, never be justified or something in between the two: *To try to get away with paying taxes if you get the chance* (rate using a grade between 1 and 10, where 1 stands for no justification and 10 for always justified).

However, the aforementioned question presents a unique advantage: It has been posed in thousands of households in many countries and in different time periods. In short, it allows us to use a huge database to draw comparative data. For this reason, the question has been added to our questionnaire but not taken into account for the assessment of the index of tax morale.

c. In a next step, we attempted to identify the main non-economic factors (societal variables) that affect tax ethics. The proposed questions presented below have exactly this purpose. For example, indicative questions that reveal the assessment of public administration by the respondents are:

Evaluate the tax authorities with the following scale (1. Excellent; 2. Quite good; 3. Medium; 4. Bad)

1. Yield justice in controls
2. Efficiency—Effectiveness
3. Assistance and information is provided to citizens

Also, the question "Some consider that tax audits conducted are non-discriminatory, while others that there is some form of financial transaction, i.e. the tax auditors accept to disguise tax irregularities or infringements for a fee. What is your opinion (tax auditors are: 1. always impartial, up to 5. non-impartial)".

By the same reasoning a series of questions that reveal the perceptions of citizens regarding the fairness of the tax system, its complexity, public confidence in the institutions, legislation, judicial system and a number of other issues that theory maintains that contribute to the formation of (a positive or negative) tax consciousness, are included in the questionnaire. The aim of these questions and findings is to acquire a more complete picture on the assessment of tax morality and the factors that affect it in Greece.

5.2 *Construction of Econometric Models: Econometric Analysis (As Future Work to Be Performed)*

In addition to the questions that are aimed at uncovering the real causes that affect tax ethics, the questionnaire contains questions that will reveal demographic information, sex, education level, income status, employment status, age, etc. As a further step to the current paper, our aim is to develop econometric models that will employ the method of weighted ordered probit model, and to examine the degree of influence of each of these factors, as well as their statistical significance. All these questions will be considered as independent variables, while the position of the dependent variable will be set to the most representative question from those used for determining the tax ethics. Through this econometric analysis it will be identified which are the main factors influencing the tax morale and tax compliance in Greece.

From the conclusions drawn from this empirical research, we aim to derive the basic material for the adoption of appropriate measures and policies that can promote and facilitate the establishment of a more positive tax consciousness.

6 Conclusions

The paper has provided the various steps toward the construction of a questionnaire survey to assess the levels of tax ethics and compliance in Greece. For the construction, use and analysis of the questionnaire other international empirical studies were considered. To assess the level of tax morale a series of questions are addressed relating to the justification or not of acts of tax evasion in particular issues. Also, based on the economic, social and cultural features of Greece, various possible working assumptions are presented which will be verified through the questionnaire survey and stratified interviews.

Acknowledgements The current paper is presented under the auspices of the THALES Research Programme. THALES Programme has been co-financed by the European Union (European Social Fund—ESF) and Greek national funds through the Operational Program "Education and Lifelong Learning" of the National Strategic Reference Framework (NSRF).

For useful constructive comments and suggestions, we are grateful to the anonymous reviewers and EBEEC 2014 Conference Participants; all errors remain ours.

References

Alm J (1999) Tax compliance and administration. In: Hildreth WB, Richardson JA (eds) Handbook of taxation. Marcel Dekker, New York, NY, pp 741–768

Alm J, Jackson B, McKee M (1992) Estimating the determinants of taxpayer compliance with experimental data. Natl Tax J 45(1):107–114

Bosco L, Mittone L (1997) Tax evasion and moral constraints: some experimental evidence. Kyklos 50:297–324

Schneider F (1986) Estimating the size of the Danish shadow economy using the currency demand approach: an attempt. Scand J Econ 4:643

Schneider F (2013) The shadow economy in Greece and other OECD countries. In: Bitzenis A, Vlachos V, Papadopoulos I (eds) Reflections on the Greek sovereign debt crisis. Scholars Publishing, Cambridge

Schneider F, Enste D (2000) Shadow economies around the world—size, causes and consequences. J Econ Lit 38(1):77–114

Slemrod J (2007) Cheating ourselves: the economics of tax evasion. J Econ Perspect 21:25–48

Torgler B (2007) Tax compliance and tax morale. A theoretical and empirical analysis. Edward Elgar, Cheltenham

Economic Crisis in Greece and the Consequential "Brain Drain"

Sofia Anastasiadou

Abstract Economic crisis in Greece had enormous impact on society and people's lives. Political corruption, cronyism, nepotism, partisanship, bureaucracy, are some of the main causes which lead to the country's plague, unemployment. "Brain drain" in Greece is inevitable. Thus, this study tries to record students' opinions towards the Greek scientist emigration. The results reveal that Greek students are extremely pessimistic that unemployment could be restrained or reversed and that they believe that both Greek politicians and European authorities are incapable of leading the country into economic recovery.

Keywords Brain • Drain • Economic • Crisis • Greece

JEL Classification Codes A14 • A22 • Z13 • Z10

1 Theoretical Framework

The analysis of brain drain phenomenon is of major importance in the domain of human resources and it has acknowledged considerable attention. In addition, it is considered as a significant topic by economists and government planners all over the world (Wong and Yip 1999). As brain drain emphasizes the flight of qualified individuals and skilled elites towards countries with higher standards of living. It is defined as an international migration of skilled and professional workers (Wong and Yip 1999). Lien and Wang (2005) defined brain drain as the flows of high skilled immigrants from developing countries to developed countries. Brain drain has the negative meaning of the loss of human capital in relation to the source country, negative welfare implications for the source country (Bhagwati and Hamada 1974) and brain gain in relation to the host country.

On the one hand Boundaryless career approach (Stahl et al. 2002), highly productive job environments, career opportunities and better wages, career and salary conditions (Biondo et al. 2012), more job opportunities and better labor market conditions (Sasser 2010) abroad, and on the other hand unemployment, job

S. Anastasiadou (✉)
University of Western Macedonia, Florina, Greece
e-mail: sanastasiadou@uowm.gr

A. Karasavvoglou et al. (eds.), *The First Decade of Living with the Global Crisis*,
Contributions to Economics, DOI 10.1007/978-3-319-24267-5_9

insecurity, income reduction, over-taxation, together with limited budgets for research institutes (Ifanti et al. 2014), small population size, domestic political instability in the 'departure' countries plus other factors like the distance from destination countries, the role of the educational institutions and the standard of living especially in Europe and the United States that are considered to be much higher than that in any other developing countries (Baruch et al. 2007), seem to be the main considerations for the brain drain phenomena.

Today, Greece faces a huge economic crisis. After 2007, the country deals with significant problems such as low rate of development, high rate of unemployment, job insecurity, political instability, tax invasion etc. Within this negative climate, Greek brain drain seems to be inevitable. According to Ifanti et al. (2014) the key factors contributing to the exacerbation of the brain drain in Greece are closely linked to the causes of the financial crisis and its striking effects on Greek society. Malkoutzis (2011) stated that it is Greek financial crisis and its impact on society which generated a mass exodus of talented and highly skilled physicians, seeking for better job opportunities and salaries elsewhere. High unemployment rates, reduced salaries, severe and austere taxes, political corruption and political instability lead to the departure of knowledgeable, talented, well-educated and skilled Greeks from Greece to another country. Ifanti et al. (2014) stated that the United Kingdom, Germany, Sweden and many other European countries offer a lot of opportunities in the labour market in the fields of healthcare, and the demand for specialized physicians is high. This is the main reason why physicians leave Greece. According to Labrianidis (2011), the Greek professionals prefer to immigrate to Great Britain, Belgium, France, Holland and the USA. Recently, the study of Holezas and Tsakloglou (2008) showed that young Greek graduates of all the scientific fields immigrate to other countries.

2 Research Methodology

This paper attempts to measure Greek students' attitude toward brain drain phenomena in Greece. Principal components analysis with Varimax Rotation produces the dimension of brain drain phenomena factors. The calculations of Principal components analysis were based on variance–covariance matrix because the research variances took values from the same measurement scale.

In order to investigate the structure of the factors measured with the questionnaire, a confirmatory factor analysis (CFA) was used. Models of structural equations were used and the development of a model indicating the relationship between the various factors was attempted, and in particular, the relationship between the observed variable and the factors. The aim of this confirmatory analysis was to reveal if the questionnaire is actually valid and suitable for the measurement of the variables it investigates. It is noted that an instrument of evaluation is valid if the existence of variation is justified in its statements. In order to test the model, the goodness-of-fit of the research model is estimated.

It is noted that the criteria of acceptance of a model is the comparative fit index (CFI) which is not dependent on the size of the sample and taken values from 0 to 1 and it must, by agreement, be CFI 0.9, the index X2/df (X2/df = chi-square to its degrees of freedom ratio) and it must be X2/df < 2. Since the ratio X2/df depends on the size of the sample the ratio NNFI (Non-Normed Fit Index) is used, which is independent on the size of the sample and it must (by agreement) be NNFI > 0.95. GFI (Goodness of Fit) is used and it must be GFIt > 0.80, AGFI (Comparative Fit Index) is used and it must be AGFI > 0.8 and NFI (Normed Fit Index) is used and it must be NFI > 0.9. In addition, the indexes RMSR (Root Mean Square Residuals) are used and it must (by agreement) be RMSR < 0.06 and the RMSEA (RMSEA = root mean-square error of approximation) and it must be RMSEA < 0.06.

For the purposes of the data analysis adaptation to the regular distributions of all the variables that participated in the analysis was completed, Multivariate Normality was checked and it was shown that all the uni-variate distributions are normal distributions, all the joint distributions of all combinations of variables are also normal and all the bi-variable scatter plots are linear and homoscedastic and finally there were no outliers. Moreover, the data were evaluated for their linearity and the examination of variance charts for each variable indicated that there was not any problem of linearity.

3 Sample

Our research sample consisted of 125 Greek students from the Department of Pre-School Education of Western Macedonia University and Department of Educational and Social Policy, of the University of Macedonia who were asked to answer the scale during the academic year 2013–2014. 125 valid questionnaires were collected. Of those, 93 students were female and 33 male.

4 Research Hypotheses

The aim of the present research study is the ascertainment of the questionnaire's validity which was designed to measure factors that have an impact on brain drain in Greece as well as the investigation of relationships between the structures/constructions of the model.

For this reason, and more specifically for the examination of the importance of each possible and feasible/latent relationship that can be investigated in this model, the following four hypotheses are examined:

H1. Political reasons have a direct effect on brain drain
H2. Economic reasons have a direct effect on brain drain

H3. Career opportunities/employment has a direct effect on brain drain
H4. Psychological reasons have a direct effect on brain drain

5 Instrument

The instrument, which is intended to measure students' attitudes in relation to the significance to pre-service teacher of fully understanding brain drain impacts' dimensions in Greece, is named BrDrs. This tool consists of 25 items. The first 24 items refer to four different attitude subscales, which were extracted following the application of Principal Component Analysis, as follows:

Political reasons (authorities/leaders' corruption, nepotism, partisanship etc): attitudes concerning the influence of political corruption, cronyism, nepotism, partisanship, bureaucracy to the brain drain tendency. The reliability of this factor is $a = 0.825$ and it is particularly satisfactory.

Economic reasons (richer countries, crisis in general, fiscal and tax reasons): attitudes concerning the flight of skilled scientists towards countries with higher standards of living, job opportunities and labor market conditions abroad, lower-taxation reality abroad. The reliability of this factor is $a = 0.801$ and it is particularly satisfactory.

Career opportunities (bigger salaries, further educational opportunities): attitudes connected with highly productive job environments, career opportunities and better wages. The reliability of this factor is $a = 0.746$ and it is also particularly satisfactory.

Psychological reasons (despondent, hopeless): attitudes in relation to hopeless effort to find a stable job. The reliability of this factor is $a = 0.711$ and it is particularly satisfactory.

The 24 items have created the above four different attitude subscales conceptually and it will be tested whether these subscales are also the results of the Explanatory Factor Analysis in order for the construct validity of the instrument to be verified.

Each item of the instrument used a 5-point Likert scale that ranged from 1-Strongly Disagree to 5-Strongly Agree. The value of the Cronbach's α coefficient for this instrument in this study's sample was 0.801.

The last item (25th), that asked whether the student will have the intention to leave Greece and apply for a job in another country, measures the brain drain issue.

6 Results

Measurement Model Fit results: The square roots of all AVEs were larger (Table 2) than correlations among constructs (Table 1), thereby satisfying discriminant validity derived. Yet, all the inter-construct correlations are below the cutoff point of 0.9, which suggests distinctness in discriminant validity.

In addition, the average extracted variances are all above the recommended 0.50 level (Hair et al. 1995), which implies convergent validity.

Compared to Cronbach's alpha equal to a = 0.823, a = 0.801, a = 0.711, a = 0.718 for the Political reasons, Economic reasons, Career opportunities/employment, Psychological axis respectively, which assumes equal weights of all the items of a construct and is influenced by the number of items, Composite Reliability relies on actual loadings to compute the factor scores and thus provides a better indicator for measuring internal consistency (Hair et al. 2005). As shown in Table 2, Composite Reliabilities are above the threshold of 0.7. Overall, the measures in this study are reliable and valid.

The hypotheses are tested through structural equation modeling technique (SEM) by LISREL 8.8, software. Model estimation was done using the Maximum Likelihood Estimation, with the item covariance matrix used as input. The indicators were identified on the basis of their loadings. These indicators are associated to their respective latent or unobserved variables to calculate the estimate. The values of SEM are given below (Table 3).

The overall analysis of the model indicates that the model is a very good fit (Table 3) (CFI = 0.95, X2/df = 1.9, GFI = 0.85, AGFI = 0.85, NFI = 0.95, NNFI = 0.96, RMSR = 0.05, RMSEA = 0.05).

Table 1 Inter-construct correlations

	Political reasons F1	Economic reasons F2	Career opportunities/ employment F3
Economic reasons F2	0.18		
Career opportunities/ employment F3	0.27	0.32	
Psychological reasons F4	0.29	0.16	0.28

Table 2 Composite reliability (CR) and average variance extracted (VE)

	Composite reliability (CR > 0.7)	Average variance extracted (AVE > 0.5)
Political reasons F1	0.894	0.624
Economic reasons F2	0.912	0.815
Career opportunities F3	0.894	0.629
Psychological reasons F4	0.938	0.691

Table 3 Structural equation modelling

Values	CFI	X2/df	GFI	AGFI	NFI	NNFI	RMSR	RMSEA
Good fit indexes	0.95	1.9	0.85	0.85	0.96	0.96	0.05	0.05

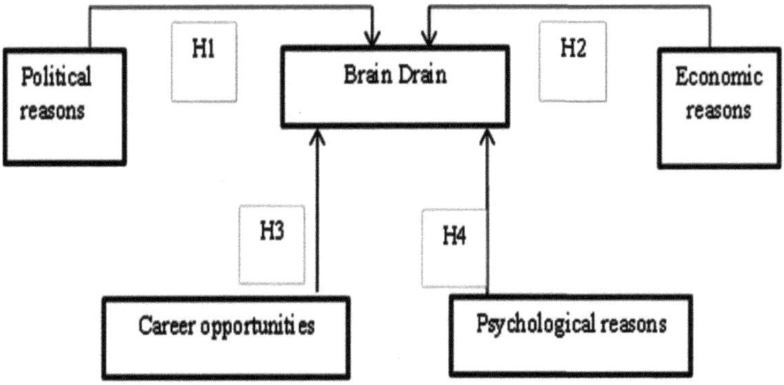

Fig. 1 The standardized path coefficients and explained variances

In summary, of the various measures of the overall model goodness-of-fit lend sufficient support to deeming the results an acceptable representation of the hypothesized constructs (Table 3). In addition, the overall model goodness-of-fit results and the measurements model assessments lend substantial support for confirmation of the proposed 4-factor model (Hair et al. 2005).

The path significance of each hypothesized association in the research model and variance explained (R2) by each path is also examined. The standardized path coefficients, and explained variances of the structure model are shown in Fig. 1.

Hypothesis H1 is supported since the effect of political reasons to the Brain Drain is significant ($\beta = 0.39$) and $R2 = 0.24$, which means that 24 % Brain Drain is explained by political reasons.

Hypothesis H2 is supported since the effect of economic reason affects significantly and positively Brain Drain ($\beta = 0.42$). In total, 43 % of Brain Drain is explained by economic reasons.

Hypotheses H3 and H4 are supported. In total, 39 % ($R2 = 0.39$) of Brain Drain and 25 % ($R2 = 0.25$) of Brain Drain are explained by Career opportunities and Psychological reasons respectively.

7 Conclusions

The basic aim of this study was the assessment of students' attitudes toward brain drain through a model. The results confirmed the value of the scale. The study showed that students' points of view relating to brain drain are influenced by political, economic reasons, career opportunities and psychological reasons. Also, a structural equation model of students' attitudes was developed that presents relations among the above domains and reveal the true impact of each one on the others. Politics and economics, that led to economic crisis paired with career deterrents reveal the danger of losing a generation that is a real bleeding for the nation. Undoubtedly, Greek people and political system should take into account the needs of the highly qualified young Greek people in order to prevent their exodus abroad, by reducing the red-tape and the imposition of further taxes so that new businesses are started. This will result in creating new jobs and in preventing this intense massive flow of students from seeking their career opportunities abroad. Moreover, the political scene must be changed. Democracy, equal opportunities, justice, reduced bureaucracy, a higher level of education, fairness in the taxation system, meritocracy, economic development, production seem to be the core elements to prevent brain drain.

References

Baruch Y, Budhwar PS, Khatri N (2007) Brain drain: inclination to stay abroad after studies. J World Bus 42(1):99–112

Bhagwati J, Hamada K (1974) The brain drain, international integration of markets for professional and unemployment. J Dev Econ 1:19–24

Biondo AE, Monteleone S, Skonieczny G, Torrisi B (2012) The propensity to return: theory and evidence for the Italian brain drain. Econ Lett 115:359–362

Hair J, Anderson R, Tatham R, Black W (1995) Multivariate data analysis with readings. Prentice-Hall International, Upper Saddle River, NJ

Hair FJ, Black CW, Badin NJ, Anderson ER, Tatham RL (2005) Multivariate data analysis. Pearson Education, New Jersey

Holezas I, Tsakloglou P (2008) The employability of graduates of higher education. Morfotiki and Anaptyxiaki Protovoulia, Athens (in Greek)

Ifanti AA, Argyriou AA, Kalofonouc FH, Kalofonos HP (2014) Physicians' brain drain in Greece: a perspective on the reasons why and how to address it. Health Policy 117:210–215

Labrianidis L (2011) Investing in leaving: the Greek case of international migration of professionals in the globalization era. Ekdoseis Kritiki, Athens

Lien D, Wang Y (2005) Brain drain or brain gain: a revisit. J Popul Econ 18:153–163

Malkoutzis N (2011) Young Greeks and the crisis: the danger of losing a generation, International Policy Analysis. Friedrich-Ebert Stiftung. Available at: http://library.fes.de/pdf-files/id/ipa/08465.pdf. Accessed 30 Nov 2013

Sasser AC (2010) Voting with their feet: relative economic conditions and state migration patterns. Reg Sci Urban Econ 40:122–135

Stahl GK, Miller EL, Tung RL (2002) Towards the boundary less career: a closer look at the expatriate career concept and the perceived implications of an international assignment. J World Bus 37:216–227

Wong K-Y, Yip CK (1999) Education, economic growth, and brain drain. J Econ Dyn Control 23: 699–726

Part III
The External Sector, National State and Development in the Balkans and Eastern Europe

The Legal Framework of European Union: Western Balkans Trade Liberalization

Odysseas G. Spiliopoulos and Dimitrios P. Petropoulos

Abstract The relations between the European Union (EU) and the Western Balkan Countries are governed by the Stabilization and Association Agreements (SAA). One of the fundamental objectives of the Association is to establish a free trade area, in accordance with WTO rules, between each of the associated Balkan states and the EU which is their largest trading partner. To this end, each of these agreements provides for the gradual establishment of a zone of free movement of goods, the introduction of a regime on the right of establishment in order to exercise an economic activity, on the cross border services supply, on current payments and capital movements. The purpose of this paper is to analyze the rules promoting the liberalization of economic transactions between the contracting parties and generally economic integration in the area concerned. Emphasis is given to the agreement concluded with Serbia.

Keywords EU • Western Balkans • Stabilization • Association • Free trade area

JEL Classification Codes F15 • F53 • K33

1 Introduction

A key element of EU policy in its relations with the Western Balkan countries (FYROM, Croatia, Bosnia-Herzegovina, Serbia, Montenegro and Albania), is the implementation since the early 2000s, of a Stabilization and Association Process (SAP) whose central objective is to create an environment of political stability, economic development and regional cooperation (Fakiolas and Tzifakis 2008). The importance of SAP consists mainly in consolidating a stable European order based both on cooperation between the EU and these countries and on regional cooperation between these countries (Grabar-Kitarovic 2010). To implement this EU

O.G. Spiliopoulos (✉)
TEI of Peloponnese, Accounting and Finance Department, 24100 Kalamata, Greece
e-mail: odspilio@yahoo.gr

D.P. Petropoulos
TEI of Peloponnese, Agricultural Technology Department, 24100 Kalamata, Greece
e-mail: d.petro@teikal.gr

A. Karasavvoglou et al. (eds.), *The First Decade of Living with the Global Crisis*, Contributions to Economics, DOI 10.1007/978-3-319-24267-5_10

strategy, negotiations for the conclusion of Stabilization and Association Agreements (SAAs) were conducted between the EU and each of these countries.[1]

The SAAs concluded between the EU and FYROM, the EU and Albania, the EU and Montenegro and the EU and Serbia have already entered into force. The last one has come into force on 1-9-2013.[2]

These agreements serve as "antechamber" for accession of these countries to the EU. In their Preambles emphasis is given to the perspective of their future accession to the EU.

Specific reference is made to "*the strong links between the Parties and the values that they share, their desire to strengthen those links and establish a close and lasting relationship based on reciprocity and mutual interest*"[3] as well as to the EU's readiness to integrate each of these countries to the fullest possible extent into the political and economic mainstream of Europe.

Particular political significance has an explicit reference to their status as potential candidates for EU membership. Actually the EU accession is envisaged once the criteria defined by the European Council in June 1993 (Copenhagen criteria) are fulfilled, subject to the successful implementation of the SAAs.

Croatia has already been a EU member state since 1-7-2013. All other Balkan states are candidate countries. In particular, Serbia, Montenegro and FYROM are official candidate countries while Albania and Bosnia-Herzegovina are potential EU candidate members.

---

[1] The Council of EU decided in June 2013 to authorize the opening of negotiations on an SAA with Kosovo. The future SAA will represent the first comprehensive contractual relationship between Kosovo and the EU and an important milestone in Kosovo's European integration process. Accordingly to the Commission, Kosovo had met all the short-term priorities identified in the 2012 Feasibility study in the areas of rule of law, public administration, protection of minorities and trade.

[2] The EU-Serbia agreement had been signed on 29-4-2008 and adopted on behalf of the EU with the 2013/490/EC, Euratom decision of the Council and Commission of 22-7-2013. The EU-Montenegro agreement was signed on 15-10-2007 and concluded on behalf of the EU with decision 2010/224/EE of the Council of 29/03/2010 (OJ L 108, 29-4-2010). The EU-Albania agreement was signed on 12-6-2006 and concluded on behalf of the EU with Decision 2009/332/EE of the Council of 26-2-2009 (OJ L 107, 28-4-2009). The EU-Bosnia-Herzegovina agreement was signed on 16-6-2008.The EU-FYROM agreement was signed on 9-4-2001 and came into force on 1-4-2004. Concerning the SAA with Serbia, see Stahl B., 2011. Perverted Conditionality: the Stabilization and Association Agreement between the European Union and Serbia. *European Foreign Affairs Review*, Vol. 16, pp 465–487.

[3] SAA between European Union and Serbia, http://eur-lex.europa.eu/legalcontent/EN/TXT/?uri=uriserv:OJ.L_.2013.278.01.0014.01.ENG. 30-3-2014, SAA between European Union and Montenegro, http://eur-lex.europa.eu/legal-content/EN/TXT/?uri=uriserv:OJ.L_.2010.108.01.0001.01.ENG. 31-3-2014, SAA between European Union and Albania, http://eur-lex.europa.eu/legalcontent/EN/TXT/?uri=uriserv:OJ.L_.2009.107.01.0165.01.ENG. 26-3-2014, SAA between European Union and Bosnia-Herzegovina, http://www.dei.gov.ba/bih_i_eu/ssp/doc/default.aspx?id=2952&langTag=en-US. 29-3-2014, SAA between European Union and FYROM, http://ec.europa.eu/world/agreements/downloadFile.do?fullText=yes&treatyTransId=602. 29-3-2014.

In the economic sector, a key pillar of the SAA is the promotion of free trade not only between the EU and each of these countries but also between these countries. The liberalization of trade covers comprehensively the movement of goods, the cross-border services supply, the establishment, the movement of capital and current payments.

Taking into account the above, it becomes clear that the objective in the field of trade is to integrate "*the Balkans into the EU's trade policy framework, by attempting to create interdependent links between these newly formed states*"(Natens and Wouters 2013, p. 11).

2 The SAAs as an Instrument Promoting Regional Economic Integration

The Preamble reflects the conviction of the parties that the SAAs will contribute to the creation of "*a new climate for economic relations between them and, above all, for the development of trade and investment, factors crucial to economic restructuring and modernization*".[4]

Article 1 of the SAAs defines the objectives of the Association established between the EU and its Member States, of the one part, and each of Western Balkan countries of the other part. In the economic sphere, the association seeks to support the efforts of these states to develop their economic and international cooperation, including through the approximation of their legislation to that of the EU, to promote harmonious economic relations and gradually develop a free trade area (FTA) between the EU and Serbia, between the EU and Montenegro, between the EU and FYROM, between the EU and Albania, between the EU and Bosnia, to foster regional cooperation in all the fields covered by these agreements.

To achieve the above objectives, and in particular for the gradual establishment of free trade areas, each of the SAA establishes specific provisions contained in a special section and in particular in Title IV on the free movement of goods[5] and in Title V on the establishment, cross-border supply services and capital movement.[6] Taking into account the aforementioned provisions of the SAAs on trade and in general on economic relations between the EU and each of the associated Balkan states, it can be noted that, apart from the fact that they promote political cooperation and institutional stability, the SAAs constitute regional economic integration agreements since they establish, at a regional level, a framework of trade liberalization and facilitation of economic activities. The provisions on trade form their

[4] See no 3.

[5] EU-Serbia, articles 18–48, EU-Montenegro art. 18–48, EU-FYROM art. 15–43, EU-Albania, art. 16–45, EU-Bosnia-Herzegovina art. 18–46. See no 3.

[6] EU-Serbia articles 49–71, EU-Montenegro art. 49–71, EU-FYROM art. 44–67, EU-Albania art. 46–69, EU-Bosnia-Herzegovina art. 47–69. See no 3.

economic component. Essentially, therefore, each SAA integrates a regional trade agreement (Cremona 2010; Brown 2012). An agreement, in order to be classified as a regional trade agreement, must fulfill the following three criteria: (a) the main objective is to liberalize or facilitate trade between two or more countries not necessarily belonging to the same geographical area, (b) trade liberalization is implemented in terms of reciprocity, (c) the result of this process is the preferential treatment.[7]

At the level of principles and declarations, there is no doubt that the parties to these agreements strongly emphasize their commitment to promote trade liberalization in accordance with the rules and principles of the World Trade Organization (WTO). According to the Preamble of all the agreements, the parties are committed to free trade in compliance with the rights and obligations arising out of the WTO membership.[8] Especially in the Preamble of the EU-Bosnia Agreement is underlined the commitment of the parties to apply these rights and obligations in a transparent and non-discriminatory way.

Furthermore, the parties recognize, via an explicit provision, the obligation to comply with the WTO legal framework as one of the general principles which underlie the association. Specifically, firstly the content of the provisions on economic integration must be fully compatible with art. XXIV of General Agreement on Tariffs and Trade 1994 (GATT 1994) and art. V of General Agreement on Trade in Services (GATS) and secondly their application shall be made in accordance with these articles.[9]

An important factor for the development of relations between the EU and each of the associated Balkan states is the commitment undertaken by each one of these to enhance cooperation and good neighborly relations with the other countries of the region including an appropriate level of mutual concessions concerning the movement of persons, goods, capital and services.[10]

In fact, the SAAs are not limited to only lay down the legal framework governing the bilateral relations between the EU and each of the associated countries of the Western Balkans but also at the same time seek to promote regional cooperation process between those related states (Title III of all the SAAs). As an appropriate

[7] World Trade Organization, 'Scope of RTAs' (2012) http://www.wto.org/english/tratop_e/region_e/scope_rta_e.html, 20-3-2014.

[8] Albania has been a WTO member since 8-9-2000, Montenegro has been a member of WTO since 29-4-2012 and Fyrom since 4-4-2003. Bosnia and Herzegovina is completing its reforms in order to bring its trade regime in line with WTO rules and is finalising negotiations on market access. As far as Serbia is concerned, in 2005, the Working Group for Serbia accession into the WTO was established by the General Council of the WTO. http://www.welcomeurope.com/news-europe/adhesion-serbie-a-omc-13956+13856.html. Negotiations at a bilateral level on customs duties for industrial and agricultural products and services supply were concluded. An important event showing that negotiations for joining the WTO have entered their final phase is the signature, on 11-1-2011, by the EU and Serbia of a bilateral agreement on Serbia's accession to the WTO.

[9] EU-Serbia art. 9, EU-Montenegro art. 9, EU-Albania art. 7, EU-FYROM art. 6, EU-Bosnia art. 9.

[10] EU-Serbia art. 6, EU-Montenegro art. 6, EU-Albania art. 4, EU-FYROM art. 4, EU-Bosnia art. 6.

instrument for the implementation of this procedure, the establishment of contractual links between the countries of the region has been chosen.

3 The Asymmetric Liberalization of Trade in Goods to the Benefit of Western Balkans

As far as trade in goods is concerned, EU is the Western Balkans countries' largest partner, accounting for about two thirds of these countries' total trade. Regarding the trade structure, the major exports from this region to the EU include manufactured goods classified chiefly by materials, manufactured articles and machinery and transport equipment while EU exports mainly include machinery and transport equipment, manufactured goods classified mainly by material, chemicals and mineral fuels.

Pending the entry into force of the SAAs, the EE has concluded Interim Agreements (IA) on trade and trade-related matters[11] with the countries of the Western Balkans given that it was necessary to apply as soon as possible the provisions of the SAAs governing trade in goods.[12] Each of these interim agreements applies until the corresponding SAA enters into force.[13] Into these agreements are incorporated both the SAA provisions governing the free movement of goods and providing for the establishment of a bilateral free trade area, the possibility of the parties to adopt trade defense measures and safeguards as well as other provisions concerning the protection of competition and customs cooperation.[14]

[11] IA between European Union and Serbia, http://eur-lex.europa.eu/legal-content/EN/TXT/?uri=uriserv:OJ.L_.2010.028.01.0001.01.ENG. 20-3-2014; IA between European Union and Montenegro, http://eur-lex.europa.eu/legal-content/EN/TXT/?uri=uriserv:OJ.L_.2007.345.01.0001.01.ENG. 1-4-2014; IA between the European Union and Albania, http://eur-lex.europa.eu/legal-content/EN/TXT/?uri=uriserv:OJ.L_.2006.239.01.0001.01.ENG. 1-4-2014; IA between the European Union and Bosnia-Herzegovina, http://eurlex.europa.eu/legal-ontent/EN/TXT/?uri=uriserv:OJ.L_.2008.233.01.0005.01.ENG. 6-4-2014.

[12] The adoption of the decision concluding specific interim agreements is based solely on Article 133 of the EC Treaty, given that they only cover areas falling within the scope of the common commercial policy and therefore fall within the exclusive competence of the EU.

[13] The EU-Albania SAA came into force on 1-4-2009 while the EU-Albania Interim Agreement (IA) had entered into force on 1-12-2006. The EU-FYROM SAA came into force on 1-4-2004 while the Interim Agreement had entered into force on 1-6-2001. The EU-Montenegro SAA came into force on 1-5-2010 while the interim agreement had entered into force on 1-1-2008. The EU-Bosnia-Herzegovina Interim Agreement came into force on 1-7-2008 while the SAA was signed on 16-6-2008 but hasn't yet entered into force.

[14] Trade-related matters notably include alignment of Serbia's customs, anti-trust and state aid rules as well as protection of intellectual and industrial property rights with the rules existing in the EU.

The EU-Serbia Interim Agreement came into force in 2010.[15] However, Serbia had already begun to implement it since 2009.

In the framework of the EU-Serbia agreement, the contracting parties undertook to establish a bilateral FTA gradually over a transitional period of 6 years[16] from the entry into force of this agreement and in accordance with the provisions of GATT 1994 and the WTO Agreement.

Firstly, our analysis will focus on the tariff liberalization regime established by the agreements.

In the sector of industrial products,[17] the agreement provides for concessions granted by both parties on a reciprocal basis. In other words, the EU grants concessions on products originating in Serbia and Serbia grants concessions on products originating in the EU.

Customs duties imposed on EU imports of industrial products originating in Serbia were abolished upon the entry into force of the agreement.

Serbia was committed to make tariff concessions but not immediately for all industrial products originating in the EU. For this reason, we can say that the liberalization of bilateral trade is asymmetric to the benefit of Serbia for both industrial and agricultural products (Moutsatsos 2007). In this way, the agreement ensures predictability by providing Serbian producers the possibility to prepare for competition from the EU.

More specifically, this country should abolish immediately upon the entry into force of the agreement, tariffs on imports of industrial products originating in the EU for some 58 % of tariff lines (46 % of total imported industrial goods). However, some products are excluded from the immediate abolition. For the industrial products listed in Annex I, the customs duties applicable on imports into Serbia, would not be removed immediately but gradually reduced according to a schedule, so that the 1 January of the sixth year after the entry into force of the SAA, all remaining duties should be eliminated. As specified in Annex Ia imports of sensitive goods, accounting for 12 % of tariff lines, should be liberalized over 2 years from the entry into force of the agreement. Imports of very sensitive products listed in Annex Ib accounting for 21 % of tariff lines should be liberalized over 4 years. Finally, liberalization of the import of the most sensitive products

[15] This agreement was adopted on behalf of the EU with the 2010/36/EC Decision of the Council of 29-4-2008, OJ L 28, 30-1-2010. The EU-Montenegro interim agreement had been concluded on behalf of the EU with the decision 2007/855/EC of the Council of 15-10-2007, OJ L 345, 28-12-2007, the EU-Bosnia-Herzegovina was concluded on behalf of the EU with the decision of the Council of 16-6-2008, OJ L 169, 30-6-2008.

[16] The transitional period for the establishment of the free trade area is 5 years under the EU-Montenegro agreements (article 18.1 of the SAA and article 3.1. of the Interim Agreement) and the EU-Bosnia-Herzegovina agreements (article 18.1 of the SAA and article 3.1 of the Interim Agreement) and 10 years under the EU-Albania agreements (article 16.1 of the SAA and article 3.1. of the Interim Agreement 3.1). See no 3 and no 11.

[17] The provisions on industrial goods cover around 6500 tariff lines.

listed in Annex Ic, accounting for 9 % of tariff lines should be completed over 5 years.

From the date of entry into force of the agreement, both parties should abolish

- any charges having equivalent effect to custom duties on imports
- any customs duties on exports and charges having equivalent effect in trade between them.

Concerning the sector of agriculture and fisheries, the EU was committed to abolish, upon the entry into force of the agreement, the duties and charges having equivalent effect on imports of agricultural products and fishery products originating in Serbia with the exception of some products defined in the agreement and in Annex IV.[18]

With regard to Serbia commitments, the customs duties applicable on imports of agricultural products originating in EU listed in Annex IIIa should be abolished upon the entry into force of the agreement, those applicable on imports of products listed in Annex IIIb should be abolished progressively in accordance with the schedule defined for each product in that Annex and those applicable on imports of agricultural products listed in Annex IIIc and d should be progressively reduced in accordance with the schedule indicated for each product in those annexes.

According to standstill clause, from the date of entry into force of this agreement, EU and Serbia should not introduce any new customs duties on imports or exports or charges having equivalent effect, in trade between them. The duties or charges having equivalent effect already applied should not be increased.

The term Non-Tariff Barriers (NTBs) include any measure or practice other than customs duties, adopted or implemented by a public institution or a private entity of a state, whose purpose or effect is to prevent the access of products originating in another state in the national market of the first state.

The liberalization regarding NTBs is achieved primarily by prohibiting quantitative restrictions on imports and exports and by establishing rules for trade facilitation in the areas of customs procedures and regulations, technical regulations and conformity assessment procedures.

Under the agreement provisions, the quantitative restrictions and measures having equivalent effect on imports into the EU of products originating in Serbia were abolished upon the entry into force of this agreement. Respectively, this country abolished by the same date the restrictions and measures having equivalent effect on imports of products originating in the EU. The two parties also committed to abolish, upon the entry into force of the agreement, any quantitative restriction on exports in trade between them.

The agreement established a standstill clause under which from the date of its entry into force, the parties are not authorized to introduce new quantitative

[18] The exception concerns mainly only a few agricultural products that are under a preferential tariff quota regime (sugar, baby beef, wine and trout).

restriction on imports or exports or measure having equivalent effect nor to make those existing more restrictive, in trade between them.

It should be recognized that in principle the tariff concessions regime established by this agreement, introduces a derogation from the Most Favored Nation (MFN) clause of Article I, § 1 of GATT. This is because its application is restricted to relations between the contracting parties something that is not compatible with WTO law, the keystone of which is the principle of non-discrimination.

However, the agreement complies with the legal system of the WTO, as it satisfies the requirements laid down in Article XXIV of GATT 1994. Specifically, it provides for a program and a plan for the establishment of a free trade area within a reasonable period that is determined in clear, definitive and unconditional terms. The establishment of the FTA is explicitly provided for and is based on binding upon the Parties provision. It isn't merely a statement of intent without legal force. In fact, the term "*free trade area*" is explicitly mentioned in the agreement. The transitional period until the complete establishment of the FTA constitutes the object of detailed provisions and regulations. In this context, the stages of its progressive realization are delineated clearly. The elimination of barriers related to the establishment of the FTA covers the essential, the important part of the trade between the parties. Finally, the agreement contains provisions providing for the granting of reciprocal trade benefits and advantages between the parties.

The liberalization of trade imposed by the detailed provisions of the agreement and implemented since 2009, led to the development of bilateral trade and especially the rise of exports from Serbia to the EU. Total Serbian exports to the EU have been rising from 3200 million euros in 2009 to 5100 million euros in 2012. Serbian exports to the EU countries account for nearly 60 % of the total Serbian exports and they continue to grow each year.[19] At the same time, EU exports to Serbia have increased from 6500 million euros in 2009 to 8600 million euros in 2012.[20]

Moreover, the agreement formed the appropriate institutional framework for the legal security and reduction of political risks, which could encourage investors to expand their economic activities in Serbia.

The other agreements (EU-Albania, EU-Montenegro, EU-FYROM) have imposed on parties trade liberalization commitments similar to those laid down by the EU-Serbia agreement.

The trade in goods between the EU and the Western Balkans is not only governed by the abovementioned agreements. In fact, EU has granted since 2000 on a unilateral basis autonomous trade preferences to all these countries. Through this preferential regime which was renewed in 2011 until 2015, nearly all products

[19] At the same time, Serbian exports to the USA accounted in 2012 for only 0.90 % of the total Serbian exports and Serbian exports to Russia accounted for 7.92 % of the total Serbian exports.

[20] Exports of agricultural products from Serbia have been steadily increasing: 640 million euros in 2009, 820 million euros in 2010, 980 million euros in 2011, to reach 1.1 billion euros in 2012.

originating in the western Balkans enter the EU market without customs duties or quantitative restrictions.

Both the conventional and unilateral instruments of liberalization have contributed to an increase in the western Balkan exports to the EU. The value of exports rose from only 1670 million euros in 2002 to 10,767 million euros in 2012.[21] The first half of 2013 the value of exports to the EU amounted to 6082 million euros.

Once applicable, the SAA would supersede the Interim Agreement providing for a much broader framework of mutual commitments concerning establishment, liberalization of trade in services and capital movement.

4 The Regime of Establishment and Cross-Border Services Supply

Before analyzing the provisions governing the right of establishment, we should clarify the meaning of the term 'establishment' according to the SAAs. The establishment includes the right of companies of one contracting party or of the other party to take up economic activities by means of the setting up of subsidiaries and branches in one party or in the other party respectively.[22] Taking the case of Serbia, establishment means on the one hand the right of a EU company to take up activities of an industrial, commercial and professional character by means of the setting up of subsidiaries and branches in Serbia and on the other hand the right of a Serbian company to take up activities of an industrial, commercial and professional character by means of the setting up of subsidiaries and branches in the EU. It also includes the right of a natural person who is national of an EU member State or of an associated western Balkan country (e.g. Serbia) to set up undertakings, in particular companies, which they effectively control.[23] With the exception of EU-FYROM SAA, according to all the other SAAs, establishment also means the right of nationals to take up economic activities as self-employed persons.

In order to facilitate the setting-up of operations by companies and nationals of one contracting party (for example Serbian companies or nationals) on the other's party territory (for example EU territory), the SAAs introduce the application on a reciprocal basis of the fundamental principles of MFN treatment and national treatment. More specifically, each associated western Balkan country is committed to grant, upon the entry into force of the SAA, concerning the establishment of EU companies in its territory, treatment no less favorable than that accorded to its own

[21] These statistics concern six western Balkan countries: Serbia, FYROM, Albania, Montenegro, Bosnia-Herzegovina and Kosovo.

[22] EU-Serbia art. 52 (d) (ii), EU-Montenegro art. 52 (d) (ii), EU-Albania, art. 49 (d) (ii), EU-FYROM, art. 47 (d) (ii), EU-Bosnia-Herzegovina art 50 (d) (ii). See no 3.

[23] EU-Serbia art. 52 (d) (i), EU-Montenegro art. 52 (d) (i), EU-Albania art. 49 (d) (i), EU-Bosnia-Herzegovina art. 50 (d) (i), EU-FYROM art 47 (d) (i). See no 3.

companies or to any third country company, whichever is the better and concerning the pursuit of economic activities of subsidiaries and branches of EU companies on its territory once established, treatment no less favorable than that accorded to its own companies and branches or to any subsidiaries and branch of any third country company, whichever is the better.[24] For its part, the EU undertake similar obligations regarding the treatment accorded to the establishment of companies from each of the associated States and (to) the operation of subsidiaries and branches of companies from each of these States established in its territory.[25]

In parallel, the agreements impose on the parties a non-discrimination obligation with regard to new regulations and measures. Under this rule, each contracting party (for example EU) is committed to adopt no new regulations or measures introducing discrimination regarding the establishment of the other party's (e.g. Serbia) companies on its territory or regarding their operation, once established, by comparison with its own companies.[26] This obligation is reciprocal with the exception of the EU-FYROM SAA under which it falls unilaterally on EU.[27]

The above rules do not apply immediately, from the entry into force of the SAAs, to the establishment of natural persons who are nationals of the parties to take up economic activities as self-employed persons. The SAAs confer on the Stabilization and Association Council the competence to determine, after a period of time from the entry into force of the agreements, the detailed arrangements to extend the above provisions to the establishment of naturals of the parties.[28]

All SAAs provide for the legal framework of intra-corporate transfers of employees. This transfer is allowed provided that specific conditions are met. At the same time, clear limitations are imposed on the exercise of this right. In the case of EU-Serbia agreement, in principle, a Serbian company established in the EU is entitled to employ, or has employed by one of its subsidiaries or branches, in the EU territory employees who are nationals from Serbia. This right is also recognized to a EU company established in the territory of Serbia. Employees who are nationals of the EU member states can be employed by this company in the territory of Serbia. The following conditions must be fulfilled: (a) such employees must be key personnel, (b) they must be employed exclusively by companies, subsidiaries or

[24] EU-Serbia art. 53.1 (a) and (b), EU-Montenegro art. 53.1 (a) and (b), EU-Albania, art. 50.1 (i) and (ii), EU-Bosnia-Herzegovina art. 51.1 (a) and (b). See no 3.

[25] EU-Serbia art. 53.2 (a) and (b), EU-Montenegro art. 53.2 (a) and (b). See no 3.

[26] EU-Serbia, art. 53.3, EU-Montenegro, art. 53.3, EU-Albania, art. 50.2, EU-Bosnia-Herzegovina, art. 51.3. See no 3.

[27] EU-FYROM, art. 48.2. See no 3.

[28] This period of time varies depending on the SAA. In the case of EU-Serbia and EU-Montenegro SAAs, this period is 4 years. Concerning the EU-Albania SAA, it is 5 years.

branches, (c) their residence and work permits must cover only the period of such employment, (d) this employment must be done in accordance with the legislation in force in the host territory of establishment.[29]

Furthermore, each SAA permit the entry into and the temporary presence within the territory of one party (e.g. EU) of senior personnel of the other party (e.g. Serbia). The recipients of this right are Serbian nationals or EU nationals who work as representatives of companies in a senior position within a company, and are responsible to set up a EU subsidiary or branch of a Serbian company or a Serbian subsidiary or branch of a EU company in a EU member state or in Serbia respectively. However, these persons are not allowed to engage in making direct sales or supplying services.[30] Moreover, the EU-Serbia, EU-Montenegro and EU-Bosnia agreements prohibit those representatives to receive remuneration from a source located within the host territory of establishment.

As far as the cross-border services supply is concerned, the liberalization is promoted by imposing at the same time both an obligation to act and an obligation to refrain from action.

Firstly, the parties should take the necessary steps to allow progressively the services supply by companies or nationals established in the territory of a party other than that of the person for whom the services are intended. These provisions should be progressively, after a period of time from the entry into force of the agreements,[31] implemented through measures adopted by the Stabilization and Association Council.[32]

Furthermore, the parties are committed to allow the temporary movement of natural persons providing the service or being employed by the service provider as key personnel, including natural persons who are representatives of a company or a national of one party (e.g. EU) or the other party (e.g. Serbia). The right of temporary entry is granted to those persons provided that their purpose is to negotiate the sale of services or to enter into agreements to sell services for that service provider. The aforementioned representatives are not allowed to be engaged in making direct sales to the general public or in supplying services themselves.

Secondly, the SAAs impose a standstill obligation according to which the parties should refrain from taking any measures or actions rending the conditions for the cross-border services supply significantly more restrictive as compared to the situation existing on the day preceding the day of entry into force of the agreements. Each contracting party may present to the other party a request to conduct consultations, in cases where the first party considers that the measures adopted by the

[29] EU-Serbia and EU-Montenegro art. 58.1 and 58.2, EU-FYROM art. 53.1 and 53.2, EU-Albania art. 55.1 and 55.2, EU-Bosnia-Herzegovina art. 56.1 and 56.2. See no 3.

[30] EU-Serbia art. 58.3 (a), EU-Montenegro art. 58.3 (a), EU-FYROM art. 53.3 (a), EU-Albania art. 55.3 (a), EU-Bosnia-Herzegovina art. 56.3 (a).

[31] For example, in the case of EU-Serbia SAA, this period is 4 years.

[32] EU-Serbia, art. 59.1 and 59.3, EU-Montenegro art. 59.1 and 59.3, EU-FYROM art. 55.1 and 55.3, EU-Albania art. 57.1 and 57.3, EU-Bosnia-Herzegovina art. 57.1 and 57.3.

other party after the entry into force of the agreement establish a more restrictive framework for services supply.[33]

Specific provisions govern the supply of transport services. In the land transport sector, the agreements provide for the application of the principle of non-discrimination and progressive harmonization of the legislation of any associated state with that of the EU[34] (EU-Serbia Protocol 4, EU-Montenegro Protocol 4, EU-Albania Protocol 5, EU-Bosnia Protocol 3). Regarding the international maritime transport, in the framework of effective implementation of the principle of unrestricted access to the international maritime markets, each party affirms its commitment to a freely competitive environment and undertakes:

(a) to abolish immediately all measures and obstacles that could have restrictive or discriminatory effects on the free services supply on this sector
(b) to grant no less favorable treatment for the ships operated by nationals or companies of the other party than that accorded to a party's own ships with regard to access to ports open to international trade, the use of infrastructure and auxiliary maritime services of the ports.

5 The Obligations of the Parties Concerning Current Payments and Free Capital Movement

The liberalization of capital movements is particularly important not only for the supply of financial services, but also for the incurrence of investments. The agreements establish a set of provisions providing for a framework of liberalization of capital movements between the Parties. It is also important to ensure the liberalization of payments on current transactions, in other words the liberalization of current payments related to the movement of goods, persons, capital and services supply between the parties. They are charged with the obligation to authorize, in freely convertible currency, any payments and transfers on the current account of balance of payments between them.

Upon the entry into force of the SAAs, the parties assume obligations concerning the transactions on the capital and financial account of balance of payments. They undertake to ensure the free capital movement relating: (a) to direct investments made in companies established in accordance with the legislation of the host country and investments made in accordance with the provisions on the establishment (Chap. II of Title V), (b) to credits related to commercial transactions or to the supply of services in which a resident of one of the parties is involved, and to financial loans and credits with maturity longer than a year.

---

[33] EU-Serbia and EU-Montenegro, art. 60, EU-Albania and EU-Bosnia-Herzegovina art. 58.

[34] EU-Serbia Protocol 4, EU-Montenegro Protocol 4, EU-Albania Protocol 5, EU-Bosnia--Herzegovina Protocol 3.

This obligation of parties also covers portfolio investment and financial loans and credits with maturity shorter than a year. However, the fulfillment of this obligation in the case of the EU-Serbia and the EU-Albania agreements will not start immediately, but a period of time after their entry into force.[35] By contrast, the EU-Montenegro provides for immediate implementation of this provision.

According to a standstill clause, the contracting parties should neither introduce new arrangements imposing restrictions on the capital movement and current payments nor make the existing arrangements more restrictive.

Facilitating the movement of capital will be the object of consultations between the parties in order to promote the objectives of the SAA. These agreements seek to promote the application of EU rules on the free capital movement in each of the associated Balkan states. They establish two phases for the realization of this objective: (a) during the first phase, the necessary conditions for the gradual application of the aforementioned rules should be created through measures adopted by the parties,[36] (b) during the second phase (it starts after the end of the first one), the detailed arrangements for full application of EU rules capital movement in each associated western Balkan country should be determined by the Stabilization and Association Council.

6 The SAAs as a Step to EU Accession

The SAA concluded between the EU and the Western Balkan countries is a decisive step to their approach with the EU and their participation in the process of European integration in order to build a stable European order. A key pillar of the SAAs is the establishment of a framework of trade liberalization at the regional level.

With regard to trade in goods, the gradual establishment of a free trade area between the EU and each of these states has contributed to the development of bilateral trade relations and especially to the increase in exports of products originating in the Western Balkans to the EU. When the implementation of all the provisions of the SAAs will be completed, the FTA will not be only limited to the movement of goods but will extend to the right of establishment, the cross-border services supply and capital movement. This evolution will create a favorable environment to attract investments especially from the EU contributing to the economic development of the whole region.

It is certain that the SAA will prepare the Western Balkan countries for the implementation of the ultimate objective of the Stabilization and Association Process which is their future accession to the EU.

[35] This period is 4 years in the case of EU-Serbia SAA and 5 years according to EU-Albania SAA.

[36] The duration of this first phase will be according to EU-Serbia SAA 4 years after its entry into force.

References

Brown C (2012) The European Union and regional trade agreements. In: Herrmann C, Terhechte JP (eds) European Yearbook of International Economic Law, vol 3. Springer

Cremona M (2010) The European Union and regional trade agreements. In: Herrmann C, Terhechte JP (eds) European Yearbook of International Economic Law, vol 1, p 250–267

Fakiolas E, Tzifakis N (2008) Transformation or accession? Reflecting on the EU's strategy towards the Western Balkans. Eur Foreign Aff Rev 13:377–398

Grabar-Kitarovic K (2010) The stabilization and association process: the EU's soft power at its best. Eur Foreign Aff Rev 12:121–125

Moutsatsos D (2007) The External trade relations of the European community. In: Maravegias N, Tsinisizelis M (eds) New European Union, organization and policies 50 years. Themelio, p 483–539

Natens B, Wouters I (2013) Mapping services liberalization commitments in European Union regional trade agreements. Working Paper No. 116 – March 2013, p 1–52

Stahl B (2011) Perverted conditionality: the stabilization and association agreement between the European Union and Serbia. Eur Foreign Aff Rev 16:465–487

Exchange Rate Volatility in the Balkans and Eastern Europe: Implications for International Investments

Alexandra Horobet, Lucian Belascu, and Ana-Maria Barsan

Abstract Our paper's objective is to study the volatility of exchange rates from the region that have not yet adopted the Euro and are not members of the Exchange Rate Mechanism II by considering the exchange rate regime and the implications of currency volatility for foreign capital flows. We model exchange rate volatility by using standard deviations of daily logarithmic changes in the exchange rates, rolling standard deviations, Hodrick-Prescott filters to detect the trends in volatility and ARIMA models. We find that currency volatility remains a strong issue for these countries and that central banks have attempted to manage it, particularly after the global financial crisis. Spikes in monthly volatility are identified for all currencies, although with some variation in time. Over the long-run, some exchange rates experienced sudden increases in volatility over the entire period, but rather quickly corrected, while others have shown an episode of high volatility at the beginning of the period and recorded a reasonable level of volatility throughout the remaining period. Exchange rate volatility "has memory", but some exchange rates are more prone to the persistent effects of shocks in volatility.

Keywords Exchange rates • Volatility • Eastern Europe • Balkans

JEL Classification Codes F31 • F37 • G17

A. Horobet (✉)
Bucharest University of Economic Studies, 6 Piata Romana, Bucharest, Romania
e-mail: alexandra.horobet@gmail.com

L. Belascu
Lucian Blaga University of Sibiu, 17 Calea Dumbravii, Sibiu, Romania
e-mail: lucian_belascu@yahoo.com

A.-M. Barsan
University of Bucharest, 24 Sfantul Stefan, Bucharest, Romania
e-mail: amy_barsan@yahoo.com

A. Karasavvoglou et al. (eds.), *The First Decade of Living with the Global Crisis*, Contributions to Economics, DOI 10.1007/978-3-319-24267-5_11

1 Introduction

The evolution of exchange rates represents a major source of concern from both a micro- and a macroeconomic perspective, given the cvasi-generalised adoption of floating rates since 1973. The choice of an optimal exchange rate regime is still an unresolved question of international macroeconomics, but recent financial history has generated a growing support for "clear-cut" exchange rate regimes—such as hard pegged rates or free floating rates—, considered more appropriated in the current framework of higher financial integration fuelled by unprecedented capital mobility at the global level. From the perspective of international investments, currency movements are highly relevant, as they influence the risk of an international investment not only directly, through their own volatility, but also through the link between foreign asset returns and exchange rate changes. In a framework of increasing international portfolio investments and of business opportunities diversification at the global level, but also of higher financial market integration, investors critically evaluate the exchange rate risk, particularly when investments are made in emerging markets, as is the case with the Balkan and Eastern European countries. A number of studies have shown that a lack of control over currency risk might put investors in the difficult position of not being able to overcome the costs of holding foreign assets with the gains obtained from foreign investments (Jorion 1985; Eun and Resnick 1994; Bugar and Maurer 2002).

The recent financial crisis had a noteworthy impact on global financial markets and under these circumstances it is critical to understand the exposure of international investors to the various risk factors abroad and, in the framework of our research, to currency risk. Various authors study the impact of global financial turmoil on exchange rate policies in 21 emerging countries between 1994 and 2009 and found that currency volatility increases more than proportionally with the global financial stress for most countries in their sample; also, the authors evidence regional contagion effects between neighbouring emerging countries (Coudert et al. 2011). Other authors investigate the group of BRIC countries and argue that high currency volatility was one of the consequences of the years of uncertainty about sustainable recovery and governments' trouble to manage their enormous fiscal deficits after 2008 (Mellet 2011).

At present, the exchange rate regimes of countries from the Balkans and Eastern Europe are rather varied, but this may be explained by the structural diversity of these countries and by their needs and past efforts to actively control inflation and exchange rate volatility. Table 1 summarizes the exchange rate regimes and monetary policy frameworks for the countries in the Balkans and Eastern Europe at the end of 2013, according to the latest report issued by the International Monetary Fund (IMF 2013).

The adoption of a specific exchange rate regime has a demonstrated impact on currency volatility. A paper that studies changes in exchange rate regimes in Visegrad countries finds that path-dependent volatility had a limited effect on exchange rate developments and that the introduction of floating regimes tends to

Table 1 De facto exchange regimes for Balkan and Eastern Europe countries, end 2013

Country	Currency	Exchange rate regime	Monetary policy framework
Croatia	Kuna (HRK)	Crawl-like arrangement	Exchange rate anchor—Euro
Czech Republic	Koruna (CZK)	Free floating	Inflation targeting
Hungary	Forint (HUF)	Floating	Inflation targeting
Poland	Zloty (PLN)	Free floating	Inflation targeting
Romania	Leu (RON)	Floating	Inflation targeting
Russia	Rouble (RUB)	Managed exchange rate arrangement	Various indicators are monitored for the monetary policy. The central bank has taken preliminary steps toward inflation targeting
Serbia	Dinar (RSD)	Floating	Inflation targeting
Turkey	Lira (TRY)	Floating	Inflation targeting

Source: IMF (2013)

increase exchange rate volatility (Kocenda and Valachy 2006). In the past two decades, some of these countries became members of the European Union—Czech Republic, Hungary and Poland in 2004, Romania and Bulgaria in 2007, and Croatia in 2013—, with direct effects on their monetary and exchange rate policies. As a fact, five of them changed their monetary policy rule by the adoption of inflation targeting regime: the Czech Republic in 1998, Poland in 1999, Hungary in 2001 and Romania in 2005. Eventually, these countries will have their currencies replaced by the Euro, but not before at least 2 years spent in the Exchange Rate Mechanism II (ERM II). Joining ERM II assumes the establishment of a fixed exchange rate of the respective currency against the Euro with a variation margin of ±15 % around the parity. Currently, only two countries are members of the ERM II (Denmark and Lithuania), while the prospects of the others to join the system remain uncertain. An important point is worth mentioning here, though: even if ERM II allowed for a rather relaxed band for the exchange rates against the Euro, in reality the effective margins for the ERM II currencies were much smaller: the Danish krone operated at a margin lower than 1 %, the Latvian lats at a 1 % margin, while the Estonian kroon and the Lithuanian litas had 0 % margins before Euro adoption. This indicates, on one hand, a serious commitment of these countries' central banks to ensure the highest possible level of stability of exchange rates against the Euro, and, on the other hand, a considerable pressure on the future members of ERM II to smooth out exchange rates fluctuations before joining the system, as moving from a highly volatile exchange rate to a rather stable one is a not on overnight process.

For what concerns the other countries in the region—Croatia, Serbia, Russia and Turkey, their characteristics in terms of monetary and exchange rate policies are diverse. Of particular concern for Croatia is the high level of dollarization of the economy, which distinguishes it from other advanced transition countries and affects its choice of exchange rate regime. The fragilities created by large quantities of foreign currency liabilities in Croatian banks' balance sheets were the main justification for making exchange rate stability the key player of monetary policy in Croatia's highly dollarized economy (Sosic and Kraft 2004). Other authors explore a number of transition economies—Poland, Czech Republic, Slovakia and the Republic of Serbia, with regard to their abandonment of the exchange rate targeting and fixed exchange rate regimes and movement toward explicit/implicit inflation targeting and flexible exchange rate regimes (Josifidis et al. 2009). In the case of Serbia, the authors find a series of obstacles for a successful inflation targeting monetary policy rule, such as a strong and persistent exchange rate pass-through and a low interest rate pass-through. Turkey is a special case among the countries in the region: since 1990s, Turkey has experienced economic declines after three major crises in 1994, 1999 and 2001, having as common denominators macroeconomic imbalances and external shocks. The 2001 currency crisis was produced by capital market liberalization and speculative attacks under the fixed exchange rate regime, which triggered the change in exchange rate regime to floating accompanied by inflation targeting in 2006. For what concerns Russia, the government debt crisis of 1998 generated a shift to a managed floating exchange rate. The exchange rate continued to be tightly managed through 2002–2005, but in 2004 less restrictive capital control regulations were adopted and, in 2005, the Bank of Russia introduced a dual-currency basket as the operational indicator for its exchange rate policy, aiming to smooth the volatility of the Rouble exchange rate vis-à-vis other major currencies. After the global financial crisis, the Bank of Russia increased the flexibility of its exchange rate policy and more flexibility is envisaged for the period to come.

Our paper aims at investigating the volatility of the exchange rates against the Euro and the US dollar for eight currencies from the Balkans an Eastern Europe that have not yet adopted the Euro and are not members of ERM II—Czech Republic, Hungary, Poland, Romania, Serbia, Croatia, Russia and Turkey. We address the trends in volatilities by taking into account the exchange rate regimes used in each of these eight countries and using daily exchange rates between 1999 and 2013. Exchange rate volatility is modelled using monthly standard deviations of daily logarithmic changes in the exchange rates, as well as rolling standard deviations with different windows, which allows us to understand short-term versus long-term changes in volatility. We apply Hodrick-Prescott filters to detect trends in monthly standard deviations and ARIMA models to investigate the exchange rates volatility response to past levels of volatility and to potential shocks in volatility. We extend here the previous works on exchange rate volatility in Central and Eastern Europe, by investigating more currencies in the region and by using other relevant instruments for understanding currency volatility (Horobet and Tusa 2007; Horobet et al. 2011).

We contribute to the research in the field with a thorough investigation of currency volatility patterns in the region, which represents, to our knowledge, the first attempt of this kind in the literature. In order to properly understand the evolution of currency volatility after 1999, we use a set of instruments that provide information on short-run versus long-run volatility patterns, as well as on volatility time-dependency and currency volatility sensitivity to potential shocks.

2 Data and Research Methodology

We use in our research exchange rates of the domestic currencies against the Euro and the US dollar of eight countries from the Balkans and Eastern Europe that have not yet adopted the Euro and are not members of the ERM II—more specifically Czech Republic (Czech Koruna—CZK), Hungary (Hungarian Forint—HUF), Poland (Polish Zloty—PLN), Romania (Romanian Leu—RON), Serbia (Serbian Dinar—RSD), Croatia (Croatian Kuna—HRK), Russia (Russian Rouble—RUB) and Turkey (Turkish Lira—TYR). Data on exchange rates was collected from the Pacific Exchange Rate Service, for the period between 1999 and 2013. The first observation dates from January 4th, 1999 for Czech Republic, Hungary, Poland, Romania, Russia and Turkey, from March 1st, 2002 for Croatia, and from September 4th, 2007 for Serbia.

Based on daily exchange rates, we calculate (1) the daily logarithmic returns with EUR and the USD, respectively, as base currencies; (2) the monthly standard deviation of the daily logarithmic returns against the EUR and the USD; and (3) the 30 days, 90 days and 360 days rolling standard deviations of daily logarithmic returns.

We apply the Hodrick-Prescott (HP) filter, which offers a smooth estimate of the long-term trend component of a series of data, to have a better view on the monthly standard deviations of daily logarithmic returns. The method was proposed by Hodrick and Prescott in 1997 to model post-war U.S. business cycles, and it uses a two-sided linear filter that calculates the smooth series S of a series Y by minimising the variance of Y around S, by taking into account a penalty parameter λ that constrains the second difference of S (Hodrick and Prescott 1997). Specifically, the HP filter minimizes:

$$\sum_{t=1}^{T} (y_t - s_t)^2 + \lambda \sum_{t=2}^{T} [(s_{t+1} - s_t) - (s_t - s_{t-1})]^2 \quad (1)$$

The parameter λ controls for the degree of smoothness of the series variance: the larger its value, the smoother the variance. We have used 14,400 as the value of λ for smoothing the series of monthly standard deviations, which is appropriate for the work on monthly data.

Autoregressive integrated moving average (ARIMA) models, popularly known as the Box–Jenkins methodology, offer an analysis of the stochastic properties of economic time series, based on the "let data speak for themselves" philosophy (Box and Jenkins 1978). An ARIMA (p, d, q) is an autoregressive integrated moving average time series, where p denotes the number of autoregressive terms, d the number of times the series has to be differenced before the series becomes stationary, and q the number of moving average terms. The ARIMA (p,d,q) model of the time series $\{x_1, x_2, \ldots\}$ may be defined as:

$$\Phi_p(B)\Delta^d x_t = \Theta_q(B)\varepsilon_r \tag{2}$$

where B is the backward shift operator, $Bx_y = x_{y-1}$, $\Delta = 1 - B$ is the backward difference, and Φ_p and Θ_q are polynomials of order p and q, respectively. ARIMA (p,d,q) models are the product of an autoregressive part AR(p) of the form:

$$\Phi_p = 1 - \varphi_1 B - \varphi_2 B^2 - \ldots - \varphi_p B^p \tag{3}$$

an integrating part of the form:

$$I(d) = \Delta^{-d} \tag{4}$$

and a moving average MA(q) part of the form:

$$\Theta_q = 1 - \theta_1 B - \theta_2 B^2 - \ldots - \theta_p B^p \tag{5}$$

While finding d in ARIMA(p,d,q) is typically implemented with the help of stationarity tests such as Augmented Dickey-Fuller or Phillips-Perron, the method of choosing values for p and q requires a careful analysis of the autocorrelations and partial autocorrelations for the times series. Still, finding the good model is usually an iterative technique where different values for p and q are given and the model diagnostic is carried out. We verify the ARIMA properties of the series of monthly standard deviations, in order to identify the time-dependence of monthly volatility—AR terms—and the influence of possible shocks in volatility—the MA terms.

3 Results

3.1 Brief Analysis of Daily Exchange Rates

Figure 1 shows the series of daily exchange rates of the eight currencies from the Balkans and Eastern Europe against the EUR and the USD, between 1999 and 2013, while Fig. 2 presents the daily logarithmic changes (or returns) of the same exchange rates. Descriptive statistics for the daily logarithmic changes are presented in Table 2. A quick look at the graphs in Fig. 1 indicates different patterns for these countries' exchange rates against both the EUR and the USD. Overall, the CZK is the only currency with an appreciating trend between 1999 and 2013 against

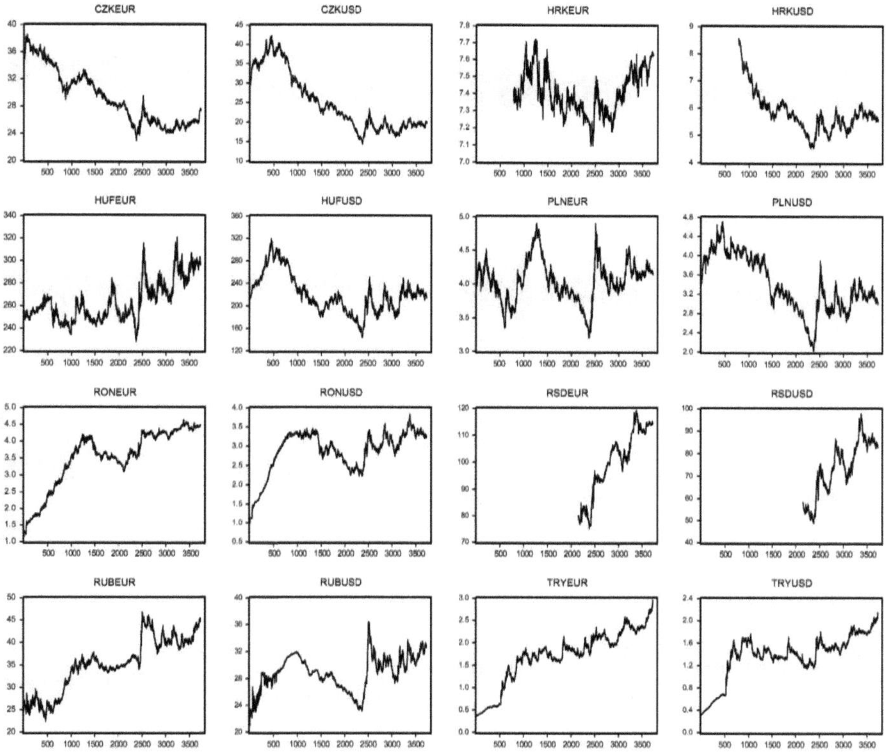

Fig. 1 Daily exchange rates against EUR and USD, 1999–2013. *Note*: The first observation is January 4, 1999 and the last observation is December 31, 2013; exchange rates are quoted with EUR and USD as base currencies

both the EUR and the USD; the RON, RSD, RUB and TRY depreciated against the EUR and USD, as a general trend, but swings in the exchange rates over these years were important, particularly in the case of the RUB and even RSD. Over the entire frame of exchange rates observations for each currency pair, the CZK appreciated by 29.2 % and the PLN by a tiny 0.06 %, while all the other currencies depreciated against the EUR, with the notable case of the TRY—a depreciation of 87.32 %. When the exchange rates against the USD are considered, three currencies recorded overall appreciations against the American currency—the HRK (54.7 %), the CZK (49.9 %) and the PLN (16.11 %). As in the EUR case, the TRY depreciated heavily, by 85.3 % overall, followed by RON, with a depreciation rate of 69.3 %.

It is worthwhile mentioning the higher stability in the RONEUR exchange rate after 2008 compared to the previous years, but which is not found in the case of RONUSD exchange rate—this is explained by the fact that on the Romanian foreign exchange market the RONEUR exchange rate is the reference rate and observed by the Romanian central bank, while the RONUSD exchange rate is determined as a cross-rate, taking into account the USDEUR exchange rate in the international foreign exchange market. By far, the HUFEUR, HUFUSD, PLNEUR,

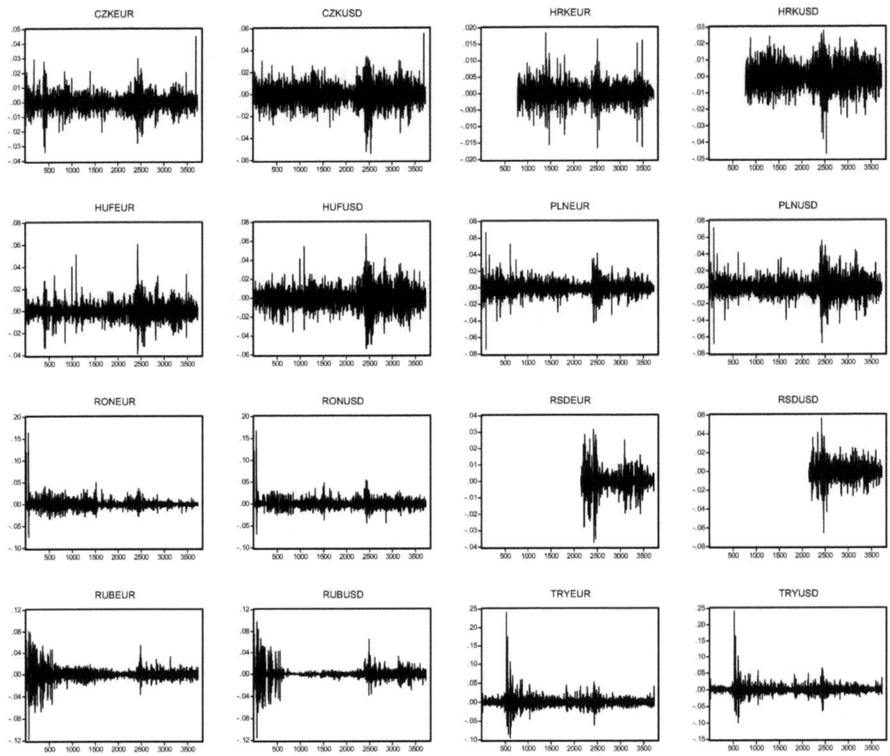

Fig. 2 Daily returns of exchange rates against the EUR and USD, 1999–2013. *Note*: The first observation is January 5, 1999 and the last observation is December 31, 2013

Table 2 Correlations between the exchange rates against EUR and USD, 1999–2013

Currency	CZK	HRK	HUF	PLN	RON	RSD	RUB	TRY
Correlation coefficient	0.6199	0.2907	0.7504	0.7261	0.7133	0.6464	0.7614	0.8459

PLNUSD and HRKEUR exchange rates display the highest volatility over the period, especially after the end of 2008. An interesting observation regards the high correlations between the exchange rates of each of the eight currencies against the EUR and the USD, presented in Table 2.

When daily exchange returns are considered, the different evolutions of exchange rates are reflected in the diverse patterns shown in Fig. 2. Again, there are exchange rates with a rather high volatility over the entire period—HRKEUR, HRKUSD, HUFUSD, PLNUSD, RSDEUR, RSDUSD, exchange rates with spikes in volatility—CZKEUR, CSKUSD, RUBEUR, RUBEUR, TRYEUR and TRYUSD, and also rather stable exchange rates—RONEUR and RONUSD. At the same time, the well documented phenomenon of volatility clustering is easily observable (Engle 1982; Bollerslev 1986; Cont 2005).

Considering the exchange rates against the EUR, an analysis of data in Table 3 shows that only one currency—CZK—appreciated, on average, against the EUR, at a rate of 0.14 % per month, while all the other currencies depreciated against the common currency—the highest average depreciation was recorded for TRY (1.11 % per month) and the lowest for HRK (0.20 % per month). The average monthly change in the value against the EUR for PLN was a surprising 0 %. At the same time, the volatility of daily returns was considerable for many currencies, either on an absolute basis (minimum and maximum values) or by taking into account their standard deviations. The most volatile exchange rates over the entire period under analysis were the TRY (a standard deviation on 5.25 % per month), the RUB (standard deviation of 4.32 % per month) and the RON (a standard deviation of 3.71 % per month), while the most stable currencies were the HRK (standard deviation of 1.09 %) and the CZK (standard deviation of 2.15 %). All exchange rate changes are non-normally distributed, with negative skewness for CZK, HRK, HUF, PLN, RON and TRY, positive skewness for RSD and RUB, and excess kurtosis—the same leptokurtic distributions are also indicated by the Jarque-Berra test of normality.

When we investigate the exchange rates against the USD (see Table 4), we observe that three currencies (CZK, HRK and PLN) recorded, on average over the period, appreciations against the USD—the highest average appreciation belongs to HRK, while all the other currencies depreciated on average against the USD—the highest depreciation was recorded for the TRY (thus confirming the results for the TRY exchange rate against the EUR). As in the EUR case, the exchange rates volatility was high, reaching 4.01 % on a monthly basis for TRY and 3.36 % per month for HUF. Daily jumps in the series of exchange rates changes are also observable in the relation to the USD—the highest were present for TRY (an appreciation of the USD of 482.8 % per month, or 24.13 % per day, on February 22, 2001) and RON (an appreciation of 335.6 % per month, or 16.78 % per day, on March 11, 2009). On average, the highest appreciations of the USD were higher compared to the appreciations against the EUR (196.3 % compared to 176.93 % on a monthly basis), as is the case with the largest depreciations of the USD (on average, the highest depreciations of the USD were 142.4 % per month, while the largest depreciations of the EUR generated an average of 121.83 % per month). The Jarque-Berra test of normality indicates leptokurtic distributions, with negative skewness for HUF, PLN, RON, RUB and TRY, positive skewness for CZK, HRK and RSD, and excess kurtosis for all exchange rate return series.

A quick look at Tables 5 and 6, which show the correlations between the logarithmic returns in the exchange rates against the EUR and the USD, indicates stronger links between the exchange rates against the USD, compared to the exchange rates against the EUR. In the case of correlations against the EUR, the highest correlation coefficient is 0.5542 between HUFEUR and PLNEUR, while the lowest is negative, with a value of −0.0118, between RSDEUR and CZKEUR. For correlations against the USD, the highest coefficient has a value of 0.8190 between HRKUSD and CZKUSD, and the lowest has a value of 0.1303 between RUBUSD and TRYUSD. The average correlation coefficient for the exchange rates against the EUR was 0.1579 and for the exchange rates against the USD was 0.5038.

Table 3 Descriptive statistics of daily returns of exchange rates against the EUR (monthly basis)

	CZKEUR	HRKEUR	HUFEUR	PLNEUR	RONEUR	RSDEUR	RUBEUR	TRYEUR
Mean	−0.0014	0.0002	0.0009	0.0000	0.0071	0.0046	0.0032	0.0111
Median	−0.0020	0.0000	−0.0040	−0.0040	0.0000	0.0040	0.0000	0.0020
Maximum	0.8980	0.3680	1.2120	1.3280	3.2760	0.6300	1.6160	4.8260
Minimum	−0.6800	−0.3300	−0.7720	−1.4820	−1.4900	−0.7440	−2.3540	−1.8940
Std. dev.	0.0215	0.0109	0.0284	0.0317	0.0371	0.0262	0.0432	0.0525
Skewness	0.2228	0.0561	0.5303	0.0805	3.8363	−0.2295	−0.2041	3.9157
Kurtosis	9.7902	10.1969	10.2694	12.5719	70.9176	9.9530	22.6156	76.5521
Jarque-Bera	7188.92	6367.97	8378.62	14,228.32	725,277.50	3192.52	59,761.47	849,410.50
Probability	0.0000	0.0000	0.0000	0.0000	0.0000	0.0000	0.0000	0.0000
Observations	3726	2950	3726	3726	3726	1578	3726	3726

Table 4 Descriptive statistics of daily returns of exchange rates against the USD (monthly basis)

	CZKUSD	HRKUSD	HUFUSD	PLNUSD	RONUSD	RSDUSD	RUBUSD	TRYUSD
Mean	−0.0022	−0.0030	0.0001	−0.0008	0.0063	0.0044	0.0024	0.0103
Median	0.0000	−0.0040	−0.0020	−0.0060	0.0030	0.0020	0.0000	0.0000
Maximum	1.1040	0.5540	1.3480	1.4340	3.3560	1.1340	1.9460	4.8280
Minimum	−1.0720	−0.9420	−1.0720	−1.3580	−1.3660	−1.3100	−2.3040	−1.9680
Std. dev.	0.0286	0.0232	0.0336	0.0326	0.0304	0.0320	0.0311	0.0401
Skewness	−0.0867	−0.1011	0.1054	0.1825	3.5556	−0.1982	0.2057	3.8914
Kurtosis	6.0587	5.1561	6.5913	8.6597	61.9480	8.0236	30.6822	77.0268
Jarque-Bera	1457.14	576.42	2009.25	4993.76	547,323.40	1669.66	118,994.70	860,168.20
Probability	0.0000	0.0000	0.0000	0.0000	0.0000	0.0000	0.0000	0.0000
Observations	3726	2950	3726	3726	3726	1578	3726	3726

Table 5 Correlations between daily returns of exchange rates against the EUR, 1999–2013

	CZKEUR	HRKEUR	HUFEUR	PLNEUR	RONEUR	RSDEUR	RUBEUR	TRYEUR
CZKEUR	1.0000	0.1480	0.4740	0.4366	0.1289	−0.0118	0.0804	0.1269
HRKEUR	0.1480	1.0000	0.1344	0.1307	0.0762	0.0661	0.1015	0.0804
HUFEUR	0.4740	0.1344	1.0000	0.5542	0.1534	0.0598	0.0640	0.2194
PLNEUR	0.4366	0.1307	0.5542	1.0000	0.2457	0.0274	0.1974	0.2545
RONEUR	0.1289	0.0762	0.1534	0.2457	1.0000	0.0305	0.1926	0.2054
RSDEUR	−0.0118	0.0661	0.0598	0.0274	0.0305	1.0000	0.0110	0.0414
RUBEUR	0.0804	0.1015	0.0640	0.1974	0.1926	0.0110	1.0000	0.1918
TRYEUR	0.1269	0.0804	0.2194	0.2545	0.2054	0.0414	0.1918	1.0000

Note: The correlations for HRKEUR and RSDEUR are calculated for the period March 1, 2002–December 31, 2013, and September 4, 2007–December 31, 2013, respectively

Table 6 Correlations between daily returns of exchange rates against the USD, 1999–2013

	CZKUSD	HRKUSD	HUFUSD	PLNUSD	RONUSD	RSDUSD	RUBUSD	TRYUSD
CZKUSD	1.0000	0.8190	0.7976	0.7273	0.4376	0.6601	0.2667	0.2905
HRKUSD	0.8190	1.0000	0.7692	0.7376	0.5969	0.7464	0.5281	0.3752
HUFUSD	0.7976	0.7692	1.0000	0.7775	0.4595	0.6484	0.2805	0.3686
PLNUSD	0.7273	0.7376	0.7775	1.0000	0.4563	0.6406	0.3106	0.3529
RONUSD	0.4376	0.5969	0.4595	0.4563	1.0000	0.6264	0.1672	0.2191
RSDUSD	0.6601	0.7464	0.6484	0.6406	0.6264	1.0000	0.4975	0.4187
RUBUSD	0.2667	0.5281	0.2805	0.3106	0.1672	0.4975	1.0000	0.1303
TRYUSD	0.2905	0.3752	0.3686	0.3529	0.2191	0.4187	0.1303	1.0000

Note: The correlations for HRKUSD and RSDUSD are calculated for the period March 1, 2002–December 31, 2013, and September 4, 2007–December 31, 2013, respectively

3.2 Analysis of Exchange Rate Volatility

We now turn our attention to the in-depth study of exchange rate volatility. After a brief analysis of descriptive statistics for the monthly standard deviations of exchange rate returns against the EUR and USD, we investigate the trends in monthly volatility using the Hodrick-Prescott filter, we observe the volatility behaviour over short-run and long-run using rolling standard deviations with various windows, and we model monthly volatilities with the help of ARIMA models. Combined, the results of these three approaches offer us a more comprehensive view over the time-dependencies of exchange rate volatilities in the Balkans and Eastern Europe.

Tables 7 and 8 provide descriptive statistics for the monthly series of volatilities for the 16 exchange rates under scrutiny. For what concerns the exchange rates against the EUR, the means of monthly volatilities range between 0.22 % for HRK and 3.91 % for TRY, with the highest monthly volatility recorded for TRY (27.55 % for February 2001) and the lowest for 0.06 % for HRK (June 2008). When the exchange rates against the USD are considered, the average monthly volatilities range between 2.72 % for RUB and 3.98 % for HUF; the highest monthly volatility belongs again to TRY (27.55 % in February 2001) and the lowest to CZK (1.36 % in June 2007). The most volatile series of monthly standard deviations were the ones for TRYEUR and TRYUSD, while the series with the lowest volatility were the HRKUSD and HRKEUR. As indicated by skewness and kurtosis, all series of monthly standard deviations show negative asymmetry and excess kurtosis, thus presenting the attributes of a leptokurtic distribution.

As a possible indication of potential shock transmission between exchange rates volatilities, we have also calculated the correlations between monthly standard deviations both against the EUR and USD (see Tables 9 and 10). The average correlation for the monthly standard deviations against the USD is 0.7127, higher than in the case of monthly standard deviations against the EUR (0.2763), thus indicating that potential shocks in the exchange rates against the USD might be transmitted quicker than the shocks in the exchange rates against the EUR. The explanation, in our view, resides in the controlled exchange rates against the EUR for many of these currencies, while the exchange rates against the USD are rather freely moving, taking into account mainly the USDEUR exchange rate in the international foreign exchange market. The highest correlation for the volatilities against the EUR is recorded for RONEUR and RSDEUR, while against the USD is found for HUF and PLN (0.9507). At the other end, the lowest correlations were −0.0835 for the monthly standard deviations of RUBEUR and HUFEUR and 0.2358 for the monthly standard deviations of RUBUSD and TRYUSD.

Controlling for the smoothness in series variance, the application of the HP filter shows three distinct patterns of evolution for the eight currencies under analysis (see Fig. 3). The first pattern is observable for CZK, HRK, HUF and PLN (except for HRKEUR): a decreasing volatility trend from January 1999 until the end of 2006, followed by increasing volatility until the end of 2009, and subsequent

Table 7 Descriptive statistics of monthly standard deviations of exchange rates returns against the EUR, January 1999–December 2013

	SD_CZKEUR	SD_HRKEUR	SD_HUFEUR	SD_PLNEUR	SD_RONEUR	SD_RSDEUR	SD_RUBEUR	SD_TRYEUR
Mean	0.0043	0.0022	0.0056	0.0063	0.0067	0.0048	0.0074	0.0391
Median	0.0037	0.0021	0.0049	0.0056	0.0059	0.0037	0.0053	0.0305
Maximum	0.0146	0.0072	0.0238	0.0239	0.0497	0.0176	0.0429	0.2755
Minimum	0.0017	0.0006	0.0013	0.0019	0.0013	0.0008	0.0014	0.0096
Std. dev.	0.0023	0.0010	0.0030	0.0033	0.0051	0.0034	0.0066	0.0346
Skewness	1.9921	1.7834	1.8777	2.3104	4.0759	1.6353	2.6069	3.9073
Kurtosis	7.7998	8.3931	9.7045	10.7258	32.1602	5.4875	10.3601	22.0575
Observations	180	142	180	180	180	76	180	180

Table 8 Descriptive statistics of monthly standard deviations of exchange rates returns against the USD, January 1999–December 2013

	SD_CZKUSD	SD_HRKUSD	SD_HUFUSD	SD_PLNUSD	SD_RONUSD	SD_RSDUSD	SD_RUBESD	SD_TRYUSD
Mean	0.0345	0.0285	0.0398	0.0379	0.0333	0.0374	0.0272	0.0391
Median	0.0322	0.0276	0.0357	0.0338	0.0299	0.0334	0.0165	0.0305
Maximum	0.1045	0.0686	0.1378	0.1434	0.2256	0.1190	0.1912	0.2755
Minimum	0.0129	0.0130	0.0148	0.0130	0.0044	0.0158	0.0012	0.0096
Std. dev.	0.0136	0.0095	0.0178	0.0192	0.0212	0.0174	0.0312	0.0346
Skewness	1.9649	1.4986	1.8577	2.0673	4.9760	2.1692	2.3760	3.9073
Kurtosis	8.7826	6.4021	8.3965	9.1878	41.5775	9.2007	9.2682	22.0575
Observations	180	141	180	180	180	75	180	180

Table 9 Correlations of monthly standard deviations of exchange rates against the EUR

	SD_CZKEUR	SD_HRKEUR	SD_HUFEUR	SD_PLNEUR	SD_RONEUR	SD_RSDEUR	SD_RUBEUR	SD_TRYEUR
SD_CZKEUR	1.0000	0.2076	0.5822	0.5465	0.2340	0.3612	0.2080	0.0698
SD_HRKEUR	0.2076	1.0000	0.1321	0.3040	0.3013	0.2091	0.3630	−0.0179
SD_HUFEUR	0.5822	0.1321	1.0000	0.4998	0.0410	0.2740	−0.0835	0.1189
SD_PLNEUR	0.5465	0.3040	0.4998	1.0000	0.3319	0.2304	0.4841	0.1819
SD_RONEUR	0.2340	0.3013	0.0410	0.3319	1.0000	0.6097	0.5627	0.2479
SD_RSDEUR	0.3612	0.2091	0.2740	0.2304	0.6097	1.0000	0.2725	0.4329
SD_RUBEUR	0.2080	0.3630	−0.0835	0.4841	0.5627	0.2725	1.0000	0.0321
SD_TRYEUR	0.0698	−0.0179	0.1189	0.1819	0.2479	0.4329	0.0321	1.0000

Table 10 Correlations of monthly standard deviations of exchange rates against the USD

	SD_CZKUSD	SD_HRKUSD	SD_HUFUSD	SD_PLNUSD	SD_RONUSD	SD_RSDUSD	SD_RUBUSD	SD_TRYUSD
SD_CZKUSD	1.0000	0.8799	0.8996	0.8839	0.8071	0.7143	0.5523	0.7551
SD_HRKUSD	0.8799	1.0000	0.8942	0.8473	0.8407	0.8040	0.5975	0.7039
SD_HUFUSD	0.8996	0.8942	1.0000	0.9507	0.8305	0.6722	0.5900	0.7488
SD_PLNUSD	0.8839	0.8473	0.9507	1.0000	0.8036	0.6074	0.5778	0.7386
SD_RONUSD	0.8071	0.8407	0.8305	0.8036	1.0000	0.7365	0.4314	0.8213
SD_RSDUSD	0.7143	0.8040	0.6722	0.6074	0.7365	1.0000	0.4161	0.6158
SD_RUBUSD	0.5523	0.5975	0.5900	0.5778	0.4314	0.4161	1.0000	0.2358
SD_TRYUSD	0.7551	0.7039	0.7488	0.7386	0.8213	0.6158	0.2358	1.0000

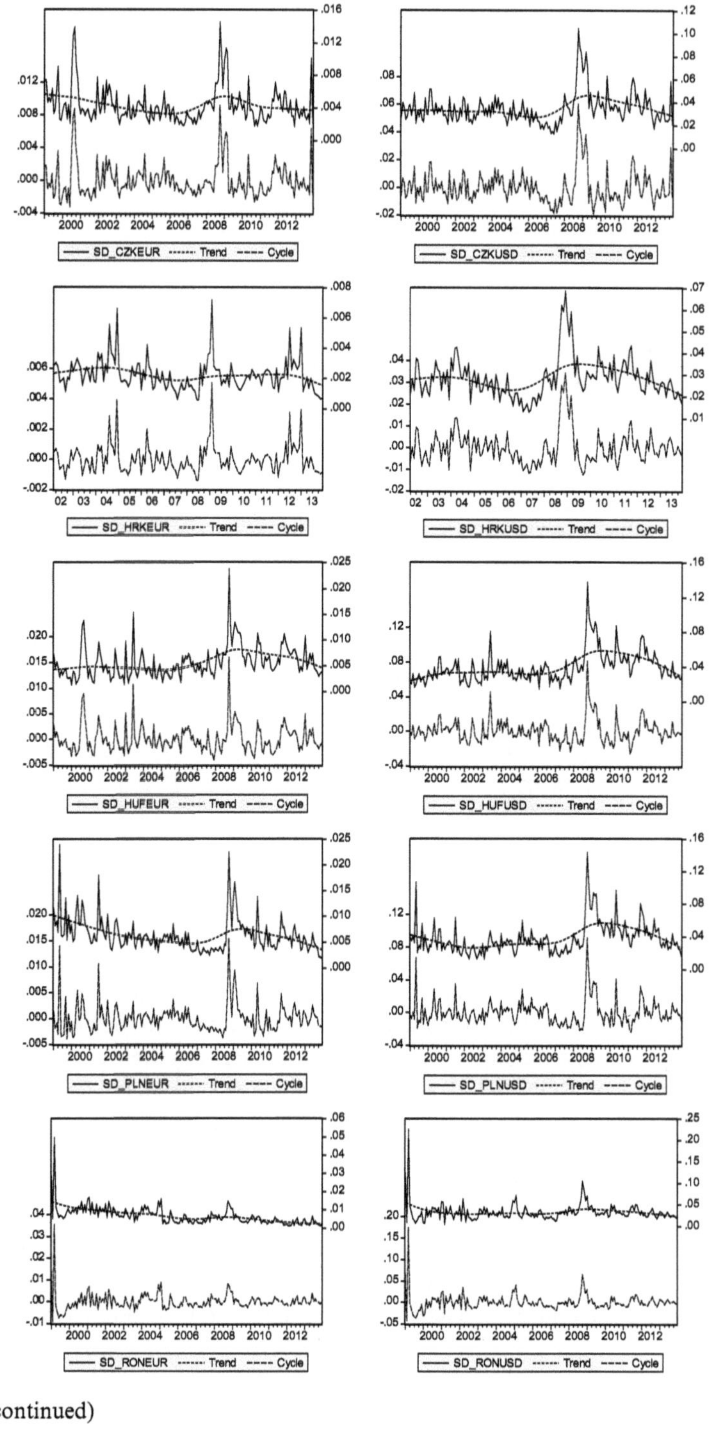

Fig. 3 (continued)

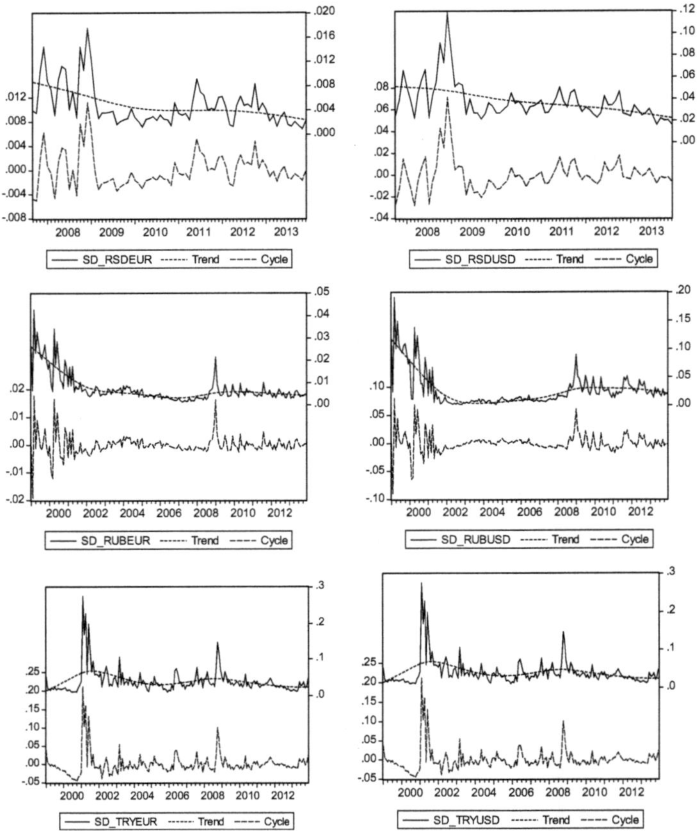

Fig. 3 Monthly standard deviations of exchange rates returns against the EUR and USD, values and HP filter, January 1999–December 2013

decline in volatilities until the end of 2013. In this group, the series of monthly volatilities were smoother for the HRKEUR, although a small increase is observable in 2008 and 2009, followed by a succeeding decline until the end of 2013. The second group of exchange rates, with a different pattern in their monthly volatility trend, is formed of RON, RUB and TRY: all three currencies had more stable monthly volatilities between 1999 and 2013, indicating the countries' central banks concern regarding the exchange rate fluctuations. The third pattern is observable in the case of the RSD (indeed, only after 2007), showing a decreasing trend in volatilities of the currency against both the EUR and USD.

The next step in our analysis focuses on the differences between short-run and long-run trends in volatility, with the support of rolling standard deviations (RSD) of daily logarithmic returns in exchange rates: the 30-days window RSD evolution

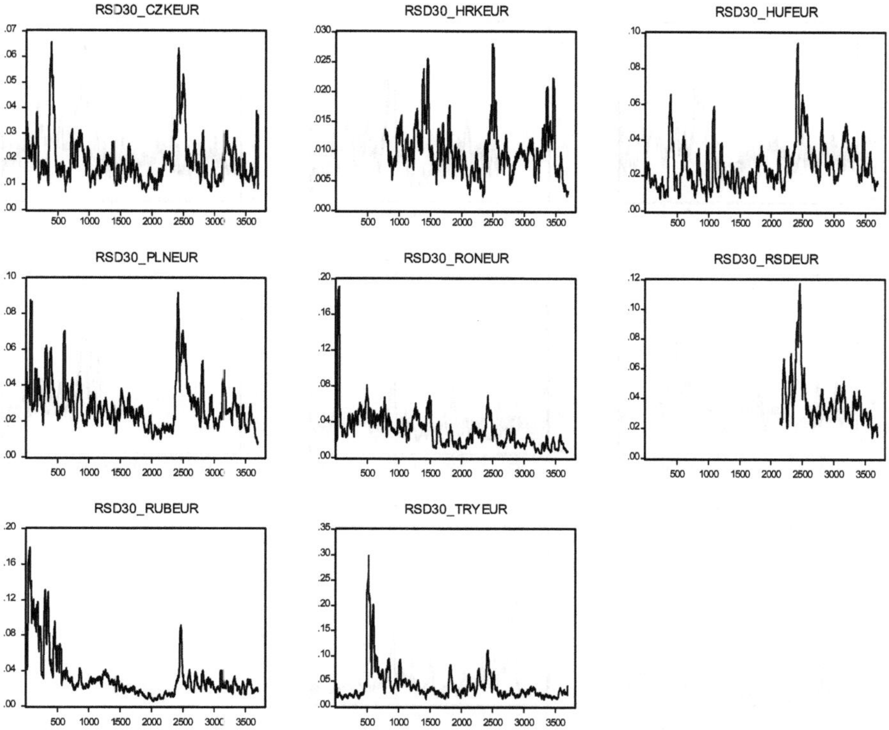

Fig. 4 (continued)

shows the short-run (1 month) shocks in volatility (see Fig. 4a, b), the 90-days window RSD shows the medium-term (3 months) shocks in volatility (see Fig. 5a, b), and the 360-days window RSD shows the long-term (1 year) shocks in volatility (see Fig. 6a, b).

A few observations are noteworthy based on our results: (1) regardless of the window length, spikes in volatility are easily observable over the entire period, particularly for some exchange rates—CZKEUR, HRKEUR, HRKUSD, HUFEUR, HUFUSD, PLNEUR, PLNUSD; (2) for other exchange rates, the spikes in volatility are present only for some months—for example, if we consider the 30-day window RSD, the RONEUR and RONUSD exchange rates have an abrupt increase in volatility at the beginning of 1999, followed by rather calm times and another (smaller) spike in 2008; the same is true for RUBEUR, RUBUSD, TRYEUR and TRYUSD exchange rates; (3) when we move from short-term to medium-term volatility, the differences between exchange rates observable in the case of short-term volatility are more obvious: on one hand, we observe exchange rates that

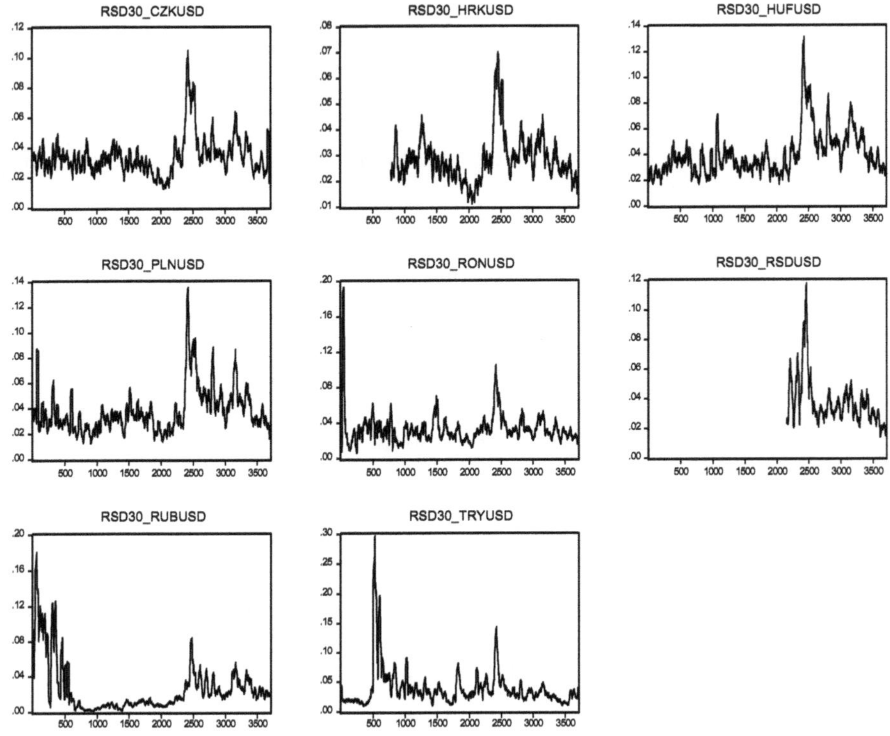

Fig. 4 (**a**) Rolling standard deviations of exchange rate returns against the EUR—30 days window, 1999–2013. *Note*: The first observation is February 15, 1999 and the last observation is December 31, 2013. (**b**) Rolling standard deviations of exchange rate returns against the USD—30 days window, 1999–2013. *Note*: The first observation is February 15, 1999 and the last observation is December 31, 2013

experienced sudden increases in volatility over the entire period, rather quickly corrected (in 3–4 months) and, on the other hand, other exchange rates that, after experiencing higher volatilities at the beginning of the period, have remained at reasonable levels of volatility throughout the remaining period; (4) the long-run RSD offers a good image of the persistency of high levels of volatility for some currencies: as one may observe, the period between 2008 and 2010 shows increased volatilities for all exchange rates that were persistent over some months before being corrected; at the same time, for some exchange rates (CZKEUR, HRKEUR, RONUSD, TRYEUR, TRYUSD) such persistency in volatility is also observable for other periods.

Table 11 presents the result of the Augmented Dickey-Fuller (ADF) and Phillips-Perron (PP) tests of stationarity for the monthly series of standard deviations for daily returns in exchange rates. All series are non-stationary in levels and stationary in the first difference—in the case of SD–RSDEUR, the ADF test

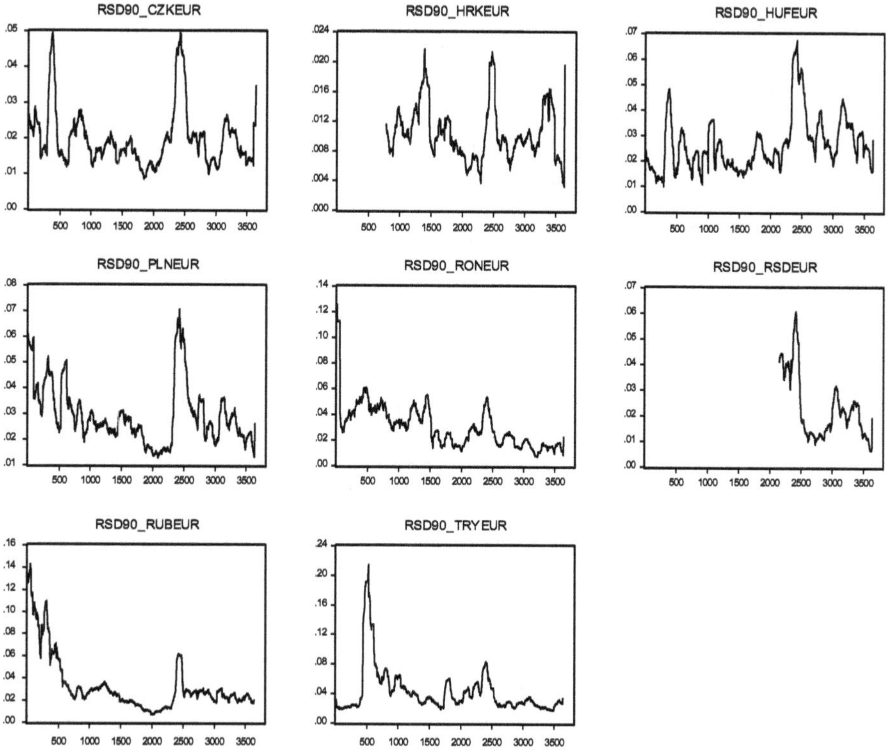

Fig. 5 (continued)

indicated stationarity in level, but the PP test confirmed non-stationarity. As a result, all SD series are I(1).

The next step in identifying a fitted ARIMA model was to study series correlogram and, based on the autocorrelation and partial autocorrelations, to try various values for p and q. We show in Table 12 the best-fit ARIMA(p,d,q) models for the monthly standard deviation series for all exchange rates, based on three model diagnostic indicators (Schwartz criterion, Adjusted R^2 and SEE). We observe that all series have AR terms, but not all of them have MA terms—MA terms are found only in the case of CZKEUR, CZKUSD, HRKEUR, HUFEUR, HUFUSD, PLNEUR, PLNUSD, RONEUR, RONUSD and RUBUSD. This result indicates, on one hand, that exchange rate volatility "has memory", sometimes even for 7 or 9 months (as is the case with HRKUSD and TRYUSD)—but all standard deviations have a memory of at least 1 month, while some exchange rates are more prone to the persistent effects of shocks in volatility (the most interesting case is the RONUSD exchange rate, where a shock in volatility seems to persistent for 4 months!).

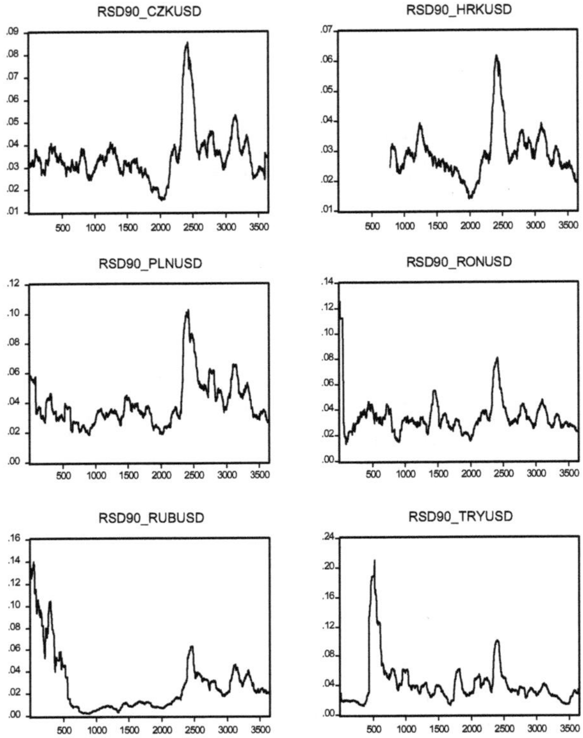

Fig. 5 (**a**) Rolling standard deviations of exchange rate returns against the EUR—90 days window, 1999–2013. *Note*: The first observation is May 14, 1999 and the last observation is December 31, 2013. (**b**) Rolling standard deviations of exchange rate returns against the USD—90 days window, 1999–2013. *Note*: The first observation is May 14, 1999 and the last observation is December 31, 2013

4 Conclusion

Our research examined exchange rate volatility for a number of eight currencies from the Balkans and Eastern Europe, with the aim of observing short-run versus long-run patterns in volatility, as well as the influence of past volatility on current volatility levels and the persistence of shocks in volatility. Our main findings point towards significant differences in volatility patterns among the currencies under investigation. First, there are currencies such as the CZK, HRK, HUF and PLN that experienced decreasing currency volatility from 1999 to 2006, followed by increasing volatility until the end of 2009 and subsequent declines in volatility until the end of 2013. Second, the RON, RUB and TRY had more stable volatilities between 1999 and 2013, which strongly indicates a serious concern of these countries' central banks regarding exchange rate fluctuations and a success of these central banks in terms of exchange rate volatility management. Third, the RSD (for which

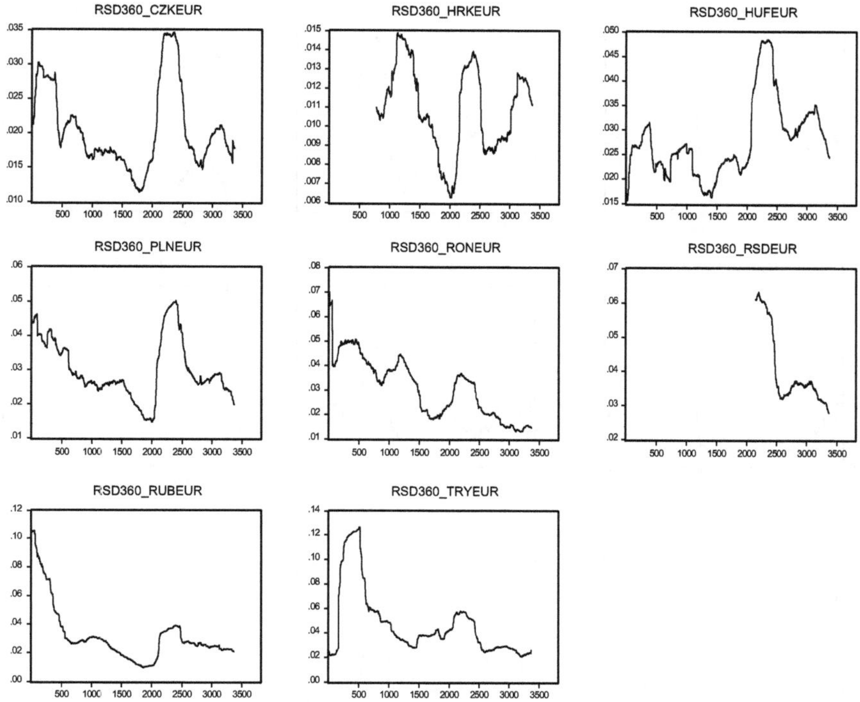

Fig. 6 (continued)

we have observations only since the end of 2007) experienced a decreasing volatility until the end of 2013.

Regarding the short-run versus long-run volatility, spikes in monthly volatility were present for all currencies, although for some of them they are observable throughout the entire period (CZK, HRK, HUF, PLN), while for others (RON, RUB, TRY) they were present in 1999–2000 and afterwards only in 2008. When long-run volatility is considered, there are exchange rates that experienced sudden increases in volatility over the entire period, but rather quickly corrected (in 3–4 months) and, on the other hand, there are currencies that, after experiencing higher volatilities at the beginning of the period, have remained at reasonable levels of volatility throughout the remaining period. The results of applying ARIMA modelling to currency volatility series indicate that exchange rate volatility "has memory", sometimes even for 7 or 9 months—but all standard deviations have a memory of at least 1 month, while some exchange rates are more prone to the persistent effects of shocks in volatility, such as the RON/USD.

Overall, our research demonstrates that currency volatility remains a strong issue for the countries in the region and that all central banks have attempted to properly manage it, particularly after the global financial crisis that emerged in 2008. At the same time, even if inflation targeting as a monetary policy rule has been adopted by almost all the countries in the Balkans and Eastern Europe, their economic

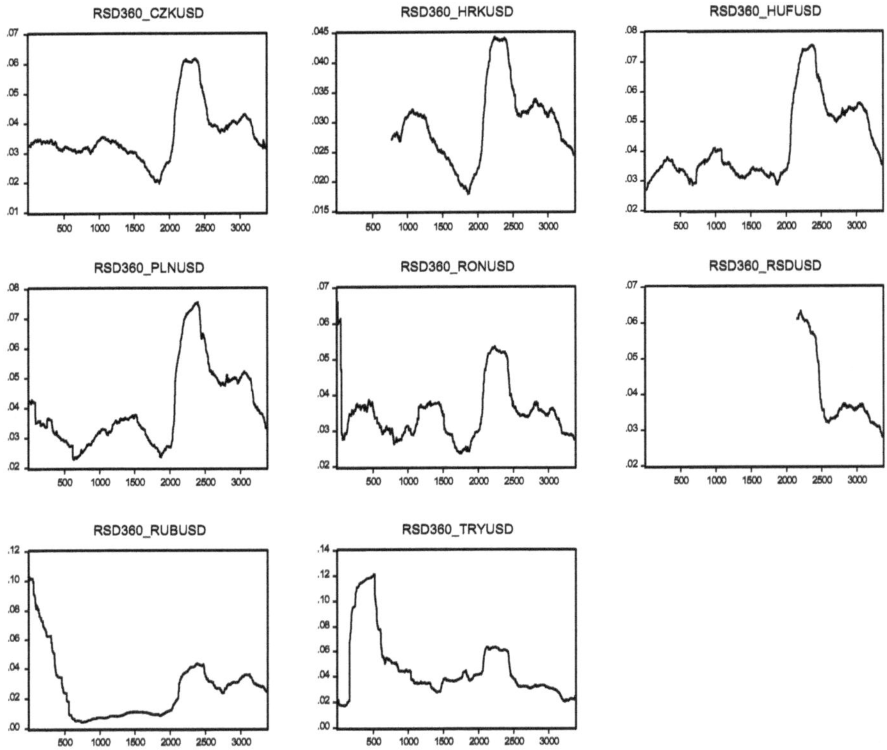

Fig. 6 (**a**) Rolling standard deviations of exchange rate returns against the EUR—360 days window, 1999–2013. *Note*: The first observation is May 26, 2000 and the last observation is December 31, 2013. (**b**) Rolling standard deviations of exchange rate returns against the USD—360 days window, 1999–2013. *Note*: The first observation is May 26, 2000 and the last observation is December 31, 2013

specificities make the adoption and implementation of a less flexible exchange rate regime that would pave the way for Euro adoption, at least for some of them, a real challenge. Our results have implications both for central banks and governments' policies, as well as for private investors that have to deal with currency risk as part of the wider range of risks they are exposed to in the region.

As any other research, our approach has limitations which can be further addressed by extending the scope of our enterprise in various directions, such as: (i) modelling currency volatility with instruments that specifically take into account the "volatility clustering" phenomenon, such as ARCH or GARCH; (ii) studying currency volatility within the overall period, during specific time intervals that are relevant for shifts in exchange rate volatility; or (iii) contrasting our results with similar results for other emerging countries, with the aim of better understanding the issue of currency volatility in a wider perspective.

Given the specific long-term endeavour of the countries in the region, which deals with the Euro adoption, another possible extension of our study might be

Table 11 Unit root tests for monthly standard deviations

	ADF		PP	
	Constant	Trend and constant	Constant	Trend and constant
SD_CZKEUR	−7.126*	−7.144*	−7.352*	−7.379*
SD_HRKEUR	−4.910*	−5.016*	−8.586*	−8.707*
SD_HUFEUR	−6.867*	−7.249*	−6.867*	−7.237*
SD_PLNEUR	−8.357*	−8.721*	−9.153*	−9.530*
SD_RONEUR	−4.456*	−6.020*	−10.779*	−12.939*
SD_RSDEUR	−1.743	−4.616*	−4.144*	−4.883*
SD_RUBEUR	−4.318*	−3.522**	−5.998*	−7.928*
SD_TRYEUR	−4.388*	−4.493*	−7.436*	−7.536*
SD_CZKUSD	−4.487*	−6.018*	−6.177*	−6.231*
SD_HRKUSD	−3.313**	−3.280***	−4.706*	−4.670*
SD_HUFUSD	−5.342*	−5.716*	−5.342*	−5.543*
SD_PLNUSD	−6.631*	−6.884*	−7.123*	−7.392*
SD_RONUSD	−5.780*	−5.766*	−12.020*	−12.004*
SD_RSDUSD	−3.732*	−4.746*	−3.662*	−4.753*
SD_RUBUSD	−3.963*	−3.752**	−5.907*	−6.115*
SD_TRYUSD	−4.388*	−4.493*	−7.436*	−7.536*

Note: ADF and PP are Augmented Dickey-Fuller and Phillips-Perron unit root tests. Test equations include either a constant or a constant and a trend. The lag length is chosen using the Schwarz information criterion for the ADF test, and the Newly West kernel estimator for the PP test
*Rejection of the null hypothesis at the 1 % levels
**Rejection of the null hypothesis at the 5% levels
***Rejection of the null hypothesis at the 10% levels

Table 12 Best-fit ARIMA models for monthly standard deviations series

	ARIMA model (p,d,q)	Schwartz criterion	Adjusted R^2	SEE
SD_CZKEUR	(1,1,1)	−9.7262	0.1762	0.0018
SD_HRKEUR	(2,1,1)	−11.0532	0.4040	0.0009
SD_HUFEUR	(1,1,1)	−9.0988	0.2098	0.0025
SD_PLNEUR	(3,1,1)	−8.8860	0.4064	0.0027
SD_RONEUR	(2,1,1)	−8.6295	0.4485	0.0031
SD_RSDEUR	(4,1,0)	−9.1031	0.3404	0.0023
SD_RUBEUR	(1,1,0)	−8.0802	0.3483	0.0042
SD_TRYEUR	(6,1,0)	−4.2102	0.2569	0.0281
SD_CZKUSD	(1,1,1)	−6.2338	0.1469	0.0103
SD_HRKUSD	(7,1,0)	−7.1370	0.1411	0.0065
SD_HUFUSD	(1,1,1)	−5.8844	0.1382	0.0123
SD_PLNUSD	(3,1,1)	−5.5072	0.3015	0.0145
SD_RONUSD	(2,1,4)	−5.7798	0.5899	0.0124
SD_RSDUSD	(3,1,0)	−5.6703	0.1009	0.0133
SD_RUBUSD	(1,1,10)	−5.3252	0.5619	0.0157
SD_TRYUSD	(9,1,0)	−4.1931	0.2757	0.0280

represented by a larger framework of analysis that would include not only monetary variables, but also socio-economical and political variables. These would allow for a better control and robustness test of our results and would permit the observation of other features of exchange rate policies in these countries.

References

Bollerslev T (1986) Generalized autoregressive conditional heteroskedasticity. J Econ 31:307–327
Box GPE, Jenkins GM (1978) Time series analysis: forecasting and control. Holden Day, San Francisco, CA
Bugar G, Maurer R (2002) International equity portfolios and currency hedging: the view point of German and Hungarian investors. Asian Bull 32:171–197
Cont R (2005) Volatility clustering in financial markets: empirical facts and agent-based models. http://www.proba.jussieu.fr/pageperso/ramacont/papers/clustering.pdf. Accessed 10 Apr 2014
Coudert V, Couharde C, Mignon V (2011) Exchange rate volatility across financial crises. J Bank Financ 35:3010–3018
Engle R (1982) Autoregressive conditional heteroscedasticity with estimates of the variance of United Kingdom inflation. Econometrica 50:987–1008
Eun CS, Resnick BG (1994) International diversification of investment portfolios, US and Japanese perspective. Manag Sci 40:140–160
Hodrick R, Prescott EC (1997) Postwar U.S. business cycles: an empirical investigation. J Money Credit Bank 29:1–16
Horobet A, Tusa E (2007) Exchange rate volatility in Central and Eastern Europe. Rev Fac St Econ Anal Univ Oradea XVI:381–385
Horobet A, Dumitrescu DG, Dumitrescu (Raileanu) AS (2011) Investors' exposure to currency risk in Central and Eastern Europe: are turbulent times Different? Bus Rev Cambridge 18:124–131
International Monetary Fund (2013) Annual report on exchange arrangements and exchange restrictions 2013. IMF, Washington, DC
Jorion P (1985) International portfolio diversification with estimation risk. J Bus 58:259–278
Josifidis K, Allegret JP, Beker PE (2009) Monetary and exchange rate regimes changes: the cases of Poland, Czech Republic, Slovakia and Republic of Serbia. Panoeconomicus 2:199–226
Kocenda E, Valachy I (2006) Exchange rate volatility and regime change: a visegrad comparison. J Comp Econ 34:727–753
Mellet A (2011) BRICS currency volatility: confusion or indecision? Stud Univ Babes-Bol 56:74–92
Sosic V, Kraft E (2004) Floating with a large life-jacket: monetary and exchange rate policies in Croatia. http://urrutiaelejalde.org/files/2012/01/Vujcic2.pdf. Accessed 11 Apr 2014

Market Volatility and Foreign Exchange Intervention

Srđan Marinković and Ognjen Radović

Abstract This paper explores unilateral interventions by National Bank of Serbia on RSD/EUR market, conducted over the period from 2004 to 2010 inclusive. We have employed a Markov-switching model that describes the time-varying nature of the exchange rate volatility. The changing nature of volatility may arise due to the process of information arrivals or being liquidity driven, but can also be a consequence of interventions. We found the probability of switching between high-volatility and low volatility states conditioned upon the intervention. The regime switching model proved to be able to indicate correctly the ex ante identified structural breaks that came from intervention policy. Moreover, our study raises doubts that the central bank intervenes also in response of detrimental past exchange rate trends rather than solely in response to excess volatility.

Keywords Central bank interventions • Exchange rate volatility • Markov switching model

JEL Classification Codes C22 • E44 • F31

1 Introduction

In the real world, we could hardly imagine a central bank protractedly absent from the exchange market. Central banks often face a challenge to manipulate the exchange rate by intervening directly on the exchange market (Calvo and Reinhart 2002). The nature of intervention differs, depending on exchange rate regime. Official exchange rate intervention in the foreign exchange market occurs when the authorities buy or sell foreign exchange, normally against their own currency and in order to affect the exchange rate (Sarno and Taylor 2001).

Intervention might be unilateral, when one central bank act on its own, or a coordinated one, when two or more central banks concert their actions in order to achieve what is considered to be a mutual goal. Interventions done by the National

S. Marinković (✉) • O. Radović
Faculty of Economics, University of Niš, Trg kralja Aleksandra Ujedinitelja 11, 18000 Niš, Republic of Serbia
e-mail: srdjan.marinkovic@eknfak.ni.ac.rs; ognjen.radovic@eknfak.ni.ac.rs

A. Karasavvoglou et al. (eds.), *The First Decade of Living with the Global Crisis*, Contributions to Economics, DOI 10.1007/978-3-319-24267-5_12

Bank of Serbia (hereafter NBS) were that of a unilateral kind, since no other central bank is interested in the local market.

According to the impact of foreign exchange (hereafter FX) intervention on money supply, it can be classified either as sterilized or unsterilized. The sterilized intervention is the type of intervention that is immediately or after some short time followed by official domestic asset transaction with an aim to offset the effect of FX intervention operation on money supply. By their very nature, a sterilized intervention's effect on domestic money supply must be ultimately neutral or close to that, since an offsetting monetary transaction restores the pre-intervention size of the monetary base. Opposite to that, an unsterilized intervention is expected to have the same impact on domestic money supply as other monetary instruments (e.g. open-market operations) might have, with the only difference that foreign, rather than domestic assets are bought or sold (Henderson and Sampson 1983). As with many central banks of the most developed countries, interventions conducted by the National Bank of Serbia belong to that of sterilized type. NBS uses repo operations to tune finely domestic money supply, apart from some other monetary tools.

Empirical literature on NBS intervention policy is nothing but a scarce. There are just a few pieces of research (Jovanović 2009; Marinković 2014), which add specific importance to this study. The basic aim of this paper is to test and validate what effects NBS interventions had over the end of 2003 through 2010.

The remaining part of this paper is structured as follows. We begin in Sect. 2 with a review of literature on the role of foreign exchange intervention, effects, economic rationale and motives behind it, proceeding in Sect. 3 with empirical findings on the effectiveness of interventions. Section 4 explores NBS intervention policy, while Sect. 5 describes dataset. Section 6 proceeds with the description of research methodology, as well as discussion of results. Finally, Sect. 7 presents a conclusion.

2 Review of Theory on Effects of Official FX Intervention

In theory of international economics, official intervention may influence exchange rate through two channels; via effects on currency structure of market participants' portfolios (portfolio balance channel) and/or through affecting market participants' expectations about future course of exchange rate fundamentals (expectation/signaling channel). For foreign exchange intervention to be effective, market participants need to substitute the asset denominated in one currency for the asset denominated in other currencies. Therefore, not only a consequence but also a precondition of any successful intervention is that market participants accept new currency structure of their portfolios. Providing that given instruments are not perfect substitutes, new portfolio currency weight scheme would be accepted only if the exchange rate has been changed so that the optimal portfolio is eventually restored (Dominguez and Frankel 1993a). This briefly explains the mechanism that helps an official intervention to have a desirable impact on exchange rate through the portfolio-balance channel.

Nevertheless, even if foreign and domestic assets were not perfect substitutes, a monetary authority might use interventions to signal to the market the information about the future course of exchange rate fundamentals (e.g. money stock, etc.), or its commitment to pursue towards the intervention goal. If the signal is trustworthy, the spot exchange rate will adjust to the expected future exchange rate (Mussa 1981). The signaling effect better explains why sometimes the desirable effects are absent, or why even the real effects ended up opposite to what is desirable. Although central banks, by choosing the side of the market to intervene, signal information about their goal to the market, it is up to other market participants to extract information about its ability and commitment to reach the goal. Signaling effect is an element according to which intervention policy has to be practically designed. If a central bank believes that an announcement of the goal may benefit the probability of reaching it, it will do so. Otherwise, it will hide it and hold the information private. With this issue, contemporary literature (Beine et al. 2009a, b; Dominguez 2006) departs from the traditional position, which suggests that secrecy about the scale of an intervention is always desirable, while secrecy about the target is sometimes desirable (Bhattacharya and Weller 1997).

The advancement in market microstructure theory brought about a new momentum in exploring the effectiveness of the official FX intervention. This branch of economic literature brings into the research focus relationship between order flow, information and price (Evans and Lyons 2002a, b). It allows the order flow to influence the price on two distinct ways. According to the inventory approach (Stoll 1978; O'Hara 2004) any disturbance in the order flow, by definition non-informative, will influence traders' price setting behavior, and consequently market clearing price (exchange rate). By searching for and posting bid and ask quotes which will help them to restore optimal inventory, competitive FX traders drive the market. Note that the inventory approach corresponds to what is known in the exchange rate theory as portfolio balance channel (Sarno and Taylor 2001). This way of influencing is likely to be as important and as strong as official interventions' distortion in the order flow. Interestingly, this channel is not always estimated as an important determinant of the quotation behavior of foreign exchange dealers. Lyons (1995) has found some evidence in favor of the inventory channel, while most recent papers (Bjønnes and Rime 2005) have not. There were several arguments in support of the latter evidence. Firstly, perhaps because FX dealers are successful in matching their books and possibly because huge distortions in the order flow (massive interventions) are out of leading central banks' regular practice.

The inventory-based approach explains market-clearing mechanism and traders' price-setting behavior that come as a consequence of stochastic deviations in the order flow. New order flow is by assumption non-informative, so that traders accommodate their bid and ask quote in order to restore optimal level of inventory. For example, if the distortion of order flow comes because a central bank sells foreign exchange, traders will manage their positions by lowering both ask and bid exchange rate quote. By acting like this, they will simultaneously encourage clients to buy and discourage clients from selling. The inventory-based approach requires that initial orders made by the central bank should have a substantial size relative to the normal order flow, to make quote readjustments necessary for portfolio rebalancing. Albeit, the intervention largely compared to market turnover is not a regular practice of the world's leading central banks. This is the case of NBS intervention, which makes inventory (portfolio) based channel an operable way of influencing the local exchange rate.

With the risk that the intervention conveys relevant information about future exchange rate fundamentals, price-setting behavior of traders becomes more complicated. It is a matter of crucial importance for trader profitability that they correctly extract information from new order flow. For example, if a selling intervention brings new information that indicates lower exchange rate, even if the transaction volume is rather irrelevant, the right response of any trader would be the same as it was in the above case of the stochastic order flow. Lower bid and ask quotes would ensure inventory optimization. However, if the trade (intervention) were mistakenly taken as informative, the old quotes would be still correct, while the new, revised quotes would attract the informed traders to buy from our trader, no matter if the central bank ceases or continues to intervene. Depending on the elasticity between price and order flow, our trader would sooner or later loose its inventory. In order to get back in business, they would have to restore their inventory by buying foreign exchange shortly afterwards from other traders at the rate higher that they had previously sold it. This would decrease its realized spread and profitability. This risk of being wrong in assessing information content of trade (as well as intervention) is known as adverse selection risk. Therefore, in order to be effective, official intervention has to convey a clear and credible signal about future stance of policies relevant for exchange rate determination. If the signal has not been communicated to the market, this will generate ambiguity amongst traders. This could be an explanation why sometimes intervention is followed with no persistent effect on the exchange rate level, but only with an increase in short-term volatility.

The second is information approach (Copeland and Galai 1983) that complies with the signaling channel. If order flow brings some new information on the exchange market, it would have some impact regardless the size of intervention. It would generate chain reaction, i.e. revisions in other participants' order flow. Thus, even small-scale official intervention is likely to generate strong effect on exchange rate, when the intervention is thought to have informational content.

The literature also differs in terms of which intervention goal is primarily studied. According to Beine et al. (2009a, b) the main objective of foreign exchange interventions is to influence the exchange rate level, reduce some undesirable trend, smooth exchange rate volatility, or intervene in favor of another central bank. Thus, there may be several intervention goals, with most of them not being mutually exclusive. If we try to simplify, there are only two directions of influence, which fully correspond to two, more or less, alternative, intervention goals; it is either exchange rate level or volatility that an official authority may attempt to tackle. The issue may get a unified framework if we take that authority, by taking any level of exchange rate as desirable at the time, actually expresses its concern about long-term exchange rate volatility. Moreover, long gradual swings in the exchange rate might have even more devastating effects on specific economy than its short-term or daily volatility. Then, continuous intervention that lasts for long periods might reveal this type of concern.

Volatility is the tendency for prices to change unexpectedly. According to market microstructure theory (Harris 2003), prices change either in response to new information about values or in response to the trading activity by uninformed traders. Therefore, in terms of its origin, there are two kinds of volatility: fundamental and transitory volatility. Fundamental volatility is caused by changes in fundamentals. The unexpected nature of changes is a crucial element of volatility. If the information (about fundamentals) were common knowledge, the change of price would have come with no trading activity between the previous and the new price level. If were not, the actors that possess information before the others would have tried to use it against the less informed. Simply, through the process of trading, the information will be spread out, together with weakening of trade activity and price converging toward the new fundamental value. It will generate prices that are more informative and consequently better resource allocation. Thus, an increase of the fundamental volatility is to be taken as an aftermath of a beneficial process in which transaction prices converge toward equilibrium value.

The part of volatility, which is a consequence of activity of uninformed traders, is called transitory volatility. The demands of impatient traders for liquidity will firstly drive the price out of fundamentals. The price will fluctuate around the equilibrium value, for some time, and eventually revert to the fundamental value. Contrary to fundamental volatility, here an initial change of price means diverging from fundamental values. By assumption, informed traders are aware of the non-informational nature of deviation and respond in a way that eventually brings the price back to the unchanged fundamental value.

The described dynamics in both cases seemingly leads eventually to market equilibrium, since it assumes that corrective market forces, i.e. informed traders, manage to stabilize the market. However, not all market situations can be explained that way. Empirical research suggests that financial market return tends to cluster between high and low volatility periods. Volatility runs in trends so that financial market return exhibits volatility clustering, that is, periods when volatility is high follow periods when volatility is low (Blake 2000). This means that financial market time series are frequently heteroscedastic, with neither mean nor volatility constant. The volatility of this nature is called episodic volatility. Often, volatility is not only episodic but also excessive, in the sense that it is not easily explainable by the Efficient Market Hypothesis. According to West (1988), excessive price volatility may be the consequence of rational or speculative bubbles, feds, or simply the computation error (e.g. small sample problem). Excessive price volatility is often taken as a leading indicator of crisis tendencies (see Chakrabarti and Roll 2002). Empirical research of volatility (Siegel 2002) suggests that excessive volatility strongly coincides with financial crises or economic slowdowns. The links between two phenomena can be plausibly explained by the fact that an increase in uncertainty about future fundamentals appears to be feature of both phenomena.

Therefore, not all volatility jumps are considered to be harmful to the economy. They may be just a consequence of the regular process in which the price reacts to new information arrivals. However, exchange rates are prices of paramount importance, especially for open economies. This is why central banks are often taken responsible to intervene in cases of excessive exchange rate volatility.

3 Review of Empirical Literature on Effectiveness of Official FX Intervention

There has been considerable debate, both in the policy arena and among academics, about whether intervention can be effective, and if so, why. For a long time since researchers claimed no effect of official FX intervention at all (Edison 1993). It clashed with the fact that intervention has been a common occurrence in foreign exchange markets. Although central banks would intervene on the weak side of the market, confronting the ongoing trend, or 'lean against the wind', econometric analyses observed even perverse responses to intervention; the domestic currency depreciates when the central bank purchases it against foreign currency. Similarly, some earlier tests (Dominguez 1998; Beine et al. 2002) indicated that intervention rather increased exchange rate volatility than moderate it.

Yet, the results of tests that were undergone before 1990s should not be taken as granted. Namely, such analyses were often not grounded on high-frequency intervention data, most likely because such data were not available to the public. It is statistics about international reserves that were used earlier to extract intervention data. This approach faces several issues. Firstly, changes in the value of international reserves that are expressed in single currency are not necessarily caused by intervention. This may appear due to changes in exchange rates or changes in currency composition of international reserves. Moreover, the large share of reserves is made of interest-bearing assets, so that any current income earned on those assets adds to the value of international reserves. Last but not least, the data on international reserves are often published quarterly, rarely monthly, and almost no piece of data are available for shorter periods. This is why such data become useless for analyzing intraday changes of exchange rate and contemporaneous effects of foreign exchange intervention.

Researchers explore effects of official intervention by using various research methods, starting from event studies (Dominguez 2003, 2006; Fatum and Hutchison 2003), through methods specific for high-frequency time series analysis, e.g. General Methods of Moment (Kearns and Rigobon 2005), ARMA (Beine et al. 2009a, b), volatility modeling, often with models from GARCH family (Beine et al. 2002). The first study that has implemented event study approach in investigating official intervention effectiveness in this sense has been Dominguez and Frankel (1993b). They were first to challenge the overly pessimistic view about the effects of intervention on exchange rate that was almost a consensus in earlier papers (see Henderson and Sampson (1983), or Edison (1993) for a review). Event studies usually regress return (continuously compounded) on a set of regressors including relevant intervention data. The variable of prime researchers' choice is interest rate differential, albeit sometimes they use purchasing power parity to represent fundamentals. Regression coefficient assigned to interventions explains effect of intervention on exchange rate, providing that return is calculated based on end-of-business day exchange rate. It is thus interpreted as a contemporaneous impact on exchange rate. Some event studies use data only from around periods of interventions. It is a way to circumvent limitations coming from unusual data-generating process, or sporadic nature of intervention. Statistical inference depends on success criteria. Intervention may be successful not only if it diverts the previous trend, but also if it moderates, or smoothes the pre-intervention trend. Based on similar methodology, but with some improvement in dataset, Dominguez (2003) and Fatum and Hutchison (2003) found the intervention operations effective, especially if they are properly conceived and executed.

All those methods are based on a single regime assumption. This assumption does not respond well to the reality of foreign exchange markets. Recently, researchers have started using methods that postulate multiple regimes. Conditional mean and conditional volatility of logarithmic exchange rate growth rates are used to define alternative states or regimes (Beine et al. 2003; Taylor 2004, 2005). We see that the variables of change that govern shift of regime from one to another are practically alternative goals of official intervention. Such analyses are used to reveal whether interventions drive shift from one to another state or regime. An interesting advance in empirical literature is Taylor (2005) study. The author employed Markov-regime switching model for the dollar-yen real exchange rate, assuming that one regime is characterized by no mean reversion and the other by mean reversion. By operating with real rather than nominal exchange rate, he was able to official interventions which induced mean-reverting behavior (by assumption equilibrium restoring) from those conducted within a small neighborhood of equilibrium. It is found that the shift to a stable state was more likely when a central bank confronts misalignments, while the opposite is true in the other case.

4 NBS Intervention Policy

At the beginning of the transition process all the way to late 2006, Serbia used an exchange rate as a nominal anchor policy. The exchange rate regime was 'dirty' floating within the exchange rate targeting monetary strategy. In this period, direct FX interventions were a regular practice. NBS intervened on a daily basis with roughly 40 % of total foreign currency supplied through interventions.

Since August 2006 (NBS 2006), NBS de facto shifted from the exchange rate targeting to the pure inflation targeting monetary strategy. Exchange rate was not anymore the variable of prime concern. According to the agreement signed with the government (NBS 2008a) and the following new memorandum, (NBS 2008b, p. 4), "NBS is expected to intervene directly on the foreign exchange market in order to (1) prevent excess daily fluctuations [with no transparent numerical threshold], while avoiding cumulating the pressure from either side of the exchange market (buying or selling) in long term sequences, (2) control financial stability risk, and (3) safeguard adequate level of international reserves".

Although seemingly straightforward, the mandate does not limit the behavior of NBS as strong as it may look at first glance. The first condition means that NBS is not expected to act against market forces. However, the second condition may be interpreted in a way that it allows confronting the ongoing exchange rate trend if the exchange rate threatens to somehow endanger the financial stability. Finally, the third condition warns about the scarcity of financial resources (international reserves) that can be used for the above purposes.

Let us get a closer look at the first two objectives. The most prominent objective of NBS official FX intervention is smoothing the exchange rate return (interpreted as daily return volatility). If the exchange rate moves in small increments (smoothly) but constantly in one direction, i.e. following a trend, it comes that the first condition for intervention is not satisfied, so that the authority has to stay away from intervention. However, if the trend is there, but the daily movements are large enough, it will activate the official response. By confronting such excessive daily oscillations, the official authority will at the same time push against the ongoing trend. In the absence of a transparent threshold, it may look as if NBS arbitrarily breaks the trend. Nevertheless, one could never say that NBS acts out of its mandate since the second condition, the financial stability, lays ground for the intervention conditioned by the level of the exchange rate. There needs to be some level of exchange rate that could act as an imaginary threshold that triggers FX intervention operations. Namely, for a small and open country, which is additionally burdened with a rather pervasive level of financial euroization, the exchange rate becomes a variable able to endanger the financial stability. NBS typically 'leans against the wind' i.e. confronts short-term trends of exchange rate. Most often, the trends are interpreted as deviation from what is considered a long-term equilibrium value.

The nature of NBS intervention differs amongst periods. Over the period of exchange rate targeting NBS intervened in long-lasting sequences with a few days with no intervention in between. In addition, NBS rarely acknowledged their own intervention operations. Over the period of inflation targeting, NBS has intervened occasionally. Episodes have generally continued to involve operations across multiple days, but with long-lasting breaks in between. From August 2006 to the end of 2010, we identified nearly 40 episodes of intervention clusters. Those operations differ in terms of transparency from the operations conducted over the first period. NBS started to routinely release information to the press, so that operations no longer caught the market by surprise. Moreover, interventions started to be more balanced, with the central bank occasionally switching its side from selling to buying the reserve currency.

Some researchers (Marinković 2014) used the event study methodology and found the official NBS foreign exchange intervention, realized during the inflation targeting period, able to generate rather temporal effects on smoothing the exchange rate return. Namely, the stabilization of the exchange rate typically did not last longer than a few days. It disappeared immediately after the intervention.

NBS intervention policy differs from that seen in the leading central banks' practice. Firstly, NBS clusters interventions in several day long sequences, while the leading central banks, in the majority of cases, do it within a single trading day. Contrary to the practice of the leading central banks, NBS interventions do not regularly cluster within a trading day. They are usually realized with a single transaction, so that the reaction time of the monetary authority is the same as the time frequency of the data. Practically, commercial banks are requested to post their firm quotes, e.g. both bid and asked, so that they would not know whether the central bank is ready to buy or sell the reserve currency in any specific episode. Then, the central bank chooses to enter the transaction with a bank that offered the most favorable quote. Secondly, interventions belong largely to that of massive-scale. Since in some periods, the scale of NBS interventions was way above the interbank turnover, the portfolio balance channel of influence may matter in this case. This is the prime reason why we will enter the intervention amount directly into the model. In some other papers intervention data are specified only as dummy, most often as trinomic variable, which may be a satisfactory rich framework only for studies solely oriented to information/signaling effect of interventions.

5 The Dataset

Data on exchange rate comprise daily logarithmic returns of spot exchange rates (Fig. 1), where spot rates are directly quoted, i.e. expressed in the number of domestic currency units per a unit of foreign currency (RSD/EUR). The data are official mid-quote closing rates provided by National Bank of Serbia. Although some researchers favored using data on deviations from equilibrium exchange rate (interpreted according to the interest rate parity or purchasing power parity conditions) instead of nominal exchange rate data, we opted for nominal data, since according to NBS mandate, the interventions are conditioned by daily volatility of the nominal exchange rate.

The intervention data enter the specifications as amounts. The intervention data used in this paper are daily cumulated (net) EUR-intervention volumes by National bank of Serbia (Fig. 4). In the period considered it was typically the case that NBS intervenes by selling the reserve currency, except in some very rare occasions where it was buying the reserve currency. All data are sampled with daily frequency. The data range from December 2003 to December 2010, delivering in total 1776 observations.

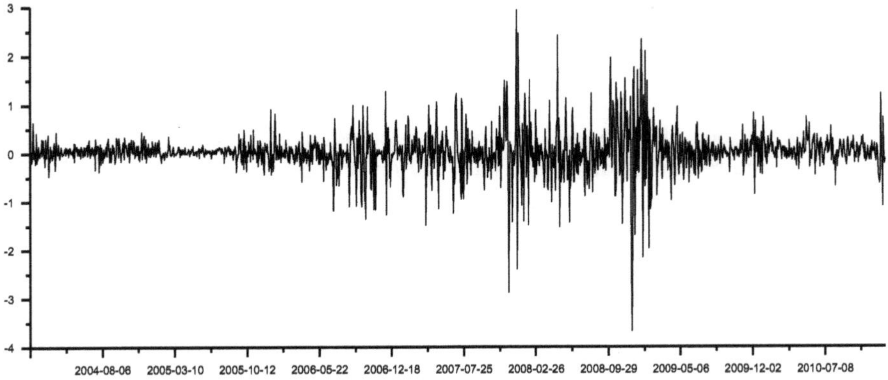

Fig. 1 Exchange rate (RSD/EUR) daily logarithmic return

The available data on NBS intervention tell us only about the volume of transaction and the size of the market that NBS takes. There is no indication on exchange rate at which NBS sells or buys foreign currency in any specific intervention occasion. Consequently, having only volume information at hand, it was not possible to examine the joint volume (order flow) and price impact on the FX market.

6 Regime Switching Modeling

There is a risk that statistical inference based on time series analysis, which does not take into account a switch in regime, leads to spurious results. Models, which ignore any change in the ambience, usually overestimate volatility persistence. If time series exhibits breaks in their behavior, associated with various events, such as financial turmoil, institutional or policy changes, the best way is to assume that there must be some imperfectly predictable forces that govern those changes.

Contrary to what was previously believed, Engel and Hamilton (1990) claim that the exchange rate follows the regime switch process, or that the model of the exchange rate evolves over time. The switch of the regime that governs the exchange rate here is taken to include not only de facto changes in the exchange rate regime, but also changes in such a way that the exchange rate responds to its fundamental determinants. Put that way, the regime switch framework is able to be used more widely, e.g. for the floating exchange rate regime.

Thus, we need a probabilistic model of what causes the change from state one to state two and vice versa. We have applied Markov regime switching volatility model of exchange rate return. The model has the ability to portray the time evolving nature of volatility. We assume that the exchange rate return is drown from one of two distributions indexed by $s_t = i$ ($i = 1, 2$). Based on the assumption that the regime indicator variable s_t evolves according to the first-order Markov chain implies that the conditional probability that the observation y_t (logarithmic exchange rate return) has been drawn from distribution or state i at time t depends on the state it has been drawn at time t−1, or:

$$P_{ii} = \Pr(s_t = i | s_{t-1} = i), \quad i = 1, 2 \tag{1}$$

The regime indicator variable is not directly observable, but it is possible to draw some probabilistic inference about regimes. This inference will take the form of two probabilities (Hamilton 2008):

$$P_{it} = \Pr[s_t = i | \Omega_t; \theta] \tag{2}$$

Here Ω_t denotes the set of observations obtained as of date t (exchange rate returns, intervention data) and θ is a vector of population parameters (e.g. variance, transition probabilities). An estimate of the value of population parameters is obtained by maximizing the sample conditional log likelihood of the observed data by numerical optimization.

Since we assume only two states (regimes) of the foreign exchange market ($i = 1, 2$), those two probabilities sum to unity by a construction. In our models state (regime) one is low volatility state and state (regime) two is high volatility state. The mean of exchange rate return does not play any role in our models, in spite of the fact that there is considerable promise in models with a much higher number of regimes. It is expected that once changed regime will change back again, which suggest that P_{22} should be less than unity.

We start with Markov switching model of volatility (MS model I) that includes no intervention data. The second model (MS model II) includes intervention data. We tested models with no autoregressive elements, since the model that includes lagged values of exchange rate return failed to generate shifts between regimes.

6.1 *Markov Switching Model of Volatility with No Intervention Data*

In this section, we present the evidence from a univariate type of Markov regime switching model (with nine estimated parameters). We assume Student's *t*-distribution. The numerical optimizations are done in Matlab, the package MS_Regress (Perlin 2014).

The volatility difference between low and high volatility states is statistically significant. The variance in high volatility states is more than 16 times the variance in low volatility states (Table 1). The high volatility state switches to low volatility state, and vice versa, rather frequently, meaning that the periods are short-lived. The expected duration of regime one (low volatility state) is 49.27 periods (days), while the expected duration of regime two is a bit shorter (29.35 days).

Table 1 Markov regime switching model without intervention data (MS model I)

	Low volatility regime (1)	High volatility regime (2)
Switching parameters (distribution parameters)		
Variance	0.002541	0.041363
SE (*p*-value)	0.0002 (0.00)	0.0050 (0.00)
Switching parameters (regressors)		
Value	0.0060	0.0016
SE (*p*-value)	0.0020 (0.00)	0.0095 (0.86)
Probability of transition (SE)		
Stay the same (P_{11}; P_{22})	0.98 (0.11)	0.97 (NaN)
Shift to the other (P_{12}; P_{21})	0.02 (NaN)	0.03 (0.13)
Expected duration (periods)	49.27	29.35
Non switching parameters		
Value 1	–0.0000	
SE (*p*-value)	0.0001 (0.94)	
Value 2	–0.0013	
SE (*p*-value)	0.0002 (0.00)	
Df	4.1645	
SE (*p*-value)	0.5197 (0.00)	
Final log likelihood	1322.36	

According to the transition probability matrix (Table 1), the regimes seem highly persistent. The probability of regime one to stay in the same regime is close to one ($P_{11} = 0.98$), which is slightly higher than in the case of regime two. Please note that the calculation of the Hessian by numerical differentiation is not guaranteed to provide a real number. When this happens, in this paper the case of SE numbers' calculation related to probability of transition, the function MS Regress Fit will output NaN (Not a Number) values for the standard errors (Perlin 2014, p. 23).

The plots (Figs. 2 and 3) describe graphically the evolution of volatility. Time is portrayed on plots' abscise. The plots do not show volatility itself but the probability that any period belongs to either of the two discrete states. Smoothed probabilities for state one and two make us able to form an inference about what regime the economy was in at date *t* based on observations obtained through a later date. If the probability comes close to 1 or 0, it means we can be fairly convinced about the volatility feature of the period. The figures are strongly conclusive about the volatility, since the smoothed probability is, more often than not, approaching its extremes.

The next figure (Fig. 4) presents conditional volatility figures delivered by the Markov regime switching model (I) together with data (normalized) on intervention, with some points marked, ex ante identified as possibly significant for explaining volatility developments. Selling interventions are presented as negative figures (lay below the horizontal axis), while those buying as positive ones (above the horizontal axis).

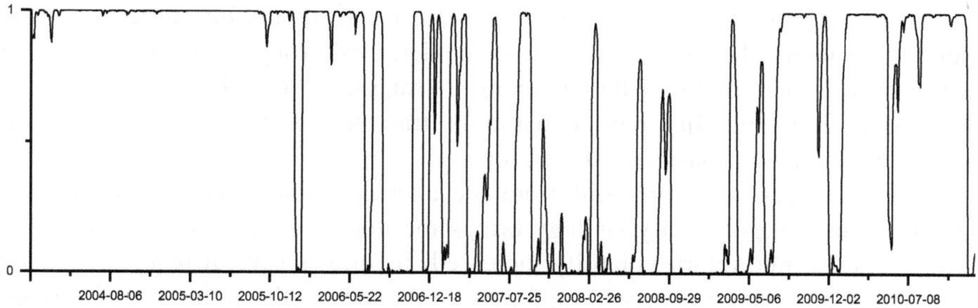

Fig. 2 Smoothed regime probability for state one (MS Model I)

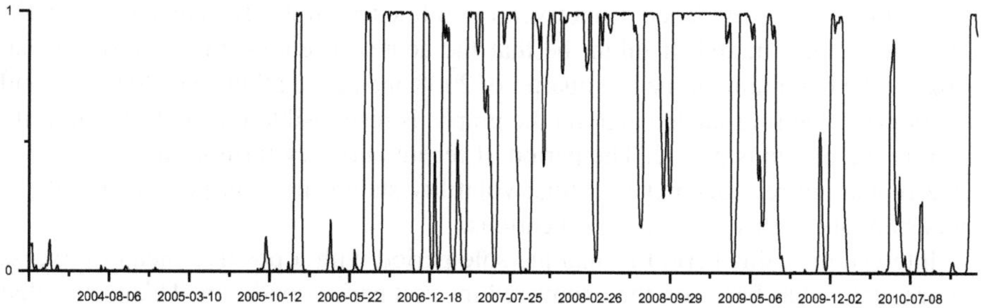

Fig. 3 Smoothed regime probability for state two (MS Model I)

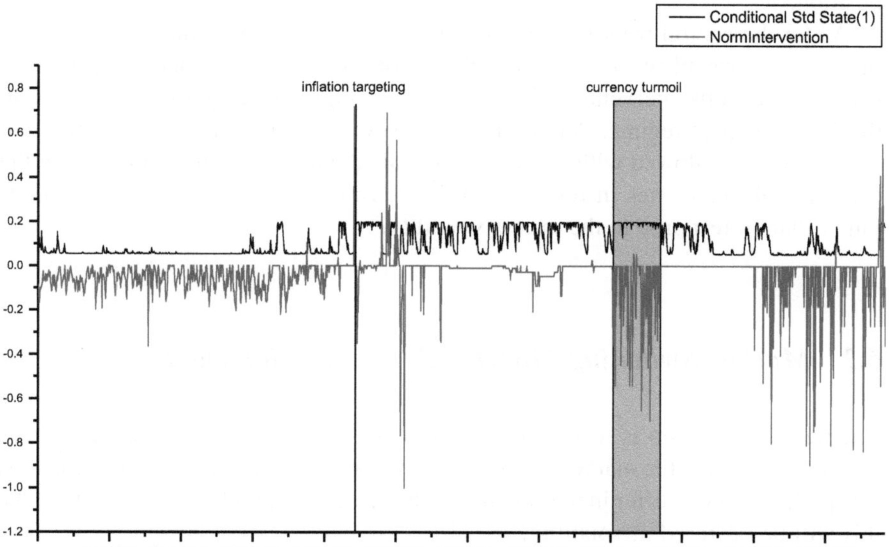

Fig. 4 Conditional volatility vs. FX interventions (normalized)

Visual inspection of the data on conditional volatility and intervention reveals some coincidence between them. The coincidence is strong during the exchange rate targeting period (from the beginning to August 2006). The whole period is marked as low volatility regime (calm or tranquil period) side by side with persistent and rather massive interventions.

From the very start, the shift from the exchange rate targeting to the pure inflation targeting monetary strategy brings the market to a high volatility state. The exchange rate return volatility increased. It follows several reversals to low volatility state. These reversals might be explained by the influence of foreign exchange interventions. Bearing in mind the announced motivation for interventions, they clearly have the potential to explain rather frequent switch to the low volatility regime. Nevertheless, during the inflation targeting period (from August 2006 onwards) the evidence of intervention influence on the exchange rate volatility is seemingly mixed. It might be that the acute currency-banking turmoil that stoke at the beginning of the last quarter of 2008 and lasted all the way to the second quarter of 2009 (the shaded area on the graph) is responsible for the lost regularity seen in the previous period. The period of recent currency turmoil (also bank run) clearly and entirely belongs to a high volatility state (turbulent period) despite of persistent and rather massive interventions.

Interestingly, this period is also the sole period with a positive mean of excess return, defined as based on the uncovered interest parity condition. This means that the market diverged from an awarding to a punishing short foreign-long domestic position. In the periods that preceded and followed the crisis, excess return had negative mean, which garnered speculative profit to actors sharing the same position.

As for the central bank response function, we see that the central bank clusters intervention around periods of both high and low volatility. It is not obvious that the central bank stops intervening after the prevalent high volatility regime switches to the low volatility regime. Additionally, there were some long-lasting periods of high volatility followed with no intervention at all. Our study raises doubts that the central bank intervenes in response to the detrimental past exchange rate trends rather than in response to the excess volatility.

6.2 *Markov Switching Model with Intervention Data*

The next logical step is to incorporate an underlying assumption that some economic forces drive the market between different states. If the entire period contains sub-periods, which differ in the way the exchange rate responds to its fundamentals, this will be mirrored in volatility.

We assume that there is a good reason for a shift between regimes, e.g. that probability of switching from one regime to another depends on central bank interventions. This assumption complies with the previously stated motivations of the National Bank of Serbia, which include preventing excess daily volatility of exchange rate, calming disorderly markets, as well as counterfeiting unfavorable exchange rate trends. The model differs from the previously tested one, since the Markov Switching model II is estimated with the intervention amount entering the transition probabilities. Instead of a restrictive assumption that transition probabilities are fixed in time, we assume that the probabilities are time varying and dependent on intervention. Thus, transition probabilities are modeled as functions of intervention amounts. Since transition probabilities must stay in the range between 0 and 1, the functional specification has to be that of the logit type (Stix 2002):

$$P_{ij} = \Pr[s_t = i | s_{t-1} = i, I_{t-1}] = \frac{e^{\beta_{i0} + \beta_{i1} \cdot I_{t-1}}}{1 + e^{\beta_{i0} + \beta_{i1} \cdot I_{t-1}}} \tag{3}$$

Where, I stands for intervention volume, and $i = 1, 2$.

Whether intervention is relevant in the two regime models can be tested for the significance of the individual parameters β_{i1}, where $i = 1, 2$.

Since regime one is a calm regime (low volatility) and regime two is a turbulent one (high volatility), a sufficient condition for interventions to be effective is that the conditional probability that the process stays in the calm regime once it is there increases ($\beta_{11} > 0$) and the corresponding conditional probability of the turbulent regime to stay the same decreases ($\beta_{21} < 0$) (Stix 2002). Transition probability parameters β_{11} and β_{21} are both estimated significantly different from zero. Furthermore, β_{11} is positive, while β_{21} is estimated negative. This indicates that interventions increased the probability of staying in the calm regime, as well as that interventions decreased the probability of staying in the turbulent regime.

The Markov switching model with intervention data delivers a slightly different transition probability matrix (Table 2) than the model without intervention data. For both low volatility and high volatility regimes persistence is lower, with the difference more noticeable in the case of high volatility regime. Transitions are more frequent (Figs. 5 and 6), which consequently gives shorter expected durations.

Table 2 Markov regime switching model with intervention data (MS model II)

	Low volatility regime (1)	High volatility regime (2)
Switching regression coefficients		
Intervention	–0.0033	–0.0087
SE (Z; *p*-value)	0.0004 (–7.6286; 0.0000)	0.0019 (–4.4734; 0.0000)
Variance	–1.9141	–0.3606
SE (Z; *p*-value)	0.0314 (–60.8936; 0.000)	0.0360 (–10.0128; 0.000)
Transition probability parameters		
β_{11}	3.2210	
β_{21}		–2.4173
SE (Z; *p*-value)	0.1963 (16.4079; 0.0000)	0.2219 (–10.8955; 0.0000)
Probability of transition		
Stay the same (P_{11}; P_{22})	0.9616	0.9182
Shift to the other (P_{12}; P_{21})	0.0384	0.0818
Expected duration	26.0551	12.2226
Diagnostics		
Mean of dependent var	0.0246	
SD dependent var	0.4199	
SE of regression	0.4128	
Sum squared residual	301.9089	
Durbin–Watson	1.4350	
Log likelihood	–205.9377	
Akaike info criterion	0.2388	
Schwarz criterion	0.2573	
Hannan-Quinn criterion	0.2456	

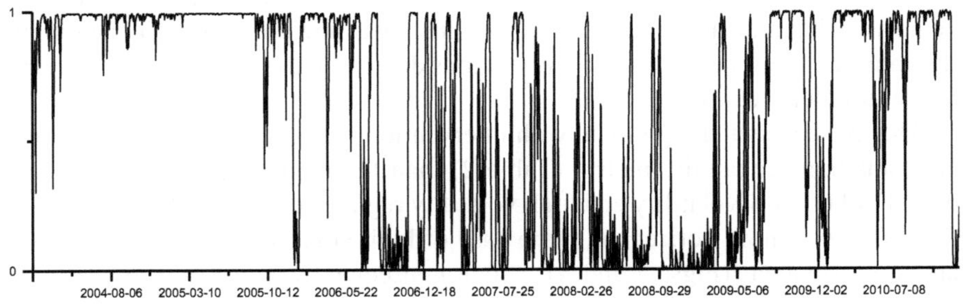

Fig. 5 Smoothed regime probability for state one (MS Model II)

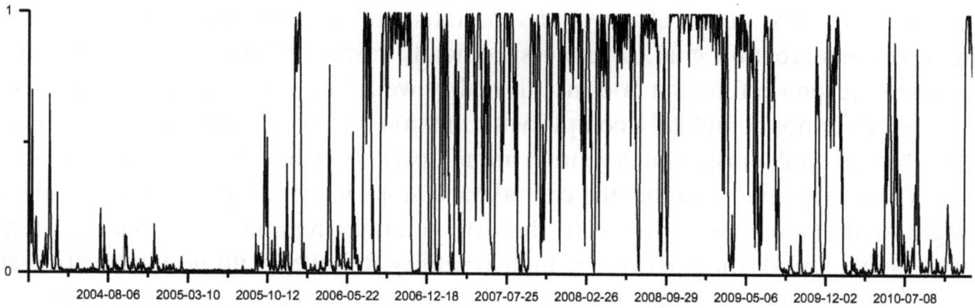

Fig. 6 Smoothed regime probability for state two (MS Model II)

7 Conclusion

The basic purpose of this study is to explore empirically the impact of the official foreign exchange interventions of the National bank of Serbia on local currency (RSD/EUR) market. We experimented with two computational procedures using Matlab and EViews 8 softwares, respectively. Both tests assume Markov switching regime, with the difference that the former does not incorporate explicitly the influence of intervention on the exchange rate dynamics, while the latter does. Unfortunately, the model with intervention data is of more restricted use since it assumes normal distribution. This is probably why probability plots differ, delivering transition probability matrices, as well as regime duration figures, that are not completely comparable.

The research findings seem straightforward in terms of the impact that interventions have on the exchange rate. The evidence of the second model indicates that interventions increased the probability of staying in the calm regime, the same as that interventions decreased the probability of staying in the turbulent regime. The findings do not clash with the event study results that indicate the ability of the NBS interventions to smooth the exchange rate return, after multiple day lasting intervention. However, the event study was based on comparisons between pre-intervention and post-intervention average return, ignoring the developments in between, i.e. while the intervention is still there. Namely, the case when the central bank is forced to push the market several days in sequence may be interpreted as its inability to reach the goal contemporaneously. The evidence from regime switching models increases the strength of arguments in favor of effectiveness of the NBS intervention.

Simultaneity is a problem that makes it difficult to study effects of intervention on exchange rate. Namely, exchange rate movements trigger intervention, while intervention per se is expected to impact the exchange rate, so that we could not state that the explanatory variable is strictly exogenous. This may limit validity of research conclusions. However, significant number of transitions among regimes, during the period considered, made it easy to estimate transition parameters accurately.

The inference about effectiveness of intervention critically depends on the assumed intervention goal, or more specifically response function. However, the assumed response function does not fit reality well. The way that the central bank reacted does not completely comply with the goal of preventing excess volatility. The central bank clusters intervention around periods of both high and low volatility. There is no evidence that the central bank stops intervening after the prevalent high volatility regime switches to the low volatility regime. Additionally, there were some long-lasting periods of high volatility followed with no intervention at all. Our study raises doubts that the central bank intervenes also in response of detrimental past exchange rate trends rather than solely in response to excess volatility.

Acknowledgement The authors are grateful to the Republic of Serbia Ministry of Education, Science and Technological Development for the funds and support that made this research possible. The data on interventions were supplied by courtesy of the National Bank of Serbia.

References

Beine M, Bénassy-Quéré A, Lecourt C (2002) Central bank intervention and foreign exchange rates: new evidence from FIGARCH estimations. J Int Money Finance 21(1):115–144

Beine M, Laurent S, Lecourt C (2003) Official central bank interventions and exchange rate volatility: evidence from a regime-switching analysis. Eur Econ Rev 47(5):891–911

Beine M, Janssen G, Lecourt C (2009a) Should central bankers talk to the foreign exchange markets? J Int Money Finance 28(5):776–803

Beine M, Laurent S, Palm FC (2009b) Central bank FOREX interventions assessed using realized moments. Int Financ Mark Inst Money 19(1):112–127

Bhattacharya U, Weller P (1997) The advantage to hiding one's hand: speculation and central bank intervention in the foreign exchange market. J Monet Econ 39(2):251–277

Bjønnes HG, Rime D (2005) Dealer behavior and trading systems in foreign exchange markets. J Financ Econ 75(3):571–605

Blake D (2000) Financial market analysis. Wiley, Chichester

Calvo AG, Reinhart CM (2002) Fear of floating. Q J Econ 117(2):379–408

Chakrabarti R, Roll R (2002) East Asia and Europe during the 1997 Asian collapse: a clinical study of a financial crisis. J Financ Mark 5(1):1–30

Copeland T, Galai D (1983) Information effects on the bid-ask spread. J Finance 38(5):1457–1469

Dominguez MK (1998) Central bank intervention and exchange rate volatility. J Int Money Finance 17(1):161–190

Dominguez MK (2003) Foreign exchange interventions: did it work in the 1990s? In: Bergsten CF, Williamson J (eds) Dollar overvaluation and the world economy. Institute for International Economics, Washington, DC

Dominguez MK (2006) When do central bank interventions influence intra-daily and longer-term exchange rate movements? J Int Money Finance 25(7):1051–1071

Dominguez MK, Frankel JA (1993a) Does foreign-exchange intervention matter? The portfolio effect. Am Econ Rev 83(5):1356–1369

Dominguez MK, Frankel JA (1993b) Foreign exchange intervention: an empirical analysis. In: Frankel J (ed) On exchange rates. MIT Press, Cambridge, MA

Edison HJ (1993) The effectiveness of central-bank intervention: a survey of the literature after 1982. Special papers in international economics no. 18, Princeton University

Engel C, Hamilton J (1990) Long swings in the exchange rate: are they in the data and do markets know it? Am Econ Rev 80(4):689–713
Evans DM, Lyons RK (2002a) Order flow and exchange rate dynamics. J Polit Econ 110 (1):170–180
Evans DM, Lyons RK (2002b) Time-varying liquidity in foreign exchange. J Monet Econ 49 (5):1025–1051
Fatum R, Hutchison MH (2003) Is sterilised foreign exchange intervention effective after all? An event study approach. Econ J 113(487):390–411
Hamilton J (2008) Regime-switching models. In: Durlauf S, Blume L (eds) New Palgrave dictionary of economics, 2nd edn. Palgrave McMillan, London
Harris L (2003) Trading and exchange: market microstructure for practitioners. Oxford University Press, New York, NY
Henderson D, Sampson S (1983) Intervention in foreign exchange markets: a summary of ten staff studies. Fed Reserv Bull 69:830–836
Jovanović M (2009) Serbian foreign exchange market during 2004–2008. SEEMHN Papers No. 19, National Bank of Serbia, Belgrade
Kearns J, Rigobon R (2005) Identifying the efficacy of central bank interventions: evidence from Australia and Japan. J Int Econ 66(1):31–48
Lyons KR (1995) Test of microstructural hypotheses in the foreign exchange market. J Financ Econ 39(2/3):321–351
Marinković S (2014) Non-parametric sign test and paired samples test of effectiveness of official FX intervention. Econ Ann 59:107–130
Mussa M (1981) The role of official intervention. Occasional Paper No. 6, Group of Thirty, Washington, DC
NBS (2006) Memorandum Narodne banke Srbije o principima novog okvira monetarne politike: Na putu ka ostvarenju ciljeva niske inflacije. Narodna banka Srbije. http://www.nbs.rs/internet/latinica/30/memorandum_novi_okvir_mon_pol_05092006.pdf. Accessed 15 Aug 2012
NBS (2008a) Sporazum o ciljanju (targetiranju) inflacije. Narodna banka Srbije. http://www.nbs.rs/export/sites/default/internet/latinica/30/memorandum_o_saglasnosti_NBS_i_Vlade.pdf. Accessed 15 Aug 2012
NBS (2008b) Memorandum Narodne banke Srbije o ciljanju (targetiranju) inflacije kao monetarnoj strategiji. Narodna banka Srbije. http://www.nbs.rs/internet/latinica/30/memorandum_monetarna_strategija_122008.pdf. Accessed 15 Aug 2012
O'Hara M (2004) Market microstructure theory. Blackwell, Cambridge, MA
Perlin M (2014) MS Regress – The MATLAB package for markov regime switching models. http://ssrn.com/abstract=1714016 or http://dx.doi.org/10.2139/ssrn.1714016
Sarno L, Taylor MP (2001) Official intervention in the foreign exchange market: is it effective, and if so, how does it work? J Econ Lit 39(3):839–868
Siegel J (2002) Stocks for the long run. McGraw-Hill, New York, NY
Stix H (2002) Does central bank intervention influence the probability of a speculative attack? Evidence from the EMS. Working paper, No. 80, Oesterreichische Nationalbank, Vienna
Stoll H (1978) The supply of dealer services in securities markets. J Finance 33(4):1133–1151
Taylor PM (2004) Is official exchange rate intervention effective? Economica 71:1–11
Taylor PM (2005) Official foreign exchange interventions as a coordinating signal in the dollar-yen market. Pac Econ Rev 10(1):73–82
West K (1988) Bubbles, fads and stock price volatility tests: a partial evaluation. J Finance 43 (3):639–656

Do Remittances Reduce Poverty in Developing Countries?

Costin-Alexandru Ciupureanu and Mihai Daniel Roman

Abstract Workers' remittances represent a lifeline for the poor, increasing income for the families left behind. They represent an important link for the study of the impact of international migration in both origin and destination countries. This paper examines the effects of remittances on poverty in Poland, Romania, Ukraine and Turkey for the period 2002–2011. The results of the panel data analysis show that per capita official international remittances significantly reduce the level and depth of poverty in the analysed countries. A 10 % increase in per capita workers' remittances will lead to a 5.3 % decline in the share of people living on less than $2 per person per day. Due to the use of informal channels for transferring money, an important share of remittances is left unrecorded. One possible way for the policymakers to deter the use of informal channels is by further creating incentives for lowering the costs for sending money back home. Also, better data and monitoring could bolster the rate of official remittances.

Keywords International migration • Remittances • Poverty • Panel data model

JEL Classification Codes F22 • F24 • I32

1 Introduction

Migration has enormous implications for growth and poverty alleviation in both origin and destination countries. In 2013, more than 230 million people across the world were migrants and the officially recorded remittances to developing countries exceeded $400 billion in 2013, an increase of about 4 % over the previous year (Ratha et al. 2014). Remittances have a crucial role on the sending and receiving countries, but due to inaccurate data, their impact is difficult to estimate. While the

C.-A. Ciupureanu (✉)
Faculty of Cybernetics, Statistics and Economic Informatics, The Doctoral School of The Bucharest University of Economic Studies, 13-15 Dorobanti Street, Bucharest, Romania
e-mail: ciupureanu_alex@yahoo.com

M.D. Roman
The Bucharest University of Economic Studies, 6 Romana Square, Bucharest, Romania
e-mail: mihai.roman@ase.ro

A. Karasavvoglou et al. (eds.), *The First Decade of Living with the Global Crisis*, Contributions to Economics, DOI 10.1007/978-3-319-24267-5_13

cost of sending money remains high, a large portion of these flows will continue to be sent through the informal channels. Development of the banking sector in the sending countries may reduce the role of the informal channels and, in this case, a key role on immigrants' decision making process is played by the time and cost for executing payment orders (Karafolas and Sariannidis 2009; Karafolas and Konteos 2010).

Remittances increase household incomes and are therefore a powerful anti-poverty force in developing countries. Also, they proved to be more resilient during economic downturns, political and civil crises in the origin countries (Ratha 2013). Altruism is one of the main reasons why migrants send money back home. Also, the propensity to remit is influenced by the level of income of migrants and the level of integration in the receiving country (Roman 2013).

In this paper we analyse the effects of remittances on poverty in Poland, Romania, Ukraine and Turkey for the period 2002–2011. After the fall of the iron curtain and the enlargement of the European Union, the level of migration of the four emerging economies has risen steadily along with the levels of remittances towards the families left behind.

The remainder of the paper is organised as follows. Section 2 summarizes some of the literature on remittances impact on poverty and growth. Some of the key aspects of the remittances inflows in the analysed countries are discussed in Sect. 3. In Sect. 4 we present the econometric analysis along with the data used and the main empirical results. In the last section we discuss the conclusions of this paper.

2 Brief Literature Review

While the literature concerning the impact of international migration and remittances on growth has mixed conclusions, there is an overall consensus that international migration and remittances help reduce poverty in the sending countries. Nevertheless, the outcomes of various studies differ in the magnitude of which the poverty of the families left behind is alleviated. For example, 1 cross-country study of 71 developing countries found that both international migration and remittances significantly reduce the level, depth, and severity of poverty in the developing world. A 10 % increase in the share of migrants in a country's population and in per capita remittances will lead to a 2.1 % and, respectively 3.5 % decline in the share of people living in poverty (Adams and Page 2005). Remittances have a significant and positive impact on the Polish economy, and this impact is expected to increase with the expected rise in the labour mobility within the European Union. In the period 1994–2010, remittances sent to Polish residents increased the average annual growth of real disposable income by 0.2 %, which in turn translates into an average annual rate of increase in household consumption by 0.1 % and 0.1 % higher annual GDP growth rate (Barbone et al. 2012). To some extent, remittances undoubtedly influence the well-being and poverty in some areas in Ukraine, but it is not reasonable to consider them the most important development drive in the country (Glazar et al. 2012). Remittances towards Turkey have decreased steadily, being observed an inverse trend of flows, i.e. the Turkish migrants that returned back home began sending money to their families back in Germany (Elitok 2013). In the case of Romania, workers' remittances promote economic growth and although their level has fallen sharply, workers' remittances have remained more resilient compared with the net inflows of foreign direct investment (Ciupureanu and Roman 2013). Panel estimates for several countries from Latin America suggest that remittances have greater impact on poorer and unequal countries affecting positively both GDP growth and poverty reduction (McLeod and Molina 2005). In another study on Latin American countries it is showed that migration and remittances have a significant poverty-reducing effect and a positive and significant impact on growth, i.e. the increase in remittances from 0.7 % of GDP in 1991–1995 to 2.3 % of GDP in 2001–2005 has led to an increase of 0.27 % per year in per-capita GDP growth (Acosta et al. 2008). Remittances have promoted economic growth in 24 Asia/Pacific countries and also helped reduce poverty, especially extreme poverty. However, remittances should not been seen as panacea, as not all poor households receive money and remittances cannot act as a substitute for official sources of capital (Katsushi et al. 2011). Remittances have a strong impact on labour participation, i.e. households with a remittance income have a higher reservation wage and reduce labour supply by moving out of the labour force (Kim 2007). Remittances are currently the second largest source of foreign exchange both in absolute terms and as a percentage of GDP. For some countries, they represent a significant form of international capital flows, exceeding export revenues, foreign direct investment and aid. Also, remittances help alleviate credit constraints on the poor, substituting for the lack of financial development, improving the allocation of capital, and therefore accelerating economic growth (Giuliano and Ruiz-Arranz 2009). For some countries, remittances represent a large share of GDP. For example, total Albanian immigrant remittances reached, in average, 13.9 % of the Albanian GDP for the time period 1994–2007 (Karafolas and Sariannidis 2009; Karafolas and Konteos 2010). In a study on 99 developing countries has been analysed the impact of workers' remittance flows during 1975–2003 on financial sector development, by increasing the aggregate level of deposits and/or the amount of credit to the private sector extended by the local banking sector. The authors found that remittances have a significant and a positive impact on bank deposits and credit to GDP (Demirguc-Kunt et al. 2006). Contrary to these findings, in an earlier study, it is found a negative impact of remittances on economic growth (Chami et al. 2003). Also, the main findings of the estimation results of a dataset for the 1970–2004 period on 84 countries is that remittances do not seem to make a positive contribution to economic growth (Barajas et al. 2008). Vasilescu and Roman (2011) analysed the internal migration effects on various economic and social aspects for Romanian case and they found that internal migration tends to reduce the revenues discrepancies between regions. Roman (2011) analysed the Romanian emigrants' motivation to migrate in various countries and to send money to the origin country. Using Data Analysis techniques he revealed different clusters of destination countries for Romanian emigrants (Latin countries, Germanic countries or North American countries etc.) and also the main influencing migration factors (unemployment rate, Gini Index, and revenues level).

3 Dynamics of Workers' Remittances Inflows in the Analysed Countries

The migration phenomenon in all analysed countries is characterized by emigration; the stock of emigrants is varying from around 13–14% of population in the case of Ukraine and Romania, to 8.2 and 5.6 % in the case of Poland and Turkey. Regarding immigration, the largest increases in international migrants from 2013 to 2010 were seen in Romania (+4.8 %) and, in Turkey (+2.8 %). Also, recent developments in Syria create the premises for more asylum seekers to come in the region (Ratha et al. 2013, 2014). In the first years of 2000 all four emerging economies have risen sharply until 2008 when they started to slow substantially on the background of the global financial crisis. Among the four emerging economies the Polish economy has been the most resilient during the crisis and has not been hit by recession. In Romania and Poland the economic activity starts to recover, but at different paces; in contrast to Romania's economy, the Polish economy is being helped by strong fundamentals. While the Turkish economy had grown by an average of 9 % over 2010–2011, the growth slowed to only 2.2 % in 2012 amid monetary tightening. Regarding Ukraine, in spite of the fact that its economy had grown by an average of 4.7 % over 2010–2011 its outlook seems gloomy due to the recent political crisis (IMF 2012).

Against this background, in all the sample countries, except for Turkey, the level of workers' remittances has risen steadily, to reach, before the global financial crisis, around 5 % of GDP in the cases of Ukraine and Romania and, 2.5 % of GDP in Poland (own calculations based on data from the Eurostat online database). Compared to their size, workers' remittances flows are comparable with the net inflows of foreign direct investments (FDI). After the crisis, workers' remittance inflows decreased dramatically, but not as much as the net inflows of FDI and in the case of Ukraine these flows already outreached the levels registered before the crisis. The reason of this outcome is twofold. First, the destinations countries of the Ukrainian emigrants are more diversified than the ones of the Romanian and Polish emigrants. The Ukrainian emigrants have emigrated mainly in Russia, Poland and the United States, while the Romanian emigrants are concentrated in Italy and Spain and the Polish emigrants have chosen mainly as their destinations the United Kingdom and Germany. The second reason for the recovery of the level of workers' remittances in Ukraine could be put on the counter-cyclicality of these monies. Ukraine being confronted with a severe political crisis, the Ukrainian emigrants are helping their families left behind in the country. In the case of Turkey, the peak of the level of workers' remittances was reached in 1998 (US$5.3 billion). Since then, their level has dropped five times in the past few years (Aydas et al. 2005; World

Bank 2012). One possible reason for this outcome could be the family reunification of the emigrants established abroad.

The use of informal channels for remitting money is deterring the correct measurement of these funds. In the past 4 years the average prices for sending money in Ukraine have risen from 5.69 % to 7.13 % and the average prices for sending money in Romania and Poland have remained steadily at around 6 % and, 8 %, respectively. In the case of Turkey, while the average prices have fallen from 10.87 % to 8.6 %, they are still way above the 5 % target established by G8 in 2009 (own calculations based on data from the online database of the World Bank). Further reducing the cost for sending money abroad would create more incentive for using the official channels for remitting money to the families left in the country of origin.

4 Econometric Analysis

In this section, using cross-country data we analyse the impact of workers' remittances on poverty in Poland, Romania, Ukraine and Turkey. The estimate equation is written as:

$$Log\,Ph(Pg) = b_0 + b_1 Log\,GDPpc + b_2 Log\,R + b_3 Gini + b_4 UN \tag{1}$$

where:

Log Ph (Pg) = natural log of poverty headcount index (poverty gap index)
Log GDP pc = natural log of per capita GDP in purchasing power parity (PPP) units
Log R = natural log of per capita workers' remittances
Log GINI = natural log of GINI coefficient
Log UN = natural log of the unemployment rate

The model assumes that economic growth and workers' remittances will reduce poverty; therefore the income variable and workers' remittances variable are expected to be negative and significant. The model also assumes that, unemployment and income inequality affects poverty reduction. The income inequality and unemployment variables are expected to be positive and significant.

4.1 Data

The data are annual and cover the period 2002–2011 for all the sample countries. All the data is extracted from The World Bank's database. The data set includes 38 observations; we have missing data for the poverty measure in 2011 for Ukraine and Turkey. The poverty is measured as the poverty headcount index and poverty gap index. The poverty headcount index measures the percent of the population living beneath $2 per person per day, while the poverty gap index measures the depth of poverty, i.e. the percentage of how far the average expenditures of the poor falls short of the poverty line. The income variable is measured as GDP per capita in purchasing power parity units. Foreign direct investment are the net inflows of investment to acquire a lasting management interest (10 % or more of voting stock) in an enterprise operating in an economy other than that of the investor. Worker's remittances follow the IMF's Balance of Payments definition and it is the sum of personal transfers and compensation of employees. Personal transfers include all current transfers between resident and non-resident individuals. Compensation of employees refers to the income of border, seasonal, and other short-term workers who are employed in an economy where they are not resident and of residents employed by non-resident entities. All the variables are estimated in log terms.

4.2 Empirical Results

This paper examines the impact of workers' remittances on poverty, for the period 2002–2011. We report regressions using two measures of poverty (poverty headcount and poverty gap). To control for fixed effects we add dummy variables to the model. The panel data analysis results are reported in Table 1, first without, and then, with dummies.

In all the models the GINI coefficient and workers' remittances variable are of the expected signs and statistically significant in all the cases. However, the income variable is not significant in all the cases and, for two of the models, is not of the expected sign (negative). Surprisingly, the unemployment variable is not of the expected sign (positive) and it is statistically significant in all cases.

Estimates for the poverty gap measure suggest that, on average, a 10 % increase in per capita workers' remittances will lead to a 4.7 % decline in the share of people living on less than $2 per person per day. Remittances will have a slightly larger

Table 1 Ordinary least square results (t-statistic in brackets)

	Dependent variable: poverty headcount		Dependent variable: poverty gap	
Constant	1	2	1	2
Log GDP pc	0.018181 (0.431296)	−0.015588 (−0.677499)	0.007161 (0.179689)	−0.020074 (−0.9239)
Log R	−0.440222 (−2.579425)	−0.619575 (−5.77286)	−0.413561 (−2.563300)	−0.536221 (−5.1116)
Log GINI	4.929014 (3.129550)	3.672258 (2.255775)	4.987532 (3.349778)	2.890426 (1.88023)
Log UN	−1.908475 (−2.577588)	−0.553135 (−1.737410)	−2.117282 (−3.024923)	−0.966158 (−3.2136)
R^2	0.419342	0.980636	0.433099	0.981137
Adjusted R^2	0.348959	0.965883	0.364384	0.966764

impact on poverty reduction when poverty is measured by the poverty headcount. For the poverty headcount measure, the estimates suggest that, on average, a 10 % increase in per capita workers' remittances will lead to a 5.3 % decline in the share of people living in poverty.

5 Conclusion

In this paper we have analysed the impact of workers' remittances on poverty reduction in Ukraine, Poland, Romania and Turkey. All four emerging economies are characterized by emigration with important inflows of workers' remittances registered after the fall of the iron curtain and the enlargement of the European Union. After the crisis, all the emerging economies started to recover, but at different paces with different future outlooks due to political crisis and anti-government movements registered in Ukraine and Turkey. For the period 2002–2011, all the countries, except for Turkey, have registered sharply increases of workers' remittances inflows, only to decline abruptly with the start of the recent global financial crisis. Also, workers' remittances proved to be more resilient than other inflows of funds, such as the net foreign direct investments. The inflows of workers' remittances are showing signs of recovery and, in the case of Ukraine, these monies already outreached the levels registered before the crisis. In the case of Turkey, the peak of the level of workers' remittances was reached in 1998 (US $5.3 billion). Since then, their level has dropped five times in the past few years. One possible reason for this outcome could be the family reunification of the emigrants established abroad. Although we cannot capture the informal flows of money remittances, the estimation results indicate that, on average, a 10 % increase in per capita workers' remittances will lead to a 5.3 % decline in the share of people living on less than $2 per person per day. Enhanced data collecting and further reducing the prices for sending money overseas could improve the statistical data on workers' remittances to better capture their effect on developing countries.

Acknowledgements This paper was co-financed from the European Social Fund, through the Sectorial Operational Programme Human Resources Development 2007–2013, project number POSDRU/159/1.5/S/138907 "Excellence in scientific interdisciplinary research, doctoral and postdoctoral, in the economic, social and medical fields-EXCELIS", coordinator "The Bucharest University of Economic Studies".

References

Acosta P, Calderón C, Fajnzylber P, López H (2008) Do remittances lower poverty levels in Latin America? In: Fajnzylber P, López H (eds) Remittances and development, Lessons from Latin America. The World Bank, Washington, DC, pp 87–132

Adams R Jr, Page J (2005) Do international migration and remittances reduce poverty in developing countries? World Dev 33(10):1645–1669

Aydas OT, Metin-Ozcan K, Neyapti B (2005) Determinants of workers' remittances: the case of Turkey. Emerg Mark Finance Trade 41(3):53–69
Barajas A, Cosimano T, Fullenkamp C, Gapen M, Montiel P (2008) Macroeconomic consequences of remittances. International Monetary Fund, Washington, DC
Barbone L, Pietka-Kosinska K, Topinska I (2012) The impact of remittances on Poland's economy, vol 12. CASE-Center for Social and Economic Research
Chami R, Jahjah S, Fullenkamp C (2003) Are immigrant remittance flows a source of capital for development. International Monetary Fund, Washington, DC
Ciupureanu C, Roman M (2013) Remittances and economic growth. A case study on Romania. Proceedings of the 12th International Conference on Informatics in Economy Education, Research and Business Technologies, Bucharest, Romania, pp 511–515
Demirguc-Kunt A, Martinez Peria MS, Aggarwal R (2006) Do workers' remittances promote financial development? The World Bank, Washington, DC
Elitok SP (2013) Remittance flows between Germany and Turkey: a reverse trend? Istanbul Policy Center, Istanbul
Giuliano P, Ruiz-Arranz M (2009) Remittances, financial development and growth. J Dev Econ 90 (1):144–152
Glazar O, Strielkowski PW, Weyskrabova B (2012) Migration and remittances in the CEECs: a case study of Ukrainian labour migrants in the Czech Republic. Charles University Prague, Faculty of Social Sciences, Institute of Economic Studies, No. 2012/19
IMF (2012) World economic outlook. Coping with high debt and sluggish growth. International Monetary Fund, Washington, DC
Karafolas S, Konteos G (2010) Choice of money transfer methods in the case of Albanian immigrants in Greece. Transit Stud Rev 16(4):962–978
Karafolas S, Sariannidis N (2009) The banking network as a transmission channel of migrant remittances: the case of Greek and Italian banks in Albania. Transit Stud Rev 15(4):674–684
Katsushi S, Gaiha R, Abdilahi A, Kaicker N (2011) Remittances, growth and poverty: new evidence from Asian countries. The School of Economics Discussion Paper Series (1125)
Kim N (2007) The impact of remittances on labor supply: the case of Jamaica, vol 4120. World Bank, Washington, DC
McLeod D, Molina J (2005) Remittances, inequality and poverty reduction: some tests for Latin America. LACEA meetings paper proceedings. AUP Paris, France
Ratha D (2013) The impact of remittances on economic growth and poverty reduction. Policy Brief no 8. Migration Policy Institute
Ratha D, Eigen-Zucchi C, Plaza S, Wyss H, Yi S (2013) Migration and remittances flows: recent trends and outlook, 2013–2016. Migration and Development Brief no. 21. The World Bank
Ratha D, Eigen-Zucchi C, Plaza S, Wyss H, Yi S (2014) Migration and remittances: recent trends and outlook. Migration and Development Brief no. 22. The World Bank
Roman M (2011) Romanians remittances and migration destination. Studii si cercetari de calcul economic si cibernetica economica 3–4:3–15
Roman M (2013) Financial effects of the international migration in Europe: modelling the decision to remit. Panoeconomicus 60(4):541–555
Vasilescu MD, Roman M (2011) Internal migration and labour market in Romania – a regional approach. Reconect 3(2):142–149
World Bank Group (ed) (2012) World development indicators 2012. World Bank

MIX
Papier aus verantwortungsvollen Quellen
Paper from responsible sources
FSC® C105338

If you have any concerns about our products,
you can contact us on
ProductSafety@springernature.com

In case Publisher is established outside the EU,
the EU authorized representative is:
Springer Nature Customer Service Center GmbH
Europaplatz 3, 69115 Heidelberg, Germany

Printed by Libri Plureos GmbH
in Hamburg, Germany